TRUSTEE FOR THE HUMAN COMMUNITY

Congo premier Patrice Lumumba listens as United Nations representative Dr. Ralph Bunche answers a reporter's question during a press conference at the premier's residence, Leopoldville, Congo, July 20, 1960. © Bettmann/CORBIS

TRUSTEE FOR THE HUMAN COMMUNITY

*Ralph J. Bunche, the United Nations,
and the Decolonization of Africa*

Edited by

Robert A. Hill

and Edmond J. Keller

OHIO UNIVERSITY PRESS   ATHENS

Ohio University Press, Athens, Ohio 45701
www.ohioswallow.com
© 2010 by Ohio University Press
All rights reserved

To obtain permission to quote, reprint, or otherwise reproduce or distribute material from Ohio University Press publications, please contact our rights and permissions department at (740) 593-1154 or (740) 593-4536 (fax).

Printed in the United States of America
Ohio University Press books are printed on acid-free paper ∞™

16 15 14 13 12 11 10   5 4 3 2 1

The title of this volume, "Trustee for the Human Community," is taken from Ralph J. Bunche's essay "U.N.—Trustee for the Human Community," in *The Will to Think: A Treasury of Ideas and Ideals from the Pages of* Think, edited by Robert Cousins (New York: Farrar, Straus, and Cudahy, 1957).

This is a project of the UCLA Globalization Research Center–Africa
UCLA Globalization Research Center-Africa

Library of Congress Cataloging-in-Publication Data

Trustee for the human community : Ralph J. Bunche, the United Nations, and the decolonization of Africa / edited by Robert A. Hill and Edmond J. Keller.
    p. cm.
  Includes bibliographical references and index.
  ISBN 978-0-8214-1909-0 (hc : alk. paper) — ISBN 978-0-8214-1910-6 (pb : alk. paper) — ISBN 978-0-8214-4344-6 (electronic)
  1. Bunche, Ralph J. (Ralph Johnson), 1904–1971. 2. Decolonization—Africa—History—20th century. 3. Africa—History—1884–1960. 4. United Nations—Officials and employees—Biography. 5. Statesmen—United States—Biography. 6. Nobel prize winners—Biography. 7. Africanists—United States—Biography. 8. African Americans—Biography. I. Hill, Robert A., 1943– II. Keller, Edmond J. (Edmond Joseph), 1942–
  E748.B885T78 2010
  341.23'3092—dc22
  [B]

2010001184

Contents

Preface and Acknowledgments   vii

Introduction
    ROBERT A. HILL AND EDMOND J. KELLER   ix

Centenary Memory Beads for Mr. Bunche
    ABENA P. A. BUSIA   xix

ONE: Bunche the Africanist Intellectual

Chapter One
    Ralph Bunche
    African American Intellectual
       MARTIN KILSON   3

Chapter Two
    Ralph Bunche and the Dawn of Africanist Scholarship
       DAVID ANTHONY   19

Chapter Three
    The Making of an Africanist
    Ralph Bunche in South Africa, 1937
       ROBERT EDGAR   25

Chapter Four
    Ralph Bunche and the Decolonization of African Studies
    The Paradox of Power, Morality, and Scholarship
       ELLIOTT P. SKINNER   42

Chapter Five
    Ralph Bunche the Africanist
    Revisiting Paradigms Lost
       PEARL T. ROBINSON   69

TWO: Bunche the Statesman for Africa

Chapter Six
    Decolonization through Trusteeship
    The Legacy of Ralph Bunche
       NETA C. CRAWFORD   93

Chapter Seven
    An Unexpected Challenge
    Ralph Bunche as Field Commander in the Congo, 1960
        JOHN OLVER   116

Chapter Eight
    Ralph Bunche and Patrice Lumumba
    The Fatal Encounter
        CRAWFORD YOUNG   128

Chapter Nine
    Ralph Bunche, Patrice Lumumba, and the First Congo Crisis
        GEORGES NZONGOLA-NTALAJA   148

THREE: Reflections on Bunche's Legacy in Global Perspective

Chapter Ten
    Africa in the Global Decolonization Process
    The Road to Postcoloniality
        RALPH A. AUSTEN   161

Epilogue
        CHARLES P. HENRY   181

Appendix
    United Nations Charter: The Trusteeship System   185

Contributors   193

Index   199

Preface and Acknowledgments

As one of the founding fathers of the United Nations and the key architect of the UN charter's trusteeship clauses as well as the first head of the UN Secretariat's Trusteeship Division, Ralph J. Bunche perfectly embodied the spirit of a world of nations, on which the UN is founded. Bunche was a key figure in the planning of the international trusteeship system that paved the way for the decolonization process in Africa and Asia following the Second World War. This momentous change, rightly regarded today as a revolution in international relations, sounded the death knell for the system of empire and imperialism that had dominated world affairs until 1945. Indeed, it would be difficult to think of another individual whose role or vision exceeded or even equaled that of Bunche's in terms of meeting the challenges of postwar decolonization as well as the issues of international security and peace and human rights.

In conjunction with and as part of UCLA's year-long commemoration of the centenary of Ralph Bunche's birth, the UCLA Globalization Research Center–Africa, in collaboration with the Marcus Garvey and UNIA Papers Project and the James S. Coleman African Studies Center, in June 2004 hosted an international conference with the aim of examining the significance of Bunche's role in meeting the historic challenge of Africa's decolonization.

In addition to recognizing and evaluating the critical importance of Ralph Bunche as a key architect and theoretician of the decolonizing process, the conference strove to reexamine the process of Africa's postwar decolonization, taken as a whole. The conference also sought to evaluate the role of the United States, and specifically African Americans, in leading the demand for African independence. Taken together, the conference attempted to provide a balance sheet for understanding the history of postindependence Africa and the important role that Ralph Bunche played in that history.

We express our profound appreciation for the efforts of the scholars who contributed to the success of the conference and whose presentations appear as essays in this volume. In addition, we acknowledge the valuable contributions made by a number of specially invited participants whose knowledge and expertise enriched the conference proceedings: Salih Booker, executive director of Global Rights, and Professors Herschelle Challenor, Charles Henry, Benetta Jules-Rosette, Ntongela Masilela, Gwendolyn Mikell, and Francis Nesbitt.

The conference was preceded by an opening banquet at which Professor Abena P. A. Busia presented her remarkable and evocative poem "Centenary Memory Beads for Mr. Bunche." It was followed by a performance of an excerpt from "The Ralph J. Bunche Suite," an original, full-length composition by jazz guitarist–composer Kenny Burrell, performed by an ensemble of student musicians from the UCLA Jazz Studies Program under Professor Burrell's direction.

The assistance of the staff of the Globalization Research Center–Africa—Charisma Acey, Tala Rezai, and Negin Avaregan—is gratefully acknowledged in the planning of the conference. Azeb Tadesse of the James S. Coleman African Studies Center and Katherine Goetz provided superb assistance in the preparation of the final manuscript of this volume.

Funding for the conference was provided by generous assistance from several UCLA entities: the Office of the Executive Vice Chancellor; the College of Letters and Science, Division of Social Science; UCLA Extension; the Graduate Division; the School of Law; the James S. Coleman African Studies Center; the Globalization Research Center–Africa; and the Center for Modern and Contemporary Studies. In addition, the Ford Foundation provided support for the preparation of the manuscript and publication of the present volume. Our deepest thanks to these sponsors for their enthusiastic support and assistance.

Introduction

ROBERT A. HILL AND EDMOND J. KELLER

IN 2003 there were worldwide centennial commemorations of the birth of Ralph Johnson Bunche—pioneering scholar, international statesman, and quintessential public intellectual. The University of California, Los Angeles, hosted public events throughout the year to mark the occasion. Bunche had been an outstanding undergraduate at UCLA in the 1920s, a gifted athlete, a brilliant student, and one of the most acclaimed UCLA alumni. This book is a product of an international conference organized by the UCLA Globalization Research Center–Africa, in collaboration with the Marcus Garvey and UNIA Papers Project and the James S. Coleman African Studies Center (June 3–4, 2004).

Over the years numerous biographies and scholarly works have been written about Bunche.[1] However, there has not been a comprehensive treatment of his pioneering contributions to the study of Africa and his equally groundbreaking efforts to lay the foundation for the emergence of viable, independent African states characterized by peace and social justice. It was the realization of the gap in Bunche scholarship that inspired the conference and the present volume of essays, drawn from the conference proceedings. The following chapters bring together contributions to the field of decolonization and African American history by viewing both through the prism and personality of Ralph J. Bunche, a major world statesman and African American intellectual-cum-policymaker on the global stage.

This volume combines different historical episodes of Bunche's life and views on his career, all from the perspective of the enduring relationship and contribution of the African American community to the struggle for Africa's independence. One important aspect of Bunche's career not discussed here was his role in mediating conflict in the Middle East, for which he won the Nobel Peace Prize in 1950, and his work during the Suez crisis of 1956. As important as these achievements undoubtedly were, it was felt that they deserved to be treated much more fully in a separate volume. The aim and scope of the present volume is to situate Bunche within African American intellectual history and within the focused world of the UN's critical role in the end of European empires in sub-Saharan Africa.

In the two first quarters of the twentieth century, Ralph Bunche was one of the foremost authorities in the world on the structure of European colonialism in Africa as well as an active participant in the discussions taking place at the time over how to bring about the decolonization of Africa under conditions of imperial rule. In *A World View of Race,* Bunche blamed European countries for "raping" Africa rather than "civilizing" it. Even though they had publicly proclaimed that their mission was to "serve" Africa, Bunche felt there was clear evidence, based on what he had seen firsthand in Africa, that greed was what led the European colonizers to brutally suppress and economically exploit the peoples of their African colonies.[2] Throughout his subsequent studies, Bunche was concerned to expose the twin scourges of racism and imperialism in the lives of African peoples. But while the language he used to discuss this issue was ideologically left of center, the alternatives he offered were always based on pragmatism rather than revolution, as Martin Kilson so adroitly explains.

How did Bunche acquire his African expertise? After graduating from UCLA summa cum laude in 1927, Bunche was awarded a tuition fellowship to study political science at Harvard University. He completed his master's degree from Harvard in 1928 and took up a faculty position in political science at Howard University. For the next seven years he divided his time between his faculty position at Howard and studies at Harvard for the PhD in political science. At the time, European imperialism was at its height and this coincided with the continuing institutionalization of white supremacy and racism in the United States. It was understandable, therefore, for Bunche to choose to study the role of race and imperialism in the European colonization of African territories. As partial fulfillment of his PhD requirements, Bunche designed a research study to attempt to evaluate different routes to the eventual decolonization of Africa. He narrowed his study to francophone West Africa and the territories of Togoland and Dahomey (present-day Benin). These two small territories were adjacent to each other, but following World War I, one territory, Togoland, was governed by the French as a League of Nations mandate; the other, Dahomey, was a colony of France. Bunche attempted to assess

Introduction

whether Africans fared better, or were better prepared to become independent states, under one regime than the other.³

Neta C. Crawford summarizes the basic elements of the League's original mandate system. After the defeat of the Germans and the Ottomans in World War I, the founders of the League of Nations grappled with how to administer the former German and Ottoman colonies throughout the world. As a solution, they developed the notion of mandate territories. Such territories were identified in the League's covenant as territories "inhabited by peoples not able to stand by themselves under the strenuous conditions of the modern world" (art. 22, par. 1). The crafters of this document declared that the well-being and development of people in this situation had to be insured by the civilized world. This was said to be "a sacred trust of civilization." What this all implied was that mandate territories would have to come under the tutelage of the League. However, the actual administration of these territories was performed by Great Britain, Belgium, France, and South Africa.⁴

Although he did not find that the League's mandate system was the ideal route to Africa's decolonization, Bunche did consider it to be, at least in the two cases he studied, better in some ways than direct colonial rule. The mandate system contained rules to guarantee certain basic rights to the inhabitants of a territory and to protect them against such colonial excesses as forced labor and unfair taxation. Moreover, inhabitants had better representation in governing their own affairs, and better access to social services such as education and health care. Nevertheless, Bunche found that the mandate system did not always operate the way it was supposed to. One of the most important weaknesses he found was that those countries that administered mandate territories were required to be monitored, but that amounted to nothing more than self-monitoring through annual reports to the League. Bunche felt that the system could be substantially improved if there could be a built-in mechanism for the impartial and ongoing monitoring of the performance of the countries responsible for administering mandate territories.

In the conduct of his dissertation research, Bunche traveled for six months in 1932–33, first to Paris and then to the West African territories he studied and then back to Paris. In addition to carefully sifting through archived colonial records, he engaged in ethnography—in-depth interviews with colonial administrators and African notables in the two territories.

Following the completion of his dissertation, and before returning to Howard, Bunche published his first book in 1936, *A World View of Race,* in many respects a radical critique of racism and European imperialism. Bunche showed he had a sophisticated understanding of the interrelationship of racism and imperialism as a global phenomenon. In order to further develop his knowledge of this subject, Bunche took several courses in anthropology at Northwestern University in preparation for his second research visit to Africa.

Between October 1937 and July 1938, Bunche studied and traveled in eastern, central, and southern Africa. The purpose of this trip was to examine the impact of European colonialism from the perspective of Africans. He began his journey in London, where he met with several black activists with whom he exchanged views on Pan-Africanism and colonialism. Once in Africa, Bunche attempted to assess the quality of black African leaders and their political potential for changing the colonial system, as described here by Martin Kilson, David Anthony, Robert Edgar, and Pearl T. Robinson. On balance Bunche did not come away with a favorable impression of African leaders. This view would carry over into his work as the United Nations envoy in the chaotic conditions of the former Belgian Congo. Bunche passionately believed that European colonialism in Africa should be ended, but at the same time he believed in the continuing need for outside tutelage.

After Bunche returned to the United States in 1938, he was drawn away from his academic interest in Africa to work with the famed Swedish economist and social scientist Gunnar Myrdal on the Carnegie Endowment–funded research project on the plight of African Americans that became Myrdal's *An American Dilemma: The Negro Problem and Modern Democracy* (1942). Bunche conducted fieldwork in the southeastern United States and wrote several important monographs for the project. He was involved with the Myrdal project for about two years.

Bunche's reputation, however, did not hinge on the work he did for *An American Dilemma* or on work that he did on African American issues generally but on international issues. By 1940 the Second World War was raging in Europe and the U.S. government was scrambling to develop its policies toward the conflict. Bunche possessed an unrivaled understanding of European colonial administration in Africa as well as the story of how the League of Nations had tried to deal with this issue. That is what attracted the U.S. government to invite Bunche

Introduction

to join the Office of Special Services in the State Department in 1941. Bunche subsequently became a part of a team that was responsible for drafting the government's policies relating to European and Japanese colonies. This in turn made him an ideal candidate for a task force charged with providing input from the U.S. government in the forming of the United Nations. In 1945, Bunche was a member of the U.S. delegation that went to San Francisco to participate in the drafting of the UN charter. There he was very involved in drafting chapters XI, XII, and XIII of the charter.[5] These chapters established the Trusteeship Division within the UN Secretariat, mandated that the colonial powers prepare their subjects for self-government, and required them to submit to "trustee agreements" with the UN. The aim of this last provision was to enable the UN to monitor the progress being made in trusteeship territories toward self-government. Bunche felt this was the best path to independence for African and Asian colonies. Although it fell short of immediate and total independence, it did put in place the monitoring guarantees that Bunche felt were lacking in the mandate system of the League of Nations.

Bunche's work in the establishment of the United Nations led to his "temporary" assignment by the U.S. government to the UN in order to facilitate the establishment of the Trusteeship Division. What was supposed to have been a six-week assignment quickly became permanent. By all accounts, through his work in the division, Bunche was able to contribute significantly to the winding up of European colonialism in Africa and Asia.

By 1947, Ralph Bunche was no longer in the employ of the U.S. State Department, but instead the United Nations. In that same year the UN General Assembly agreed to the partition of Palestine. That led to an escalation of the conflict between Arabs and Israelis in the territory. Ralph Bunche was delegated by the UN secretary general to be his personal envoy and to serve as the special assistant to the mediator assigned to negotiate a truce in the conflict, the Swedish count Folke Bernadotte. In September 1948, Bernadotte was assassinated by combatants in an Israeli extremist underground organization, and Bunche was appointed by the UN secretary general as his successor. Within three months of becoming acting mediator, he had hammered out a deal that at least temporarily brought about a cessation to the hostilities.

Over the next ten years, through quiet diplomacy Bunche continued his work in trying to use UN influence to assist the decolonization process in Africa. This is what led arguably to his most difficult assignment, representing the UN in finding a peaceful solution to the Congo crisis in the aftermath of Belgian rule. This was a period in which the cold war rivalry between the Western allies and Russia was intensifying, and there was growing concern in the West that the UN should do its part to halt the spread of communism, particularly in what was perceived to be the vulnerable, newly independent African states. In the Congo, Bunche viewed his responsibility as primarily providing advice to the UN on how to meet this challenge. Ultimately, he called for the use of a UN-sponsored peacekeeping force, the first of its kind. However, he constantly found himself at odds with the Congo's elected prime minister, Patrice Lumumba. Lumumba saw Bunche more as an agent of the United States and less an impartial representative of the UN. This view was reinforced when Bunche refused Lumumba's request to send UN forces to the Katanga region to halt its secession. At this point, the collision between assertive nationalism and political trusteeship became unavoidable.

Rather than focus on the totality of Bunche's scholarly and diplomatic careers, the present collection concentrates on his development as an Africanist academic and on his diplomatic involvement and mediation in the decolonization process of Africa.

Part 1 examines Bunche's career as an Africanist. Martin Kilson (chapter 1) carefully sketches Bunche's ideological and political beliefs as represented in his writings about European colonial rule in Africa. Kilson describes Bunche as a complex individual who was dedicated to the empowerment of African Americans while at the same time seeing their struggle as only one part of global struggle between the oppressed and the agents of imperialism. Bunche was a radical but not a revolutionary. Kilson emphasizes that he had the definite mindset of a pragmatist.

David Anthony (chapter 2) focuses on Bunche's evolution from Africanist academic into international civil servant, dedicated to the total decolonization of the African continent. Robert Edgar (chapter 3) concentrates on Bunche's 1937 visit to South Africa in his effort to understand how black Africans viewed their situation in that country and to assess whether they were preparing themselves to alter their plight in a system increasingly characterized by white supremacy. Bunche

Introduction

is said to have come away with the impression that the conditions under which blacks in South Africa lived were worse than the situation of African Americans. Also, Bunche criticized South Africa's black leadership because of what he saw as poor political organization.

Elliot Skinner and Pearl Robinson focus on Bunche's contribution to the creation of African studies as a scholarly pursuit. Skinner (chapter 4) attempts to show the linkage between the discrimination suffered by African Americans in the early twentieth century and the solidarity they developed with their sisters and brothers in colonial Africa. He paints a picture of a person who wanted not only to understand the world but to change it. Providing yet another insight into Bunche's global perspectives, Skinner notes that Bunche believed that African studies had to go beyond colonial studies and to situate Africa and Africans within the context of the world community of peoples.

Robinson (chapter 5) provides another perspective on Bunche's evolution as an Africanist scholar, noting that he saw economics and politics intimately intertwined in the European colonial project. Again, as in the previous four chapters, Robinson highlights Bunche's belief that intellectuals were spearheads of the process of decolonization as well as postcolonial reconstruction and development. She attempts to show how Bunche, rather than using his academic training to engage in scholarly writing, used his research to support the development of his career as a public intellectual.

Part 2 is organized around Bunche's contribution as a statesman and international civil servant. Neta Crawford (chapter 6) begins with an analysis of Bunche's first encounter with European colonial institutions in Africa and of his dissertation research in Togoland and Dahomey. In the process of that research Bunche came to understand not only colonial institutions and practice but also the newly created institution of "mandate territories" by the League of Nations. This understanding prepared him well for his career as an international public servant when he helped draft the charter of the United Nations, particularly those articles that laid the foundations for the UN's Trusteeship Division. Crawford suggests that in characteristic fashion, although he would have preferred a much more direct route to decolonization in Africa, Bunche was willing to compromise and support the implementation of the trusteeship system. Crawford concludes by considering what Bunche might think of the tendency in international circles to favor a reintroduction of some of the elements of the trusteeship concept in present-day "transitional administration systems." She suggests that Bunche would have been as critical of this system as he had been of the mandate system because its administrators are not held accountable for their actions.

Subsequent chapters engage in a lively debate about the significance of Bunche's activities, as a UN representative, in the former Belgian Congo in the early 1960s. This was a very difficult assignment and Bunche at times seems to have been overwhelmed by a cauldron of political agendas (nationalist, leftist, communist, economic, political). John Olver (chapter 7), a former aide to Bunche in the Congo, describes him as having a narrow view of the UN's mission in the Congo: peacekeeping. Bunche negotiated the exodus of the Belgian military from the Congo and the entry of the UN forces and, as a consequence, did not want the UN to get involved in the civil war in Katanga. He made it clear that UN forces should treat the Congolese with respect and not with paternalism and condescension.

Crawford Young and Georges Nzongola-Ntalaja focus specifically on the relationship between Bunche and Lumumba. Young (chapter 8) shows Lumumba as a hero of African independence who had the potential to be a strong leader; however, he became the victim of his own personality flaws as well as the volatile situation around him. Bunche is described as despising Lumumba because of his abrasive and often undiplomatic approach to dealing with problems. Young suggests that the poor relations between the two resulted in a blemish on Bunche's otherwise stellar career of international service.

Nzongola-Ntalaja (chapter 9) picks up on this theme, describing Bunche as having been hostile to nationalism and having a negative opinion of Lumumba even before he arrived in the Congo on the eve of independence. The fiasco in Katanga and the UN's refusal to send its forces to support the Congolese army in putting down the secessionist rebellion there, as well as Lumumba's turning to the Soviet Union for military assistance, further strained the relationship between the two men. Nzongola-Ntalaja suggests that the UN's commitment to halting the spread of communism was reinforced by Bunche's own biases and this to a large extent contributed to Lumumba's demise.

Throughout Bunche's writings one can identify a global perspective. Part 3 illuminates the legacy of Ralph Bunche in the study of postcolonial Africa and the field of African studies. The final chapter elaborates on this in its treatment of colonialism's demise and its aftermath on the continent. This piece is reminiscent of Bunche's critique

Introduction

of imperialism and racism. Ralph Austen (chapter 10) traces the connection between globalization and colonial rule in Africa. He notes that despite public justifications to the contrary, the colonization of Africa was driven by the economic motivations of the European colonizers. The colonialists were seen as interested in exploiting Africa's resources until they perceived their presence there as too costly. Austen explains the emergence of African nationalism and the development of new relationships between countries of the European metropole and their colonies in the 1960s and 1970s. He sees Africa, at this moment in the process of globalization, as poised to remove the last vestiges of the colonial hangover, and it is up to Africans themselves to seize the moment.

In his epilogue, Charles Henry concludes that despite Bunche's failure to create an enabling environment for development and democracy in Africa, his contributions to Africa's decolonization were undoubted and go a long way toward contributing to his brilliant legacy as a distinguished scholar, statesman, and the quintessential public intellectual in the second half of the twentieth century.

Ralph Bunche died on December 9, 1971.

Notes

1. For example, Charles P. Henry, *Ralph Bunche: Model Negro or American Other?* (New York: New York University Press, 1999); Benjamin Rivlin, *Ralph Bunche, The Man and His Times* (New York: Holmes and Meier, 1990); Brian Urquhart, *Ralph Bunche: An American Life* (New York: Norton, 1993).

2. Ralph J. Bunche, *A World View of Race* (Washington, DC: Associates in Negro Folk Education, 1936), 38–39.

3. Ralph J. Bunche, "French Administration of Togoland and Dahomey" (PhD diss., Harvard University, 1934).

4. The African territories concerned were Togoland, Cameroons, Tanganyika, Ruanda-Urundi, and South-West Africa, all former German possessions. Other mandate territories outside Africa were Iraq, Palestine and Transjordan, Syria, Lebanon, New Guinea, Nauru, Samoa, and the Marshall, Caroline, and Mariana islands.

5. The text of the UN charter dealing with trusteeship and non-self-governing territories was drafted by Bunche; those excerpts can be found in an appendix to this volume.

Centenary Memory Beads for Mr. Bunche

ABENA P. A. BUSIA

For Mr. Ralph Johnson Bunche, on the centenary of his birth—
what can be the generation of memory?
The stories are so many and so few,

From Pacific halls west to Atlantic plazas,
if we encircle the globe,
what story beads can we tell?

What does it take to recollect a legacy so large,
to honor and to keep in mind
decades of public labor so invisible and private?

Let's tell the first bead for the ancestors:

Offspring of the free of spirit
whether slaves or freemen, maids or schoolmasters,
his was an American life—

His inheritance a fierce love
that nurtured dignity and taught
the pride of doing all things well

And left as sweet and lasting legacy
a simple admonition
never to abandon faith, hope, and dreams.

Let's tell the second bead for the orphaned boy:

Who dreamed he'd walk the mountains
and claimed the whole broad world
his schoolroom;

For the twice valedictory dutiful son who learned well
the lessons of his worth
that no barred swimming pools and closed honor clubs

And segregated dining cars
could dishonor.
What rites of memory can we perform?

Let's tell the third bead for the scholar-athlete:

Who loved hoops and laughter
and stowed away on ships
who laid carpets, shelled peas,

And learned to sing the toreador's song
as well as the cabin boy's call.
Who upheld his life long the dignity of labor,

And early claimed an Olympian call
of overarching sympathy
that like love creates new worlds from old.

So let's tell the fourth bead for the visionary:

Who first in so many things,
through silent protests and quiet pickets
and early direct action

Trekked across this land
and voyaged around the world
for all our civil rights and freedoms.

From D.C. to London, from Togo to Cape Town,
from Nairobi to Palestine, and back again,
what moments are there, for us to recall?

We'll tell the fifth bead for the scholar:

Who took a world view on race,
and laid bare the foundations of this American dilemma
that ruled the nation and controlled the world.

Centenary Memory Beads for Mr. Bunche

What mementoes can be garnered
by those who never knew him.
What rite of memory can be performed?

When memories begin to fade or falter coast to coast—
from towering building to sculpture park—
What is it they aim to recall?

Let's tell the sixth bead for the visionary diplomat:

Who helped transform the League of Nations
into a more lasting union
when the world had had enough of war,

Who believed like the prophet we could indeed
beat swords into ploughshares
and spears into pruning hooks.

What rite of memory can we implore
for a lifetime ensuring
we should study war no more?

So let's tell the seventh bead for the international servant:

Strong in spirit and bold of mind
whose métier was words
forged in chambers, bedrooms, and conference halls

To wake the nations,
some to rise and claim their seats
and some to lay their armor down.

What rites of memory can recall
the faithful Trustee whose negotiations were directed
toward mutual respect among peoples?

So tell the stories of the eighth bead of sacrifice:

For the man who knew both early and grown
too many losses
of sudden deaths too young,

Who mourned mentors, colleagues, children, friends,
In the exacting toll of service
and never told the price he paid

For other peoples' treaties—
Who wrestled a truce with words, a new colossus
bestriding ancient gulfs.

So let's prize the ninth bead of the man of peace:

And the nobility of his prayer—
that there may be freedom and equality and independence won
for the brotherhood of nations;

That coming generations
may find the path to the simple hope
of a good life for all peoples,

And the right to walk with dignity
on all the world's great boulevards
"to make full use of the great good that is in us."

So we can call the last bead in simple dedication:

For Mr. Ralph Johnson Bunche, on the centenary of his birth.

© Abena P. A. Busia
Los Angeles, California, June 3, 2004

PART ONE

Bunche the Africanist Intellectual

CHAPTER ONE

Ralph Bunche
African American Intellectual

MARTIN KILSON

I WANT to discuss the analytical trajectory along which the young Ralph Bunche—during his graduate studies in political science at Harvard University in the late 1920s and early 1930s—arrived at an intertwined leftist-and-pragmatic characterization of the political system of twentieth-century European colonial governance in African societies. The main source for my discussion is Ralph Bunche's Harvard University PhD dissertation titled "French Administration in Togoland and Dahomey" (1934), which was produced under the direction of several Harvard Department of Government professors, including senior adviser Professor Arthur Holcombe and junior adviser Assistant Professor Rupert Emerson.

Bunche's Leftist-Pragmatist Persona

Bunche's PhD dissertation was unique insofar as it was the first political science dissertation at an American university that was based on fieldwork in African societies. To my knowledge, the only other American political science scholar who, by the 1930s, had preceded Ralph Bunche in undertaking on-the-ground research relating to colonial governance in Africa was Raymond Leslie Buell. As an assistant professor in Harvard's Department of Government in the 1920s, Buell conducted fieldwork in a large swath of African colonial territories, which resulted in two classic volumes titled *Native Administration in Africa* (1927).

As I'll point out later, through several analytical stages in Bunche's dissertation on European imperialist rule in Africa his analysis fluctuates between Marxist and pragmatist perspectives, with the pragmatist perspective eventually prevailing. The roots of Bunche's Marxist perspective were associated with his quest as a second-generation member of the twentieth-century African American intelligentsia to fathom the dynamics of racial-caste marginalization of peoples of African descent in American society. The sources of Bunche's pragmatist perspective were rooted in the political science curriculum Bunche experienced (a curriculum fashioned by liberal political science scholars like Arthur Holcombe, John Gaus, Raymond Leslie Buell, and Rupert Emerson), and also rooted in the intellectual dynamics Bunche experienced as a Harvard graduate student. Several progressive-oriented African Americans were graduate student peers of Ralph Bunche, among whom were John P. Davis (a Harvard Law School student), Robert Weaver (an economics student), and John Hope Franklin (a history student).

American Aspects

As those of you know who have read the writings of John Kirby on the black American intelligentsia in the New Deal era, William Banks's seminal probe of the quest for black responsibility among the twentieth-century black intelligentsia, or the marvelous biographies of Ralph Bunche by Brian Urquhart and Charles Henry, the ideological and political attributes of the young Ralph Bunche were on the left of the American political spectrum. And Bunche shared this intellectual trait with other black intellectuals during the years between the two world wars. Among others, that second-generation group of twentieth-century black professionals with whom Bunche shared a leftist worldview include John Aubrey Davis Sr., political scientist on the faculty of Lincoln University; John P. Davis, NAACP labor lawyer; St. Clair Drake, anthropologist on the faculty of Dillard University; Langston Hughes, poet; Thurgood Marshall, NAACP civil rights lawyer; A. Philip Randolph, head of the Brotherhood of Sleeping Car Porters; Ira Reid, sociologist on the faculty of Fisk University; Robert Weaver, economist for the National Urban League; and economist Abram Harris, psychologist Kenneth Clark, civil rights lawyers Charles Houston and James Nabrit Jr., and sociologists E. Franklin Frazier and Doxey Wilkerson, all on the faculty of Howard University.

Bunche shared another key intellectual-formation trait with his leftist black intellectual peers. They all stood on the broad radical-democrat shoulders of William Edward Burghardt DuBois—that great trailblazer of intellectual progressivism among the early-twentieth-century African American intelligentsia. Influenced by the great Alexander Crummell of the American Negro Academy and of Wilberforce University, DuBois fashioned and propagated what I call a black-ethnic commitment orientation for early twentieth-century black intellectuals. Writing in 1903 in his great tome *The Souls of Black Folk,* DuBois observed that black-ethnic commitment among the evolving twentieth-century black intelligentsia "must insist continually ... that voting is necessary to modern manhood, that color discrimination [racism] is barbarism, and that black boys need education as well as white boys."

For DuBois, then, the black intellectual committed to his own people should be engaged in facilitating the development of a modern social system and citizenship rights for the African American working class. He argued that black intelligentsia who failed to advance these goals were "shirk[ing] a heavy responsibility,—a responsibility to themselves, a responsibility to the struggling masses, a responsibility to the darker races of men whose future depends so largely on this American [Negro] experiment."[1]

The young Ralph Bunche, however, tended to locate an independent turf for himself on the shoulders of DuBois. The young Bunche's leftist thinking exhibited a firm belief in the Marxist view of the Western working class as a multicultural radical force. Accordingly, in the 1930s, when a major section of Bunche's black leftist peers were fashioning civil-rights activist organizations to challenge white supremacist practices such as not hiring blacks in white-owned businesses located in urban black communities (in New York, Cleveland, Chicago, Richmond, Philadelphia, Washington, D.C., and elsewhere), Bunche did not join this Don't Buy Where You Can't Work movement.

The organization was called the New Negro Alliance (NNA), organized in Washington, D.C., in 1933 and active until 1940. Its leading members included John Aubrey Davis, Belford Lawson, lawyer; James Nabrit, Albert DeMond, and William Hastie, civil rights lawyers; Elmer Henderson, lawyer for the National Urban League; H. Naylor Fitzhugh, accounting professor at Howard University; and Charles Houston, civil rights lawyer and dean of Howard Law School, among other Washington-based black professionals.

Bunche's kind of American Marxist faith in white working-class radicalism meant that Bunche wanted black civil rights activism to be organized and conducted in a manner that accommodated the white working class. In Bunche's vision, therefore, it was a mistake for the NNA to base its antiracist activity primarily among black citizens. As John Aubrey Davis informed me of the alliance's relationship with the young Ralph Bunche in the mid-1930s: "Bunche was never a member, only a critic.... Bunche attacked the NNA because he feared the division of the [American] labor movement on the basis of race. He saw the only good in the organization was that it taught public protest, solidarity, and direct action."[2]

Other 1930s true-believer Marxist-oriented black intellectuals adopted Bunche's independent posture toward civil rights organizations based on black community mobilization, such as E. Franklin Frazier and Abram Harris, each of whom kept organizational distance from Washington's New Negro Alliance. Interestingly, neither Bunche, Frazier, nor Harris fashioned and tested an alternative civil rights activist organization with important white working-class participation. And for good reason: the dominant body of white working-class Americans in the era between the two world wars clung to racist values and practices. The white working class made this brutally clear during those seemingly highly patriotic World War II years. It violently and viciously attacked the courageous efforts of Bunche's 1930s leftist peers like James Nabrit, Charles Houston, John Aubrey Davis, George Crockett, Elmer Henderson, Clarence Mitchell, Robert Weaver, and others who became major federal-government technocrats administering the fair-labor practices of Roosevelt's Fair Employment Practices Committee (created by executive order) at local levels in the industrial North and South. White workers fomented many violent and vicious riots against black FEPC officials' courageous efforts to gain wartime industrial jobs for African American workers.

African Aspects

The interesting intertwining of leftist and pragmatist elements in the mindset of the young Ralph Bunche stands out in his writings on the nineteenth- and twentieth-century European colonial system in Africa. His main works on this subject were his Harvard doctoral dissertation, "French Administration in Togoland and Dahomey," and a small but very important book, *A World View of Race*.

Bunche's leftist-pragmatist persona was rooted in the values and norms of the Enlightenment, which had delineated the groundwork of the knowledge revolution and the economic revolution that fashioned the European nation-state. The young Bunche considered this extraordinary metamorphosis out of the feudalistic era a momentous opportunity for advancing humanitarian and egalitarian processes for all people, regardless of race, religion, gender, and political origins. Writing in *A World View of Race,* just two years after completing his dissertation, Bunche embraces the Enlightenment legacy:

> The concept of human equality and the doctrine of natural rights were cradled in the modern Western World. These ideals embodied the political promise of the future; indeed, they formed the warp and woof of the most modern political institutions. There was no limit to the promise which such doctrines held forth to peoples and classes which had been abused and oppressed for centuries. The "civilized" West of the nineteenth and twentieth centuries became a great testing ground for these principles which were counted upon to free the great masses of people from suffering and bondage.[3]

This respect for values and structures of progress inspired by the Enlightenment was not, however, uncritical or one-dimensional. Quite the contrary. The young Bunche had a naturally critical mindset, and thus a gift for realpolitik. If not fully present at Bunche's initial encounter with a new idea, policy, or system, this critical mindset would nevertheless soon surface, lending a pragmatic bent to Bunche's thinking and behavior. This, then, is what I mean when I refer to the "pragmatist" feature of the young Ralph Bunche. Although he embraced the generic importance of the Enlightenment legacy, what might be called the young Ralph Bunche's gut-level sense of realpolitik regulated his fidelity to the European Enlightenment legacy. Accordingly, for the young Bunche the dynamics of the real world required skepticism toward one's fealty to the Enlightenment legacy. This, I think, is precisely what Bunche had in mind when he writes in *A World View of Race,*

> In the practical history of our modern world, the ideal doctrine of the "equality of man" . . . has fallen upon hard times. True, we continue to pay lip service to the "sacred" concept of the "natural rights of man" and its international corollary, the "rights of people."

> But the dominant peoples and powerful nations usually discover that such concepts cut sharply against their own economic and political interests. So with these favored groups, who know well how to use them for their own profit, such doctrines come to assume a strange role. (1)

This theme of tension between ideals and the realities of power engaged the young Bunche throughout the 1930s. He entertained an especially strong preference for what might be called the cosmopolitan side of Enlightenment values—so much so that in *A World View of Race* (1936) Bunche even describes possible "cosmopolitan-type" patterns of class conflict evolving among oppressed groups influenced by what he called "the principles of equality and humanitarianism advocated by [Marxist rulers in] the Soviet Union." Whatever their ideological roots, democratic or authoritarian, it seems that for Bunche class patterns trumped ethnic or race patterns when it came to political mobilization. As the young Bunche put it,

> If the oppressed racial groups, as a result of desperation and increasing understanding, should be attracted by the principles of equality and humanitarianism advocated by the Soviet Union (and it is both logical and likely that they will) then racial conflict will become intensified. In such case, however, racial conflict will be more directly identified with class conflict, and the oppressed racial groups may win the support of . . . previously prejudiced working-class groups within the dominant [white or European] population. (36)

There was, then, a perpetual pushing and pulling between the ideal and realpolitik elements in the young Bunche's intellectual metamorphosis, meaning that Bunche-as-political-actor was continually shifting between leftist and bourgeois-pragmatist political contours. Above all, this dynamic pervaded Bunche's intellectual posture toward the European imperialistic mode of transferring the capitalist political economy to African societies.

Bunche's Cost-Benefit View of Colonial Rule in Africa

In Bunche's prize-winning Harvard dissertation we gain a thorough understanding of the interplay of contending leftist and bourgeois-pragmatist patterns in his posture toward the impact of European colonial rule in nineteenth- and twentieth-century African societies. One might posit two stages in Bunche's interaction with the politics of modern colonial rule and the global implications of that politics: the political analyst stage (1930s to mid-1940s) and the crisis manager–diplomat stage (late 1940s through 1960s). Throughout the political analyst stage, Bunche's perception of colonial rule's metamorphosis in African societies vacillates between emphasizing the price exacted by colonial rule (his leftist outlook) and emphasizing the Western-type objective advantages transmitted by colonial rule (his bourgeois-pragmatist outlook). A critically candid young Bunche characterized colonial rule in his most assertively leftist published work, *A World View of Race*. Here he observes that the European imperialist process from the late nineteenth century onward crudely categorized the globe as either "advanced" or "backward" peoples, the latter being viewed as helplessly underdeveloped and incapable of keeping in step with the modernizing Western industrial societies. The young Bunche saw such theoretical classification of the world's peoples as mere deceit: an attempt, he wrote, "to mask [Europe's] cruelly selfish motives under high-sounding titles" (38)

Aware that the rhetoric of power is seldom the reality of power, the young Bunche recognized that the powercentric essence of colonial rule in Africa was plain enough:

> Powerful industrial nations have raped Africa under the false pretense of shouldering "the white man's burden" . . . ; to convert [Africans] to the Christian religion and to expose them to the benefits of an advanced European culture. . . . [However,] the backward peoples bitterly learn that the "blessings" consist of brutal suppression, greedy economic exploitation of the natural and human resources of a country which is no longer their own, forced labor, the introduction of previously unknown diseases, vice and social degeneration. (ibid.)

Now, we can gain another perspective on the young Bunche's interface with colonial rule in Africa if we ask, why colonial rule in Africa in the first place? The young Bunche's two mindsets—the leftist and the pragmatist—responded in different yet overlapping ways to this query. In the 1930s, Bunche's leftist mindset resorts to rather conventional Marxist-Leninist wisdom to illuminate this query:

> Imperialism is an international expression of capitalism. The rapid growth and expansion resulting from the development of industrialism and capitalism led the peoples of industrial countries to seek raw materials and new markets all over the world. This led to more general group contact and, because of the base motives of imperialism, to more widespread racial conflict . . . the accumulation of "surplus capital" and the resultant demand for overseas investments, all tended to force European imperialist nations to invade completely the African continent. (*World*, 40–42)

When the same question about colonial rule in Africa is addressed by the young Bunche's bourgeois-pragmatist mindset, the response is more reflective. That is, it is less ideologically assured, evincing less operational closed-endedness and thus entertaining some operational open-endedness toward colonial capitalist metamorphosis in Africa:

> Perhaps its [colonial rule's] greatest significance is found in its possibilities as a fine proving ground in human relationships—social, economic and political. Here is one place in a troubled world where mistakes previously committed may be corrected, where, indeed, a new and better civilization may be cultivated, through the deliberate application of human intelligence and understanding.[4]

Here the young Bunche's bourgeois-pragmatist mindset articulates the belief that, despite its crudely self-serving, wealth-expanding, and power-enhancing purposes, the colonial state in Africa might also entertain enough flexibility and creativity in form and ideas to permit institutional experimentation, in Bunche's words, to forge "a new and better civilization . . . through the deliberate application of human intelligence and understanding." But Bunche also understood that for colonial rule in Africa to make what might be called this "momentous political moral transformation" (the replacement of colonial capitalist authoritarianism with responsible and accountable governance), European colonial elites must recognize the generic salience of Africans as human beings. As Bunche put it in his dissertation, "French Administration in Togoland and Dahomey": "After all, great though her natural resources are, the vital wealth of Africa is in the humanity that dwells within the sweltering continent. . . . The solution of the problem of the future of Africa is to be found in the determination of the eventual relationships that will prevail between the Africans and [European] peoples" ("French," 2ff.).

Shaping Accountable Colonialism through an African Elite

Now, in regard to the issue of a leftist black American intellectual arriving at a pragmatist outlook toward the possibility of achieving democratic-type spheres within racist colonial rule in Africa seventy years ago—nearly four generations ago—the young Bunche fashioned for himself a shrewd analytical perspective on how to remedy what his leftist mindset defined as the wealth-and-power-grubbing character of European colonial rule in Africa. In his Harvard dissertation, I suggest that Bunche employed what might be called a twofold system-remedial perspective. The first part of this system focused on the role of the small stratum of educated Africans—the budding black African bourgeoisie, let us say. The second focused on the process of regime accountability within colonial rule, which is to say, on the possibility of expanding participatory practices under colonial rule, such as legislative councils in British African countries, local administrative districts, or cantons, in French African countries, and the role of international organizations like the League of Nations and its so-called mandate system for supervising former German African colonies.

At the same time, however, the young Bunche's bid for a pragmatist perspective toward racist colonial rule in Africa was continually checkmated by his leftist mindset. Thus what I call his quest for a system-remedial perspective was cautious—cautious but brave. As Bunche put it in his dissertation, "Though the time when the West African will be able, in the words of the League [of Nations] Covenant, 'to stand alone in the strenuous conditions of the modern world' is probably many generations removed from the present day, he should be serving an apprenticeship in the art of self-rule under the tutelage of his immediate [colonial] rulers.... It must be made possible for him now to acquire the experience and develop the leadership essential to good government everywhere" (388).

As a black American leftist intellectual, the young Bunche was quite certain that the governing precepts at the foundation of colonial rule in Africa were both mistaken (as ideas out of the European democratic tradition) and unworkable or crisis prone (as political blueprints). Asking himself, "By what devices is the African governed?"

Bunche responded, "Two extremes of policy have been applied to him. The one, based entirely on greed, regarded him as essentially inferior, sub-human, without a soul, and fit only for slavery. The other, based entirely on sentiment, regarded him as a man and brother, extended to him the equalitarian principles of the French Revolution and attempted to 'Europeanize' him overnight. Both were unscientific and devoted little attention to the needs and desires of the Africans" (*World*, 46).

Not only were the governing precepts of colonial rule in Africa flawed, they never even contemplated an endgame scenario. For the young Bunche, the importance of an endgame scenario was that it predisposes steps and stages—however minuscule—through which a terminus in colonial rule is reached. Anything less than this was, in Bunche's analytical schema, a political recipe for systemic confusion and crisis. As Bunche wrote in *A World View of Race,* "French and English alike are in Africa primarily for economic exploitation and not for motives of philanthropy.... Both powers intend to retain control of their respective possessions and their subject populations indefinitely." Accordingly, the young Bunche firmly chastises European colonial rulers for what might be called power-class myopia: "England and France [are] not thinking in terms of native independence or self-government for the West Africans" (47).

However, whenever the European colonial rulers arrived at a system-remedial perspective owing to internal or external crises, Bunche believed that that would spark serious thinking in terms of endgame scenarios. In his understanding of endgame dynamics, the young Bunche was keenly perceptive. For by 1933 fascism reigned in Europe—especially in Italy, Germany, Austria, and Spain—and the war that was required to smash fascism involved massive system-remedial implications for European colonial rule in Africa.

It was, of course, the optimistic, pragmatist facet of the young Bunche's intellectual persona that sparked his understanding that an educated African cadre under colonial rule would be a necessary feature of the emergence of endgame scenarios. Bunche observed that this development must "show a definite program for native development which will lead the native toward an ultimate specific political and social status.... The only sound objective of African colonial policies should be to prepare the Africans for membership in the community of the civilized world" (*World,* 46–47).

Accordingly, in what I call Bunche's system-remedial analytical perspective, he recognized a crucial reformist conveyor-belt role under colonial rule for the fledgling African educated class. In his dissertation, Bunche informs us that the embryonic African educated stratum that he observed during his fieldwork in West Africa in the early 1930s was composed of all notable members of the native community—chiefs, wealthy merchants, government clerks, members of [traditional] village councils of elders ("French," 96). Furthermore, the young Bunche gave French colonial rulers the edge in regard to recognizing a role for the embryonic African educated sector in a system-remedial process: "Beyond doubt, the French know the native better, they come into closer contact with native life, while the English stand aloof" (129).

In his more assertively leftist *A World View of Race,* Bunche also writes favorably (though perhaps naively) about the French cultural openness toward Negro peoples as compared to either the British or white Americans:

> There is no color line in France and none in her colonies, though individual instances of prejudice and discrimination may be encountered in both places. The French attitude is strikingly evident on the boats of the French lines. . . . Here there is to be found a genial cordiality among the French and their elite associates of the darker races. . . . The genuine warmth of the association between these groups of upper-class black and white, the apparent lack of any race consciousness on the part of either, is quite startling when contrasted with similar groups on board the English and German vessels engaged in the same [Africa] service. On the latter most of the practices of segregation and aloofness common to the United States, its attitude toward its Negro population, are in evidence. (52)

Moreover, in numerous sections of his dissertation, Bunche discusses what he viewed as extensive efforts by French colonial rulers to cultivate access for a select cadre of Africans to posts in the governing regime. These posts included seats on municipal councils and on functional commissions, such as water commissions, school boards, and sanitation boards. Bunche also identified what he called "subaltern positions" in central government departments, representation in decision-making colonial assemblies, and even a few top-level positions in Paris relating to French colonial rule.[5]

MARTIN KILSON

Aspects of Bunche's Discourse on Endgame Scenarios

Throughout his writings on African affairs in the 1930s, the young Bunche was of several minds in regard to the role of the African educated elite in transforming colonial rule. In his dissertation, he writes, "The formation of the [African educated] elites is at once the most cardinal and the most debatable point in the present French policy.... The members of this elite above all others are to be bound to the French state and, through absorption of French culture, will become assimilés [assimilated]" (96).

Put another way, while on the one hand Bunche's pragmatist mindset led him to recognize the system-remedial role that the embryonic African educated stratum could play under colonial rule, on the other hand his leftist mindset would not let him be uncritical about this important issue. Indeed, Bunche even speculates that "the presence of an elite group in the native community ... may be a condition viciously inimical to the best interests of the [African] masses" ("French," 97).

The young Bunche's dilemma in regard to the potential system-remedial role of the embryonic African educated elite became a testy issue in his dissertation. Referring to an anxiety on his part about "the [educated] elite native [becoming] a black Frenchman" (98), Bunche enters a delicate discussion of a leading highly educated Senegalese who functioned as a provincial administrator and in Paris as undersecretary for the colonies. That Senegalese was the famous Blaise Diagne. Bunche was disdainful about what he viewed as Diagne's hedonistic display of the wealth and influence he derived from his connection to French colonial rule. (Such display marks an African predatory-elite pattern whereby political power and wealth expansion are intertwined, a situation that has tragically plagued African ruling elites during the past forty years of independent African nation states). From the vantage point of his leftist mindset, the young Bunche reflected harshly on Diagne's career as a top-level Senegalese administrator under French colonial rule: "It is a matter of serious doubt that the celebrated Senegalese Diagne now has much honest concern with things African extending beyond the African bric-a-brac of his elaborate and ornate Paris apartment. Already many of his native constituents have hurled the epithet 'traitor' at him" ("French," 131ff.).[6]

I myself have been intellectually sympathetic to the crucial analytical role played by the young Bunche's leftist mindset in tilting

Bunche toward the negative features of his keen pragmatist recognition that by the 1930s European colonial rule in Africa required the preparation of endgame scenarios. It was, I suggest, this leftist facet of Bunche's analysis of European colonial rule in Africa that led him to emphasize the crucial importance for future independent African nation states of autonomous African elites, or what today, in the era of the postindependent African state, we would refer to as non-neocolonialized African elites.

I consider it fascinating that the young Ralph Bunche had the kind of keen and deep perceptiveness about the cross-cultural interplay of the corrupt, underside values and patterns among European elites on the one hand and the embryonic modern African educated elite on the other. Bunche was also keenly perceptive about modernizing development patterns in colonial African countries that would assist what might be called the corporateness of the African educated elite. That is, modernizing elements would minimize the dysfunctional impact of deep-rooted fissiparous cultural and ethnic forces among the emergent African-educated elite—fissiparous forces that we know today, nearly a half century after decolonization in Africa, have contributed tragically to too many "failed states" in Africa. As Bunche puts it in his dissertation, "Tribal lines are being cut across as a result of improved means of communication and travel, and tribal authority has been broken down deliberately by the French. This may prove to be a blessing in disguise to the native, however, for it will make it possible for him to ultimately present a united front in his demands for an increasing share in the control of his own country. This he could not do so long as tribal rivalries, jealousies, and isolation persisted" (422).

In these perceptive and profound formulations on the possible impact of modernizing elements under colonial rule on future independent African countries, the young Bunche shrewdly anticipated by thirty years Karl Deutsch's famous social-mobilization thesis for explaining post–World War II nationalist movements in the non-Western world.[7] In 1936 Bunche also anticipated Immanuel Wallerstein's famous capitalist world-system analysis: "The African native today is comparable with the peasants and workmen of England and France of a century ago, and with other workers and peasants today in less advanced countries of the modern world."[8]

Finally, in one observation on the keen analytical perception exhibited in the young Ralph Bunche's writings on colonial rule in Africa, I take issue with him. At the end of what I term Bunche's endgame-scenario analysis of colonial rule in Africa, he clearly anticipated the post–World War II African nationalist movements, although to my knowledge he never actually penned the words *nationalist movement*. However, toward the end of his 1934 PhD dissertation, Bunche is fully aware of what he calls variously "troublesome" movements and "weapons of effective resistance": "The [colonial state] cannot limit the experience and sophistication which inevitably come to the native along with the exploitative forces of Western civilization; these lead him to desire independence and self-assertion, making him 'troublesome' to the [colonial] administrators.... [Educated Africans] have news of the powerful weapons of effective resistance to abuses, employed by the oppressed in the Western world" (421).

Among the "powerful weapons ... of resistance" Bunche refers to in his dissertation, he mentions "the boycott" and "the general strike," all of which, he suggests, could be aggregated through "a strong movement of passive resistance [that] could make the white man's presence in West Africa futile" (423). Of course, it was precisely this transnational flow of rebellious political ideas and methods that in the post–World War II era proved fundamental to the continentwide upheaval of African nationalism.

Interestingly, while toward the end of *A World View of Race* the young Bunche refers to the "Pan-African nationalists," he does so in a snide manner. Bunche entertained a gut-level antipathy to this mode of educated African leadership political mobilization against colonial rule. He considered the "Pan-African nationalism" methodology rooted in dysfunctional manipulation of ethnic and racial patterns. Accordingly, the young Bunche was downright contemptuous of the educated African leadership associated with "Pan-African nationalism": "There are those, like the Pan-African nationalists, who feel that the darker peoples of the world must band together and gird their black and yellow loins for the oncoming world conflict between the races. The stakes in this little fracas are supposed to be world supremacy" (*World*, 92).

Shaped by his bourgeois-pragmatist mindset, Bunche's put-down perspective toward Pan-African nationalists was off the mark and overly dogmatic. In fact, Bunche exaggerated and distorted the character and purposes of the Pan-Africanist sector among the emergent African educated leadership, and as far as I can determine he never produced the names of specific personalities who propagated what he viewed as a hyperxenophobic Pan-Africanist discourse.

Formulators of Pan-Africanist discourse in anglophone colonial Africa such as the brilliant Fanti barrister J. E. Casely Hayford in the Gold Coast—now Ghana—who helped found the National Congress of British West Africa in the early 1920s, were decidedly not purveyors of xenophobic or race-chauvinist nationalism.[9] Hayford's nonxenophobic or pluralistic approach to Pan-Africanist discourse is apparent in his seminal contribution to this discourse—*Ethiopia Unbound: Studies in Race Emancipation* (1911), which presumably the young Ralph Bunche didn't consult. Nor were contributors to Pan-Africanist discourse among the early twentieth-century educated African stratum in South Africa who organized the African National Congress, purveyors of xenophobic or race-chauvinist nationalism.[10]

In short, the young Ralph Bunche failed to understand that while no doubt a potential existed among the emergent African educated leadership for hyperxenophobic uses of Pan-Africanist discourse (as, say, in the hands of President Robert Mugabe in the postcolonial Republic of Zimbabwe), a potential also existed for systemically functional applications of Pan-Africanist discourse. This was the case in the 1920s to 1940s with the Gold Coast's and Nigeria's National Congress of British West Africa, and also with Ghana's first president, Kwame Nkrumah. It was similarly the case with the African National Congress in the Republic of South Africa, especially in the postcolonial government fashioned by its first African president, Nelson Mandela.

Put another way, the young Ralph Bunche's put-down perspective toward Pan-Africanism as an anticolonial mobilization methodology was misguided. He failed to grasp the valid nonxenophobic political mobilization role of Pan-Africanist discourse, or what I sometimes call black-peoplehood mobilization discourse in the African colonial situation. Bunche's preference for a kind of hyperpragmatic rationalism on the part of the emergent educated African power contenders under colonial rule was a version of wide-eyed idealism too removed from the oppressive specificity of the imperialist process in many parts of Africa.

Be that as it may, Bunche's particular critique of the Pan-Africanist anticolonial mobilization methodology was a minor analytical weakness in his brilliant dissection of the intricately dialectical character of colonial rule in late-nineteenth- and early-twentieth-century Africa. The young Ralph Bunche's Harvard dissertation was a remarkable analytical achievement. It exhibited his incredibly unique skill at conceptually intertwining the leftist mindset and the bourgeois-pragmatist mindset that constituted his intellectual persona. Above all, a keenly humanitarian and egalitarian worldview was fundamental to the young Ralph Bunche's masterful analytical contributions to social science knowledge of colonial rule in Africa.

Notes

This chapter is taken from the keynote address for the UCLA Globalization Research Center–Africa conference commemorating the centenary of the birth of Ralph J. Bunche.

1. W. E. B. DuBois, *The Souls of Black Folk* (Chicago: A. C. McClurg, 1903), 54–55.

2. See Martin Kilson, "John Aubrey Davis: Black Intellectual as Activist and Technocrat," chap. 11 of *The Making of Black Intellectuals: Studies on the African-American Intelligentsia* (forthcoming).

3. Ralph J. Bunche, *A World View of Race* (Washington, DC: Associates in Negro Folk Education, 1936), 1. Hereafter cited in text as *World*.

4. Ralph J. Bunche, "French Administration in Togoland and Dahomey" (PhD diss., Harvard University, 1934), 2. Hereafter cited in text as "French."

5. Bunche treats attributes of the emergent African educated elite stratum in the following sections of his 1930s writings: "French," 95ff., 103ff., 318ff., 388ff.; *World,* 46–49, 50–56, 57–65.

6. See also 95–105.

7. Karl Deutsch, *Nationalism and Social Communication: An Inquiry into the Foundations of Nationality* (Cambridge: MIT Press, 1953).

8. Bunche, *World View,* 63. See Wallerstein's analysis in *The Political Economy of Contemporary Africa,* ed. Peter Gutkind and Immanuel Wallerstein (Beverly Hills: Sage Publications, 1986).

9. I probe this development in Martin Kilson, "The National Congress of British West Africa," in *Protest and Power in Black Africa,* ed. Robert Rotberg and Ali Mazrui (New York: Oxford University Press, 1970).

10. For a contemporary variant of the young Bunche's view of Pan-Africanist or black-peoplehood political mobilization by a black analyst, see K. A. Appiah, *In My Father's House: Africa in the Philosophy of Culture* (New York: Oxford University Press, 1992), chap. 1, "Invention of Africa," chap. 2, "Illusions of Race." I present a critique of Appiah in *The Transformation of Black American Intellectuals* (forthcoming). A version of this critique will appear in a forthcoming issue of *The Black Scholar,* "The Black Rejectionist Intellectual: Critique of K. A. Appiah's *In My Father's House.*"

CHAPTER TWO

Ralph Bunche and the Dawn of Africanist Scholarship

DAVID ANTHONY

THE ACHIEVEMENTS of Ralph Johnson Bunche can scarcely be contained within the covers of the volumes that have sought to treat his life and work. Bunche occupied several divergent realms at once, as a scholar of modern social thought, movements, and change, all of which drew him to late-colonial Africa. Experience gained through two periods of fieldwork, one in eastern Africa and another in southern Africa, helped give texture to a nascent discipline. He would be neither the first nor the last scion of the African diaspora to contribute keenly to this intellectual endeavor. Even as his world was fraught with profound contradictions, it was also a world in which identities and relationships, especially between Old and New World Africans, wrestled with institutional ignorance, neglect, and invisibility. Bunche became among the first Africa scholars whose own ability to straddle these continents, crossing water in his own right, helped to solidify a field.

The Accidental Africanist

Bunche was steered into African studies by Edwin R. Embree of the Rosenwald Fund in 1932 to prevent him from pursuing a potentially radical study comparing racial mixing in Brazil and the United States with a view toward understanding differences between two groups of African-derived peoples.[1] Instead, Bunche viewed two French-run territories, ex–German League of Nations mandate Togoland (now Togo) and nearby colony Dahomey (now Benin), balancing a trio of months in repositories in Britain, France, and Switzerland with an equivalent time in each dependency, preparing a dissertation for Harvard in 1934.[2]

Edgar reminds us that Bunche then taught and chaired political science at Howard University during the 1933–34 academic year beside such faculty luminaries as Abram L. Harris, E. Franklin Frazier, Doxey Wilkerson, William Alphaeus Hunton, and Sterling Brown, for a time sharing the left-wing proclivities of several members of that group. Absorbed in 1935 by the Joint Committee on National Recovery, which led in 1936 to the founding of the National Negro Congress, Bunche resumed his Africanist career in the spring of that year by organizing a conference, "The Modern Crisis of Imperialism and the Far East," and publishing a string of articles based on his West African work. As was true of his predecessor and one of the unsung founders of African studies, W. E. B. DuBois, Bunche's writings also reflected contemporary knowledge in colonial political economy, yielding a sophisticated critique of the bankruptcy of colonial capitalism.

Again intending to undertake research tackling African oppression at its root, Bunche was led in a somewhat different direction, this time by Donald Young of the Social Science Research Council, who structured another comparative project that included apprenticeships with Melville Herskovits at Northwestern University, Bronislaw Malinowski at the London School of Economics (LSE), and Isaac Schapera at the University of Cape Town. Edgar indicates that Bunche held his own in each of these encounters, not being shy about areas of disagreement with these mentors.[3] A larger point here is that by the late thirties, Bunche, already distinguished as a leading Africanist, increased his expertise through further fieldwork in eastern and southern Africa.

Fieldwork

A core value for Africanism or African studies as a discipline was collecting field data pioneered by anthropology. Such data differentiated between evidence mined strictly in archives and scholarship largely derived from primary and secondary research by others. Anticipating by a full three decades cleavages distinguishing rival British and American schools of Africanist history, manifested in reliance on archival research in the former and a mix of library work and field interviews in the latter, again Bunche showed in his eastern and southern African studies the need for familiarization with the milieu under investigation, for which other than in-country residence there could be no real substitute. Indeed this is one of the great lessons provided by his field notes, which, as Bob Edgar has shown, also provided a window into South African "non-European" politics in 1937.

In sum, an integral characteristic of the field approach to the study of Africa later popularized in the 1960s and 1970s in African studies programs at the University of Wisconsin and UCLA, grounded in anthropological methods, therefore, had already been honed if not to perfection then certainly to a high level of sophistication by Bunche. Here it is apposite to mention another neglected example of interwar era Africanist scholarship done by an African diasporic intellectual, Eslanda Goode Robeson, also studying at the LSE, who produced the brilliant eastern and southern African memoir *African Journey*.[4] From a methodological standpoint, much distinguished Bunche's tack from that associated with the questionnaire-and-script social science style. Bunche depended on systematic analyses utilizing an unusually wide range of informants with whom he spent hours in both formal and informal sessions of participant observation.

Africa for the Africans

Bunche's findings led him in more than one direction. An intellectual of breadth and depth, he nevertheless was also politically engaged. Even though certain features of that engagement were to change with time, most notably the appeal held for him by the orthodox left, the sense of commitment to social change remained a consistent feature of his life. He took this along as a core element in problem solving in the United Nations. At an early stage in his Africanist career, indeed while still a grad student, he was already clear about the fragility of the colonial role and the inevitability of its eventual demise. While this did not make him a Garveyite, it certainly crystallized his belief in self-determination far beyond the rhetorical niceties of the Woodrow Wilsonian dodge deemed inapplicable to "the darker races" in the aftermath of World War I. By contrast, Bunche and many other diaspora intellectuals familiar with *la gabegie coloniale* (the colonial mess) knew its days were numbered. This belief in self-determination distinguishes him among Africanists, many of whom then and later kept their distance from taking stands deemed harmful to their objectivity. Even though, like many diasporic scholars, he was himself a product of his era and upbringing and thus not immune from the distortions of Africa and Africans prevalent in his day (or ours, for that matter), he did his best to transcend them by seeking identification with the masses, their educated-elite vanguard, and progressive sectors of opinion among whites. These associations convinced him that colonialism was a system whose days were numbered.

Africanism for the Africanists

It is also clear that at a particular moment in his life Bunche was susceptible to influence from organizations whose objectives included reforming and democratizing Europe's hold on its imperial and colonial possessions. One such example was that of the International Committee on African Affairs (ICAA), founded in 1937 in New York and London by Max Yergan and Paul Robeson, in which Bunche was one of several intellectuals with African experience co-opted by Yergan, a former YMCA missionary to South Africa, and Robeson, then living in London and in touch with several continental African and Afro-Caribbean intellectuals then residing in the seat of the British Empire. While this organization eventually ceased to be of interest to Bunche for its association with what in Britain was termed the hard left—especially after 1940, when Yergan became the second president of the National Negro Congress in what was widely seen, not least of all by Bunche himself, who witnessed and documented it, as a coup against A. Philip Randolph—his initial involvement in it was motivated by a desire not only to understand the world, but to change it.[5]

In this regard Bunche's decision to become an international civil servant rather than a full-time professional Africanist intellectual deserves attention on its own. It may even relate at least to the aspiration of the Council on African Affairs (as the ICAA came to be known in 1940) to move U.S. foreign policy regarding Africa in a more favorable direction. Whatever reservations he held about the CAA (motivated primarily by his suspicion that its independence had been compromised by the presence within its leadership of people closely affiliated, formally, informally, or both, to the Communist Party), both career options had in common the desire not only to comprehend reality but to change it. Bunche's grasp of that reality was of great appeal to Yergan and Robeson, as they sought to cultivate him for membership and participation in the council. Bunche, however, had bigger fish to fry, electing to go to the head of the class, making change from within the establishment, taking his expertise with him.

As long ago as "the Year of Africa," 1960, George Shepperson recognized the African American contribution to African studies. In an article surveying the historical links between certain key individual Afro-Caribbean and black American intellectuals with long-standing African interests, he disclosed the existence of a hidden history of African partisanship, engagement, and advocacy involving a remarkably wide array of actors. As we revise and broaden that list of influential persons representing what has sometimes been called the African interest, it seems critical to find space for Ralph J. Bunche, the Africanist. Although this never became his full-time activity, his contributions to the field were of considerable importance. Though trained as a political scientist, Bunche's work is still profitable reading, not only for historians and social scientists such as sociologists and anthropologists, but also for jurists, lawyers, and legal scholars.

Moreover, Bunche's association with the leading Africanist intellectuals of his time involved a cross-fertilization of ideas, not only on the individual level but also in both collective and institutional terms, for these ideas filtered back into other research designs contemplated and later executed by other scholars undertaking similar field projects. Further, in both the classroom and as an academic and subsequently as a governmental and UN mentor to scores of students and disciples, Bunche was able to transmit not only a body of knowledge accumulated within his studies but also ways of looking at international social problems, influenced to some degree by his Africanist training and field research. It is fitting, therefore, to consider what Ralph Bunche gained from and gave back to the world of African studies, adding to a well from which we all draw.

Notes

In this chapter I am representing my own perspective and research design, but my work here is also part of a book being prepared for Ohio University Press and coedited by Robert Edgar, Robert Trent Vinson, and myself called *Crossing the Water: African American Historical Linkages with South Africa.*

1. Ralph J. Bunche, *An African American in South Africa: The Travel Notes of Ralph J. Bunche, 28 September 1937–1 January 1938,* ed. Robert R. Edgar (Athens: Ohio University Press, 1992), 5.

2. Ibid., 5–6.

3. Ibid., 12–14.

4. Eslanda Goode Robeson, *African Journey* (New York: John Day, 1945).

5. Here I am paraphrasing Karl Marx on philosophers (in his second thesis on Feuerbach).

CHAPTER THREE

The Making of an Africanist
Ralph Bunche in South Africa, 1937

ROBERT EDGAR

> One can do "placer" field-work here, just run a bit of water over the surface and the material pops out at you.
>
> —Ralph Bunche to Melville Herskovits, while traveling through South Africa in November 1937

ONE OF a handful of American academics, white or black, interested in African issues before World War II, Ralph Bunche stood out because he actually conducted research in Africa on several occasions: first, in West Africa for three months for his Harvard doctorate in 1932, and then in South Africa and East Africa in late 1937 and the first half of 1938 while learning anthropological field methods. This chapter examines one phase of Bunche's maturation as an Africanist and social scientist—his extraordinary experiences and insightful observations on race and segregation in South Africa.

Bunche's initial exposure to Africa came through his dissertation research, in which he compared the impact of French colonial administration on Africans in Dahomey, a colony directly under French rule, and Togoland, a French-administered territory under a League of Nations mandate. After becoming the first African American to receive a doctorate in political science (1934) and returning to Howard University to resume chairing its department of political science, he concentrated his scholarship on American and African American politics. However, he kept up his interest in global and African issues. In 1936 he organized a major conference at Howard, "The Crisis of Modern Imperialism in Africa and the Far East," and he published a provocative booklet, *A World View of Race,* that pinpointed global capitalism as the driving force behind the European conquest of Africa.

Excited by his first bout of research in Africa, he also began seeking backing for a return visit. This time Bunche planned to turn his dissertation study on its head and examine the impact of colonial rule and Western culture on Africans from the ground up, that is, from the perspective of Africans. One person he approached, with the assistance of Melville Herskovits, was Donald Young, the secretary for fellowships at the Social Science Research Council (SSRC), who explained that the council's priority was not to conduct primary research but to build up researchers' methodological skills.[1] Instead, he recommended that Bunche take up a two-year fellowship that would give him training in anthropological field methods with three eminent practitioners—Herskovits at Northwestern University, Bronislaw Malinowski at the London School of Economics, and Isaac Schapera at the University of Cape Town—and acquire on-the-ground training in anthropological fieldwork methods in South Africa and East Africa.[2] He would then have the opportunity to study colonial and European rule in South Africa, East Africa, and Indonesia.

Bunche had commented positively in his dissertation about the contributions social anthropology could make to research in Africa, so it was not a stretch for him to shift his focus and frame his study in the prevailing academic jargon of his time. He proposed to investigate "the *effect* of imperial rule on retarded people." Bunche's use of *retarded people* is striking, given his reputation as a radical analyst, but he was prepared to tailor his grant application to meet Young's terms. Bunche was a pragmatist when necessary. Since he was seeking a respite from his heavy teaching and administrative responsibilities at Howard, he understood, based on his experiences with foundation officials during his dissertation research, how to accommodate their agendas. And he was not about to insist on his own research project if it meant losing a two-year grant. In public Bunche was a model of tact and cooperation when dealing with the gatekeepers at foundations. However, in private his comments were biting. He sarcastically reflected on the profiles of the few black men who were in a position to take a round-the-world trip—a valet, a mechanic or stoker on a ship, a slave, a delegate to a missionary or YMCA conference (most likely in India), and in Bunche's case, a foundation "fellow." And he mused that "the philanthropist who set up the foundation might turn in his grave if he knew that a 'nigger' was traveling on his money."[3]

Although Young steered Bunche's study in a different direction than he desired, he may have done Bunche a favor in the long run by giving him intimate, firsthand experience in different regions of Africa that few other American academics would have until the late 1950s and 1960s, when African studies took off in the United States.

London

After spending a semester with Herskovits at Northwestern University, Bunche and his family arrived in London in early 1937. Besides participating in Malinowski's legendary seminar, he sought out prominent members of London's small black activist community, Essie and Paul Robeson, George Padmore (whom Bunche had taught at Howard), T. Ras Makonnen, C. L. R. James, Jomo Kenyatta (Bunche's Swahili tutor), Eric Williams, and I. T. A. Wallace-Johnson. Bunche engaged in extensive discussions with them on Pan-Africanism (which Bunche had severe reservations about) and colonial rule in Africa, and attended meetings and rallies on the Spanish civil war and protesting the Italian invasion of Ethiopia. Bunche had actively participated in a committee supporting the defense of Ethiopia on the Howard campus, and he considered but decided against taking a side trip to Ethiopia after realizing how dangerous it would be.[4]

Bunche's stay in London coincided with the coronation of King George VI following the shocking abdication of his brother Edward VIII in late 1936. Reporting on the events to Howard's president, Mordecai Johnson, Bunche commented incisively on the British government's calculated orchestration of the celebrations. The coronation came at a time when Stanley Baldwin's Unionist government was on the defensive because of disruptions to London's bus service and the threat of a nationwide coal strike and the lessening of the British Empire's prestige because of the Italian invasion of Ethiopia, the Spanish civil war, and the ascendancy of the fascist regimes in Italy and Germany. The British government seized the occasion by carefully scripting a patriotic pageant that silenced even its most vocal domestic critics. Through the "stage-props of pageantry, wealth, military might and glamour," the script called for an imperial makeover of the new king, whom Bunche considered to be "singularly lacking in personality and popular appeal," transforming him into a "super-man."[5] Indeed so much funding was devoted to the spectacle that Bunche believed the expenses rivaled, if not exceeded, those of the celebrations surrounding Queen Victoria's Golden Jubilee.

The highlight was the coronation parade, which provided Bunche with a window into the rituals of empire. Bunche and his wife landed seats in front of Buckingham Palace with a bird's-eye view of a procession that showcased the mystical ties that bound the empire together.

> The vast power of the Empire was amply demonstrated and every Englishman burst his waistcoat buttons with pride. There were many black troops too—a flashing, brilliant Indian contingent, another from Burma, and a small body of fez-topped, sandaled Africans. There could be no question but that this must have been adequately impressive to the petty rulers of the great dark populations of the Empire—the rajahs, the sultans and the African chiefs and kings—who came to pay homage to their sovereign and incidentally to get an eyeful of the military power which is wielded in his name.[6]

The unity of the empire had limits, though. Bunche contrasted the experiences of the white troops from the dominions, who were given free rein to go wherever they wanted, and the black soldiers from the colonies, who were carefully monitored and not allowed to roam freely. At a reception for Indian troops, a British commander even issued an order forbidding women from attending.[7]

Preparing for his South African trip, Bunche consulted a range of people who advised him on whom to see and what to visit in South Africa. Max Yergan, a YMCA missionary in South Africa from 1921 to 1936, and Essie Robeson, Paul Robeson's wife and an anthropologist who briefly visited South Africa in 1936, were two African Americans with firsthand experience on how to navigate South Africa. Jack Simons and Julius Lewin, two graduate students at the London School of Economics, William Macmillan, a historian who had taught at Witwatersrand University, in Johannesburg, and Leonard Barnes, an ardent anticolonial critic, also provided contacts. Hence, when Bunche landed in Cape Town in September 1937, he had easy entry into a world of liberal and left-of-center blacks and whites wherever he moved in the country.[8]

Although armed with a network of contacts, Bunche still had to negotiate an entry permit to land in Cape Town from South African embassy staff in London. The South African government had long held reservations about allowing African Americans to enter the country freely and thus carefully scrutinized Bunche. After behind-the-scenes interventions from people like Schapera and Jan Hofmeyr, the South African minister of the interior finally secured him a permit, and embassy officials enjoined him not to give speeches or indulge in political activities while he was traveling around South Africa.

Bunche also received advice, especially from "kindly disposed" liberal white South Africans, on how to act when he was in South Africa. They instructed Bunche, according to notes he titled a "Black Man's Guide," "If you are 'tactful,' you'll get along all right." "That is your cue," he would respond, "to win enthusiastic approbation by saying: 'All one needs is a sense of humor'—that's your great shot." He added: "You will unquestionably be told by those more sophisticated whites that Aggrey was a grand fellow—he knew how to get along in Africa—so read about Aggrey."[9] His reference to James E. K. Aggrey is meaningful because when the Ghanaian-born educator had traveled through South Africa in 1921, preaching racial cooperation as part of a Phelps-Stokes study commission on African education, he became the standard for how a black professional should properly act. One could receive no greater accolade in white liberal circles than that one acted in the manner of Aggrey.

South Africa

After arriving in Cape Town in late September, Bunche began thinking through what exactly he would do for the next three months in South Africa. He was attracted to the idea of studying the racial parallels between the United States and South Africa, but after meeting Schapera and discussing how he could most profitably spend his time, they agreed that he should carry out "an investigation of the status and problems of the South African non-European peoples under current South African governmental policies."[10] Hence, Bunche was given license to roam about South Africa looking at "problems, institutions, organizations, attitudes and reactions of the non-European groups—natives, Colored and Asiatic."[11]

Based on his experiences with American segregation and racism, Bunche had an instinctive feel for South African society and its racial complexities. Soon after he embarked from his boat in Cape Town, he noted "Negroes so mixed up here the place looks like Harlem."[12] He also observed the affinities between South African and American segregation. He related to Herskovits, "The Jim Crow set-up is quite familiar to me, of course, I get nostalgic every time I see a sign 'For Europeans Only.'"[13] He recognized the same kinds of racial attitudes and stereotypes that whites held of black people (that they were happy, childlike primitives), that blacks carried the white man's economic burden, whether in the cotton fields of the American South or the gold mines of South Africa, and that antagonisms between groups of whites—Yankees and Southerners and Afrikaners and English—influenced the brands of racism that they practiced. He took note of an escape psychology among African Americans and South African Coloureds that manifested itself in a preoccupation with skin color differentiation within their own groups. However, he asserted that there was a basic and ultimately a decisive difference—that blacks were a numerical majority in South Africa and that inevitably meant they would ultimately come out on top, but the white's minority status meant that they would develop a psychosis that would make them hysterically fearful of giving up power. Bunche also concluded that for all of America's Jim Crow laws, South Africa was a far worse society for black people: "South Africa is an entire country ridden by race prejudice—unlike U.S. in that there is no escape at all for these black and colored people."[14]

Bunche's rich observations on South African segregation covered an array of issues: government policy toward Africans, race relations, black living conditions in the African rural reserves, mines, and townships, African political and trade union leaders and organizations, health and mental care, sports and music, social life, business, education, religion, and the legal system. He provided perceptive and acerbic insights on the nature of racial oppression and the absurdities of the system. Noticing a white policeman throwing a discus at an athletic field and a black prisoner fetching it, Bunche acidly commented, "South Africa is a good place for white men. Africans do everything but move their bowels for them."[15] He was especially scathing when commenting on South Africa's official policy of "civilized labor," a South African version of affirmative action with a vengeance that guaranteed government jobs for low-income whites. He was told about a situation where white laborers on a road crew under "civilized labor" devoted part of their wages to hiring much cheaper black workers to do their jobs.[16]

Although a rigid racial caste system was well entrenched in South Africa, Bunche acknowledged ambiguities in segregation. Meeting with James Moroka and Silas Molema, two of a handful of African medical doctors, at their practices in rural communities, he learned that both had white patients who made discrete visits to consult them on sensitive issues such as venereal disease and abortions that they could not raise with European doctors. Moroka even placed labels without his name on prescription bottles so his patients could not be linked to him.[17] Despite having white patients and owning a nursing home and a surgery in Mafeking, Molema was still not allowed to live in town.

Bunche also learned that many South African blacks admired the accomplishments of African Americans, whom they regarded as "paragons of virtue" in the face of racism, a blueprint for how South African blacks could advance in a white-dominated world. The industrial-education philosophy of Booker T. Washington attracted a large following in both black and white South African educational circles, while the message of Jamaican-born Marcus Garvey and the Universal Negro Improvement Association resonated with many Africans in the rural reserves. Many South African blacks closely followed the accomplishments of African American sportsmen and entertainers such as Joe Louis, Henry Armstrong, Jesse Owens, Duke Ellington, Fats Waller, and Paul Robeson. Bunche wrote to Robeson, "Paul, you surely are an idol of the Bantu [Africans] . . . when one mentions American Negroes they all chorus 'Paul Robeson and Joe Louis.' . . . The rumor still persists that you are coming down to the Union soon; if you do the black folk will mob you with enthusiasm."[18]

Although Bunche had given his word not to make public speeches in South Africa, he regarded blacks in South Africa as so demoralized that he felt compelled to give a series of impromptu pep talks to black groups highlighting the advances made by African American professionals as civil servants, judges, lawyers, scientists, educators, and businessmen in the face of discriminatory barriers. Although he likely was not conscious of it, Bunche's message of uplift and progress echoed African American AME and Baptist missionaries who had given speeches in the same vein to black South African audiences for many decades. Both black South Africans and African Americans subscribed to the image of the African American as an exemplar of modernity.[19] Hence Bunche came to the realization that "every black American in South Africa is a missionary whether or not he willed it." Since he was not a person of faith, he added, "But he doesn't have to be a *religious* missionary."[20]

Bunche's most penetrating observations were about the state of black politics in South Africa. His visit came at a time when black South African politics was undergoing a crisis prompted by the passage in 1936 of several bills that Prime Minister J. B. M. Hertzog and his National Party had been lobbying for since the mid-1920s. The Native Land and Trust Act provided for an additional 6 percent of South Africa's land to be gradually added to the approximately 7 percent already set aside for rural African reserves. The Representation of Natives Act abolished the qualified franchise for African male voters in the Cape Province. Since the Cape African vote was one of the protected clauses in the 1910 constitution, it took a two-thirds vote of Parliament to overturn it. Although African voters represented only 1.2 percent of all voters in the country, they were an important factor in half a dozen Eastern Cape constituencies and could tip the balance in close national elections. Since they usually voted for Hertzog's principal rival, the South Africa Party, he was anxious to get rid of the African vote. He finally secured the necessary majority in Parliament when the National and South Africa parties merged in 1934 to form the United Party.

To soften the impact of the abolition of the African vote, the act provided for several alternative ways of conveying African opinion to the government. The first was the creation of European "native representatives" in Parliament—three in the House of Assembly directly elected by Cape African voters and four in the Senate indirectly elected nationally—who were supposed to voice African perspectives and views in Parliament. The second was the establishment of a Native Representative Council (NRC) made up of indirectly elected and appointed delegates that met annually to deliberate on so-called native affairs issues and to pass on recommendations to government representatives.[21]

The prospect that the Hertzog bills might be passed provoked and unified black opinion in a way that few other issues had done since 1910. In 1935 delegates representing black organizations from all over the country converged on Bloemfontein to rally against the Hertzog bills. This conference saw the establishment of the All African Convention (AAC), and its founders were optimistic that they could sustain the energy and revitalize black politics that had largely lost their direction in the 1930s. In particular the ANC president Pixley Seme regarded mass protest with deep suspicion.[22]

Bunche attended the opening sessions of the NRC in the fittingly named Pretorius Hall at Pretoria's city hall.[23] The NRC was composed of a mix of appointed European officials who were involved in the administration of native affairs as well as appointed and indirectly elected African members. Some elected members such as R. V. Selope Thema, Alexander Jabavu, Richard Godlo, C. K. Sakwe, T. M. Mapikela, and John Dube were already well-known figures in black political movements and gave the NRC a measure of credibility. The NRC was supposed to serve as a conduit for channeling African views and feelings on native affairs to the government. However, it was clear to Bunche and other critical observers that the government, through the NRC's chair, Douglas Smit, carefully scripted the NRC's deliberations. The opening statements by European officials and African representatives were ritualistic expressions of faith in the work of the Native Affairs Department and fealty to the government. Of all the speeches Bunche took the greatest offense at, Mpondo chief Victor Poto's topped the list. Poto delivered what Bunche deemed an "asslicking" speech expressing his "shame" for the September 1937 riots in Vereeniging, in which African residents protested against police raids searching for illegal visitors and beer brewers.[24]

Smit, the secretary of native affairs, tightly controlled sessions, and Bunche wondered how the NRC, which was supposed to probe and question government policy, could be chaired by a man whose department was supposed to be under scrutiny. Although the tone and manner of officials was paternalistic, Bunche concluded that Smit's objective was to reinforce white control by wielding "steamroller" tactics to push through items on his agenda and splitting African councilors along provincial lines. The NRC's European members similarly "treat[ed] the native councilors as though they are schoolboys and talk to them sometimes patronizingly and sometimes crossly."[25] For instance, Smit pounced on several African councilors who arrived late for a session and "reprimanded ... them like domestic servants."[26] Among those scolded was Alexander Jabavu, the highly respected editor of *Imvo zabantsundu,* an Eastern Cape newspaper. Despite encouragement from one of the European native representatives, Jabavu refused to stand up to Smit. The "timidly" fashion in which NRC delegates deferred to white officials dismayed Bunche.[27]

A week later, Bunche moved on to the annual conventions of the AAC and African National Congress (ANC), held traditionally in Bloemfontein.[28] But he found the caliber of black leadership sorely lacking there, too. The AAC had steadily declined since its founding, so when Bunche arrived on the second day of the AAC conference, he found only one hundred delegates in attendance (compared to seven hundred at the conference that founded the AAC in 1935). He listened to a series of reports on African business, farm labor, education, African youth and social ills, and labor and trade unions. He noted the presence of some of the European native representatives, such as Margaret Ballinger and Carl Malcomess, who made regular interventions during deliberations. Malcomess counseled Africans to be patient with the NRC and work with the European representatives to discuss issues and "to be moderate" and keep African issues from being raised in the coming [white] elections. Bunche called Malcomess's advice the "tactics of delay."[29]

Bunche did observe a small radical faction in the AAC made up of people like Goolam and Jane Gool who contended the AAC made a grievous error by participating in the NRC elections instead of boycotting them. They maintained that the whites elected as native representatives were little more than a "sop" for government propaganda. The result was that the AAC had lost its mass support. However, conference delegates received Goolam Gool's suggestion that the AAC should lead a campaign against passing laws to reinvigorate mass support with "unreserved mirth."[30]

As the conference wound down, this small group of radicals caucused to discuss what had to be done to reinvigorate the AAC.[31] They criticized the AAC for betraying the people and its leaders for their "lack of initiative." The radicals specifically blamed the European native representatives for their attempts to keep the AAC from becoming a mass organization. Bunche drew the same conclusion based on his observations of the interventions of the European native representatives at the conferences: "The role of the European reps. [representatives] is a dangerous one—they are now counseling extreme moderation among the natives.... They can't see that anything they do of significance for the native is bound to offend the reactionaries and that it is impossible to please both sides. They lack the courage to take a strong stand."[32]

To Bunche, two occurrences at the end of the conference confirmed his view of the limitations of the AAC. One was that Jabavu, reelected over Dr. A. B. Xuma (who became the ANC's president in 1940), left the conference before it officially adjourned on the evening of December 15. The second was that AAC delegates voted for a resolution that it would not meet annually but every three years.

Bunche's estimation of black leadership did not improve with the opening of the ANC's silver jubilee conference the following day. December 16 was a special day in South Africa. In the Afrikaner community, it was commemorated as the Day of the Covenant, in remembrance of the Voortrekker defeat of Zulu King Dingane's army on December 16, 1838, at the Ncome (known to Europeans as Blood) River. Dingane's day had a completely different meaning in the African community; it was a time for honoring heroes of the resistance to European conquest and rule. Because this was the silver anniversary of the ANC's founding in January 1912, the first day of the conference was devoted to prayers of thanks, homilies by black and white clergymen and politicians, and festivities. The ANC, Bunche noted, had no money to pay for organizers but found the money to pay for the slaughter of two oxen.[33]

At that evening's ANC dance and concert, Selope Thema related a fable about an inspection tour that God took around the world. God found things working smoothly in North America and Europe, but he was taken aback at the primitiveness and lack of industriousness in Africa as black people were "singing, dancing and drinking Kaffir beer." God was so revolted by this situation that he sent white people there to put things on the right course. Bunche and Jack Simons were so appalled by Thema's story that they contributed their own versions of the fable. Bunche's version had it that God was so shocked at South Africa, a country in which blacks provided all the labor and whites made all the profits, that he exclaimed, "My God, what kind of country is this?" Bunche stressed that South Africa would be in the hands of black people if they would recognize that they "*actually* had the country back now." He counseled that it was "the duty of organizations to make them realize and employ his power."[34]

Bunche's mood did not improve on the conference's second day, which started fitfully as an organizer rummaged around for speakers while a program was slapped together. ANC officials even sent an emissary to Bunche asking him to speak, but this time he flatly refused. Despite his concern about the ANC being overly dependent on outsiders, he felt compelled to intervene at one session to restore order after a major row erupted over the Cape provincial delegation's credentials.

Bunche's appraisal of ANC leadership was scathing. He observed that they were prone to looking back on past achievements rather than addressing current issues. He was especially scornful of ANC president Pixley Seme, elegantly decked out for the opening procession in a "frock coat and white spats, a stovepipe hat, [and] morning pants."[35] One of the founders of the ANC, Seme had received his AB degree from Columbia University, where he won a prize for oratory, and had gone on to study law at Oxford University. Bunche, who noted the allegation that Seme was usually arrested for bad debts every time he showed up at one of these conferences, described Seme as "a *hesitant* speaker, without force or personality" who presided over sessions "looking scared as a rabbit."[36]

Seme's tenure as ANC president since 1930 had achieved little, so by the time of the 1937 conference, the organization was virtually moribund. Bunche picked up the growing dissatisfaction of ANC delegates with Seme's leadership. Hence, it was not surprising that Rev. Z. R. Mahabane, a former ANC president, defeated Seme's bid for reelection at the conference to a three-year term by a vote of twenty-two to nine. Seme did not dispute the outcome and was relieved that a moderate rather than a "fire-eater" was replacing him, since the ANC president would have to work cooperatively with whites.

Bunche's research notes are essential reading for anyone desiring to understand how black politics unfolded over the next several decades. Certainly his perceptive eye captured the mood of black politicians and politics at a critical juncture, as the Hertzog bills of the mid-1930s issued a challenge to black politicians either to accommodate government "native" policy by participating in the NRC or move in a radically new direction. The old guard was prone to compromise and working within the system, while others—largely from the younger generation—totally rejected government policy and began to work toward cultivating a mass organization and militantly challenging the government.

Based on Bunche's personal asides in his notes, he would have instinctively sympathized with the latter. He likely would have supported a complete boycott of government-controlled institutions for blacks, and he would have advocated a move to mass action in the form of boycotts and protests. Moreover, he was deeply suspicious of white liberals, especially European native representatives, believing they were splitting blacks and moderating their demands. These were all elements of the ideology the ANC Youth League embraced when it was founded, in 1944.

At the time of the 1937 ANC conference Bunche attended, the young men who eventually made up the Youth League, many of whom had grown up in African reserves and were moving to the Johannesburg area, had not been radicalized. For instance, one future Youth Leaguer who attended the conference was A. P. Mda.[37] Although there is no mention of the twenty-one-year-old Mda in Bunche's research notes, Mda did note the latter's presence in his conference account published in an Eastern Cape African newspaper. At this juncture Mda uncritically accepted the worldview of Cape African liberals like his father, Charles, a government-appointed headman who had the right to vote and believed in bringing about change through working within the system. Hence, A. P. did not share Bunche's critical assessment of Jabavu and the AAC. Mda was still enamored of how the "Giant Congress" of 1935, which established the AAC, had unified black people and fostered a oneness of spirit. Although he rejected the idea that the AAC should take a backseat to the ANC because it was the senior organization, he regarded the Hertzog legislation as a rude rebuke to Africans that had shut the door on their aspirations to citizenship and equality.

After moving to the Johannesburg area several years later, Mda began critically examining his previous views and shifting to a position in which African political organizations operated on their own and shunned alliances with non-African groups. Mda's answer was for African leaders to close ranks around the banner of African nationalism. He joined others, such as Anton Lembede, Nelson Mandela, Oliver Tambo, and Walter Sisulu, who shared his vision of African nationalism when they founded the ANC Youth League in 1944. The Youth League's manifesto contained a scathing indictment of the compact that black and white leaders had maintained for decades. The underlying principle was trusteeship, the idea that whites had a god-given role to rule over their black wards and slowly advance them along the path of civilization. The dilemma was that even though leaders of organizations like the ANC criticized discriminatory laws and policies, they had become locked into accommodating whites through institutions like the NRC. Even though they used the NRC as a forum for criticizing government policy, they were distancing themselves from popular sentiments and were "suspicious of progressive thought and action." They had become "gentlemen with clean hands,"[38] more concerned about losing their few privileges than with organizing the black masses and leading a frontal assault on the edifices of white power.

The Youth League's goal was to transform the parent ANC into an organization that worked to the advantage of Africans through their own efforts and not with the assistance or collaboration of outsiders—either well-meaning whites or members of Coloured or Indian organizations. They promoted the boycott of the NRC and advisory boards in urban black townships. They advocated that the ANC align itself with popular protest and work to create a mass organization. The ANC's senior leaders effectively stymied the Youth League's agenda until the National Party took over the reins of government in 1948 and began implementing its apartheid policies. The tightening of racial oppression gave the Youth League the opening it needed to press the ANC to adopt the Program of Action at its 1949 conference.

While Bunche likely would have agreed with the Youth League's analysis of the ANC and their calls for mass action, he would have differed with them on how they defined African nationalism. Bunche took a dim view of a narrow African nationalism that excluded Coloureds and Indians from participating in their movement. He had observed the tensions between Africans and Coloureds and Indians at the 1937 conference when a proposal to open up the AAC to all "non-European" groups had been put forward. Some delegates expressed their misgivings about adopting that resolution and initially defeated it. He labeled their efforts "a grave mistake and a victory for bigoted, black chauvinism which played directly into the hands of the divisive policy of the government."[39]

―❧―

After leaving South Africa in January 1938, Bunche spent the next five months studying chieftainship and the British policy of indirect rule in East Africa.[40] He then journeyed through Asia to study Dutch colonial rule in Indonesia before finally returning to the United States in late 1938. He resumed teaching at Howard and successfully applied for a fellowship to write up his South African notes for a proposed book, "An Analysis of the Political, Economic, and Social Status of the Non-European Peoples in South Africa." However, administrative and teaching duties consumed much of his time at Howard, and before he could begin drafting his South African study he was invited in early 1939 to prepare extensive essays assessing the state of African American politics for Swedish economist Gunnar Myrdal, who was preparing to research what became his monumental study, *An American Dilemma*.

Although Bunche never returned to his study of South Africa, he continued to be involved with South Africans and South African issues. Working for the Office of Strategic Services during the Second World War, he maintained communication with some of the South Africans he had met in 1937. After the war, he invited Julius Lewin to join him for a year at the United Nations Trusteeship Council. In 1952–53, Z. K. Matthews, a leader of the ANC on a visiting professorship at the Union Theological Seminary, in New York City, renewed his friendship with Bunche at a time when the ANC had launched the Defiance Campaign against Unjust Laws and was engaging in more militant protest.

In March 1953 the Afro-Asian caucus put a proposal before the UN General Assembly to create a study commission on South Africa's racial policies, and Bunche was one of three persons invited to serve on it.[41] The South African government agressively opposed the commission and threatened to deny visas to any member of it who tried to visit South Africa. However, the UN secretary general, Trygve Lie, prevailed on Bunche to turn down the post, leading to charges by the Afro-Asian caucus that Lie had pressured Bunche not to join the commission. Bunche's official statement was that he already was shouldering too many responsibilities on the Trusteeship Council. In addition, he was president-elect of the American Political Science Association. Bunche's decision was also likely influenced by Joseph McCarthy's witch hunt. That same month Bunche was appearing before the U.S. Senate's internal security subcommittee to refute allegations that he had been associated with the Communist Party.[42]

Although Bunche never returned to his South African study, his travels through South Africa and East Africa in 1937 and 1938 were pivotal experiences that reinforced and deepened his understanding of the realities of colonial rule and gave him a foundation for dealing with decolonization issues when he began working for the Trusteeship Council at the United Nations a decade later.

Notes

1. A professor of sociology at the Wharton School at the University of Pennsylvania, Young was a specialist on minority groups and race relations. He edited a volume that featured contributions from dozens of African American intellectuals: *The American Negro* (Philadelphia: American Academy of Political and Social Science, 1928); he also wrote *American Minority Peoples: A Study in Racial and Cultural Conflicts in the United States* (New York: Harper and Brothers, 1932). He later served briefly as president of the SSRC before becoming president of the Russell Sage Foundation after World War II. In 1939, Young introduced Bunche to Gunnar Myrdal, who recruited Bunche as a social scientist for the Myrdal study, as described in Charles Henry, "An African American Dilemma" in *Ralph Bunche: Model Negro or American Other?* (New York: New York University Press, 1999), 92–93.
2. Ralph J. Bunche, *An African American in South Africa: The Travel Notes of Ralph J. Bunche,* ed. Robert Edgar (Athens: Ohio University Press, 1992), 10–12.
3. Ralph Bunche, "How a Black Man Is to Take a World Tour," box 63, Ralph Bunche Papers, Special Collections, Young Research Library, University of California, Los Angeles. This undated document was written on Bunche's study tour.
4. Bunche, *African American,* 15.
5. Bunche to Mordecai Johnson, May 22, 1937, Ralph Bunche Papers, Manuscript Division, Schomburg Center for Research in Black Culture, New York Public Library.
6. Ibid.
7. Ibid.
8. Both Lewin and Simons soon returned to South Africa to become law professors, but their political philosophies radically differed. Lewin was an advocate of liberalism, while Simons was a staunch supporter and theoretician of the South African Communist Party and served on its executive board.
9. Ralph Bunche, "Black Man's Guide," box 63, Ralph Bunche Papers, UCLA.
10. SSRC, John Anisfield grant for race relations study during 1939, box 12, Ralph Bunche Papers, UCLA.
11. Ibid.
12. Bunche, *African American,* 54n2.
13. Bunche to Herskovits, October 7, 1938, Melville Herskovits Papers, Northwestern University.
14. Bunche, *African American,* 249.
15. Ibid., 191.
16. Ibid., 245.
17. Ibid., 149–50.
18. Bunche to Essie and Paul Robeson, January 11, 1938, correspondence files, Manuscripts Collection, Paul and Eslanda Robeson Papers, Moorland-Spingarn Library, Howard University.
19. See Ntongela Masilela's essays on this theme, "New Negroism and New Africanism: The Influence of United States Modernity on the Construction of South African Modernity, *Black Renaissance Noire* 2, no. 2 (1999): 46–59; see also Masilela, "The 'Black Atlantic' and African Modernity in South Africa," *Research in African Literatures* 27, no. 4 (1996): 88–96.
20. Bunche, *African American,* 137.
21. Peter Walshe, *The Rise of African Nationalism in South Africa: The African National Congress, 1912–1952* (Berkeley: University of California Press, 1971), 114–33; Thomas Karis and Gwendolen Carter, eds., *Hope and Challenge, 1935—1952,* vol. 2 of *From Protest to*

Challenge: A Documentary History of African Politics in South Africa (Stanford: Hoover Institution Press, 1973), 4–12.

22. Ibid.

23. Ibid., 229–37.

24. Baruch Hirson, *Yours for the Union: Class and Community Struggles in South Africa, 1930–1947* (London: Zed Books, 1989), 63–73.

25. Ibid., 234.

26. Ibid., 237.

27. Ibid.

28. Ibid., 256–69, 272–82.

29. Ibid., 265.

30. Ibid., 263.

31. This group of radicals eventually created a new organization, the Non-European Unity Movement, which called for a complete boycott of government-created institutions such as the NRC.

32. Ibid., 274.

33. When Dr. A. B. Xuma was elected ANC president in 1940, he used his personal funds to pay for the ANC's first salaried organizer.

34. Ibid., 275.

35. Ibid., 273.

36. Ibid., 274.

37. Robert Edgar, "A. P. Mda and the ANC Youth League," in *South Africa's 1940s: Worlds of Possibilities*, ed. Saul Dubow and Alan Jeeves (Cape Town: Double Storey Books, 2005), 149–69.

38. J. Matthews, "A New AMC," *Spark* 29 (1952): 2.

39. Bunche, *African American*, 265.

40. Henry, *Ralph Bunche*, 84–85.

41. *New York Times*, March 24, 25, 1953.

42. Henry, *Ralph Bunche*, 178–79.

CHAPTER FOUR

Ralph Bunche and the Decolonization of African Studies

The Paradox of Power, Morality, and Scholarship

ELLIOTT P. SKINNER

> True, we continue to pay lip service to the "sacred" concept of the "natural rights of man," and its international corollary, the "rights of people." But the dominant peoples and powerful nations usually discover that such concepts cut sharply against their own economic and political interests. So with these favored groups, who know well how to use them for their own profit, such doctrines come to assume a strange role.
>
> —Ralph Bunche, *A World View of Race*

WHEN RALPH Johnson Bunche won the Toppan Prize for his brilliant doctoral dissertation from Harvard University, "French Administration in Togoland and Dahomey,"[1] he had taken a giant step in the decolonization of African studies and a career that would lead to world renown. In the process, the academic world would recognize that he was the driving force behind Gunnar Myrdal's classic *American Dilemma*, about race relations in the United States. Ralph Bunche's enduring fame arises from his service to the U.S. government and to the United Nations. As an adviser to the Department of State and to the military on Africa and colonial areas of strategic military importance during World War II, Bunche moved from his first position as an analyst in the Office of Strategic Services to the desk of acting chief of the Division of Dependent Area Affairs in the State Department. He also discharged various responsibilities in connection with international conferences of the Institute of Pacific Relations, the

UN, the International Labor Organization, and the Anglo-American Caribbean Commission. In 1946, UN secretary general Trygve Lie "borrowed" Bunche from the State Department and placed him in charge of the UN's Department of Trusteeship and Information from Non-Self-Governing Territories to handle problems of the world's peoples who had not yet attained self-government. From June 1947 to August 1949, Bunche worked on the most important assignment of his career—the confrontation between Arabs and Jews in Palestine. He was first appointed as assistant to the UN Special Committee on Palestine, then as principal secretary of the UN Palestine Commission, which was charged with carrying out the partition approved by the UN General Assembly. In early 1948, when that plan was dropped and fighting between Arabs and Israelis became especially severe, the UN appointed Count Folke Bernadotte as mediator and Ralph Bunche as his chief aide. Four months later, on September 17, 1948, Count Bernadotte was assassinated, and Bunche was named acting UN mediator on Palestine. After eleven months of virtually ceaseless negotiating, Bunche obtained signatures on armistice agreements between Israel and the Arab States. He returned home to a hero's welcome. New York gave him a ticker tape parade up Broadway, and Los Angeles declared a Ralph Bunche Day.[2]

When the Norwegian Nobel Committee awarded him the coveted Peace Prize in recognition of his brilliant diplomacy in achieving an armistice amid the dangerous conflict in the Middle East, Bunche became the first American Negro and first non-European so honored. He thus fulfilled a prophecy made half a century earlier by W. E. B. DuBois at the inaugural meeting of the American Negro Academy: "If the Negro is ever to be a factor in the world's history—if among the gaily-colored banners that deck the broad ramparts of civilization is to hang one uncompromising black, then it must be placed there by black hands, fashioned by black heads and hallowed by the travail of 200,000,000 black hearts beating in one glad song of jubilee."[3] That day would signal the end or the beginning of the end of the tendency to consider the issues concerning peoples of African origin primarily under the rubric of colonial studies.

Born in Detroit, Michigan, on March 4, 1904, Ralph J. Bunche was heir to a cruel dilemma. The young child was designated a Negro primarily because of the colonization and subjugation of Africa and its peoples. The result, said DuBois in *The Souls of Black Folks,* was after the Egyptian and Indian, the Greek and Roman, the Teuton and Mongolian, the Negro is a sort of seventh son, born with a veil, and gifted with second-sight in this American world,—a world which yields him no true self-consciousness, but only lets him see himself through the revelation of the other world. It is a peculiar sensation, this double-consciousness, this sense of always looking at one's self through the eyes of others, of measuring one's soul by the tape of a world that looks on in amused contempt and pity.[4]

All over the colonized world and in areas dominated by Europeans, such as the United States, this person always felt his "twoness,—an American, a Negro; two souls, two thoughts, two unreconciled strivings; two warring ideals in one dark body, whose dogged strength alone keeps it from being torn asunder."[5] The only salvation for such a person who wished to "attain self-conscious manhood" was to "merge his double self into a better and truer self." The dilemma for such persons was that they often wished neither of their older selves to be lost. DuBois asserted that the Negro, especially in the United States, hesitated to "Africanize America, for America has too much to teach the world and Africa." Yet, "he would not bleach his Negro soul in a flood of white Americanism, for he knows that Negro blood has a message for the world. He simply wishes to make it possible for a man to be both a Negro and an American, without being cursed and spit upon by his fellows, without having the doors of Opportunity closed roughly in his face." The goal of such persons was to be "a co-worker in the kingdom of culture, to escape both death and isolation, to husband and use his best powers and his latent genius."[6]

What made Bunche's Negroness crucial was that he was born at the beginning of the twentieth century, which Henry Luce called "the American Century,"[7] a period among whose major problems for humanity was "the color line,—the relation of the darker to the lighter races of men in Asia and Africa, America and the island of the sea."[8]

The dilemma that faced the young Bunche was no better illustrated than at his graduation ceremony in 1922, when the well-meaning Principal Fulton of Jefferson High School said to Nana, his maternal grandmother, "Mrs. Johnson, we are very sorry to see Ralph leave Jefferson. We like him here. He has been a good student and a good athlete. In fact, Mrs. Johnson, we have never thought of Ralph as a Negro." To which Nana replied, "You are very wrong to say that. It is an insult to Ralph, to me, to his parents and his whole race. Why haven't you thought of him as a Negro? He is a Negro and he is proud of it. So am I. What makes you think that only white is good?" And with a few more well-chosen words, she said a tart 'Good day' and left."[9]

By Nana's lifetime, Africa, if not deliberately denigrated, had become a land of "Drums and Shadows."[10] It was there and it was not there, and while present its meaning varied in rhythm, sounds, and silences. Peoples of part African descent could not decide in whose interest it would be better to be known as African, colored, or Negro, since danger lurked in any identification. It is therefore not clear whether the boy's grandmother ever explained why she treasured this Africa-derived sobriquet, a title of a "maternal clan" or honored name. Yet she could have passed for white, and her brother "passed" into the white ethnic group. Nana insisted on the identity of Negro, thereby accepting and using the "one-drop rule," then in vogue for those persons of African origin in the United States and generally in the New World.[11] Nana certainly did not wish her Africanity to be completely bleached in a flood of white Americanism, or to permit her grandson's culture and the powers of his mind and body to be "strangely wasted, dispersed or forgotten."[12]

Despite being constantly reminded about the power of the Europeans and their contempt for the people and culture of Africa and its descendants across the globe, those in the African diaspora in the Americas early recognized the link between racism, colonialism, and their homeland. They understood that the concept "Negro" or variations of it had emerged in many European languages, for the descendants of enslaved "Wolofs, Temne, Dioula, Corormantees, Whydahs, Igbos, Angolas from the 'Dark Continent,'" and had become the bane of the existence of black people the world over. For example, Linnaeus, in his *Systema naturae* (1735) placed African peoples at the bottom of the humanlike portion of the Great Chain of Being.[13] All major European philosophers denied the intellectual ability of black people. British philosopher David Hume argued, "There never was a civilized nation of any other complexion than white, nor even any individual eminent either in action or speculation. No ingenious manufacturers amongst them, no arts, no sciences.... Such a uniform and constant difference could not happen, in so many countries and ages, if nature had not made an original distinction betwixt these breeds of men."[14]

Hume dismissed as nonsense the report that an African slave in Jamaica had exhibited remarkable intellectual ability.[15] In a manner reminiscent of Hume, Wilhelm Friedrich Hegel added, "[Africa] is no historical part of the world; it has no movement, or development to exhibit. Historical movements in it—that is in its northern part—belong to the Asiatic or European world. Egypt—does not belong to the African Spirit. What we properly understand by Africa, is the Unhistorical, Undeveloped Spirit, still—on the threshold of World History."[16]

As Europe expanded on world conquest in the fifteenth century, what became significant for African peoples was that Europeans needed them and all their attributes to help build empires in the "Jerusalems" named severally as New Spain, New France, New England, Port of Spain, New London, and New Amsterdam. Thus despite their biological, cultural, and especially economic contribution to the New World, Africa's descendants long remained an unwelcome presence.[17] Thomas Jefferson's views in his *Notes on the State of Virginia* showed that he had serious doubts about the humanity of African peoples even when confronted with the genius of Benjamin Banneker and with his own alleged relations with Sally Hemmings.[18] The views of Jefferson and his peers grew out of white belief in what came to be called manifest destiny. Historian Henry Steele Commager declared that quite early, whites incubated an "American mind," an identifiable set of principles and values that they felt were inherited from their forebears and were superior to all others.[19] On a visit to America in 1782, Frenchman Hector St. Jean de Crèvecoeur, who found that Americans believed in a symbolic estate, expressed the sentiment that in America "individuals of all [white] nations are melted into a new race of men, whose labors and posterity will one day cause great changes in the world. Americans are the western pilgrims, who are carrying along with them that great mass of arts, sciences, vigor and industry, which began long since in the east. They will finish the great circle."[20]

This notion was to have a devastating impact on the rest of the world, especially on Africa and its peoples. Rudyard Kipling and Theodore Roosevelt both believed in the white man's burden and duty to conquer, dominate, and civilize the lesser breeds beyond the law, and did not care even if they had to exterminate these peoples in the process.[21]

On the other hand, the resistance of African peoples who were captured, transported, enslaved, and oppressed by the Europeans under the banner of colonialism never ceased, and neither did their defense of their attributes and of their continent.[22] Even before Olaudah Equiano, African peoples resisted enslavement and colonialism and employed all regnant paradigms to assert their equality with the rest of humankind. Almost every subsequent generation of African scholars felt it their duty to contest the assertions and beliefs in the inferiority of black people. For example, the protestations of Banneker against the beliefs of Jefferson have come down to us.[23] Later on, like Paul Cuffe, Rev. Lott Carey declared, "I am an African, and in this country [America], however meritorious my conduct, and respectable my character, I cannot receive the credit due to either. I wish to go to a country where I shall be estimated by my merits and not by my complexion, and I feel bound to labor for my suffering race."[24]

African peoples in the New World were determined to assert their right to equality in the family of nations and not to be viewed forever as serfs and colonials. For example, Henry Smyth, who fought in the American Civil War and was later appointed American consul general in Monrovia during the Scramble for Africa, defended his Africanity as being naturally human. In a revealing telegram to Secretary of State Frederick T. Frelinghuysen, Smyth asserted that he felt honor bound to help Liberia maintain its independence from the imperial designs of Britain and France:

> Race allegiance is compatible with patriotism, with love of the land [America] that gave us birth....
>
> ... The sentiment, the something stronger than sentiment which makes an English American proud of his connection with Britain, a French American proud of his connection with La Belle France, and a German American fondly attached to the memories of the fatherland, and all European races of their Aryan descent, has something that partakes of the moral sublime.[25]

In a postscript to one of his cables to the Department of State, Smyth wrote to the secretary, "The civilized Negro in Africa under foreign domination, as the civilized Negro out of Africa under like control, suffers in his liberty, because it has not the element of imperium. 'Imperium et Libertas' must be the motto and practice of the Negro, if he is to have self respect; if he is to merit the respect of others."[26]

Thus, to "decolonize" the views about Africans and African peoples was very much part of the complex views about the Negro that Nana undoubtedly passed on to the young Bunche, even during the unbridled notion of white supremacy that asserted itself during his childhood, when America's Great White Fleet sailed the oceans asserting his country's emerging dominance.[27] As a child in Detroit surrounded by primarily European immigrants seeking a better life in the United States, and for whom this was the land of the free and the home of the brave, Nana constantly admonished Bunche to "let them, especially white folks, know that you can do anything they can do." But since there were few persons of African origin in Detroit, "in his early years Ralph knew very little about the 'Negro problem' and racial prejudice, although he heard all sorts of hostile racial epithets applied to Italians, and later, in Albuquerque, to Mexicans and Indians. Nana was suspicious of foreigners, but as recorded by Ralph, laid down a firm family line on the matter. 'Negroes have no business running down anybody. Anyhow, people who can sing and like tomatoes and bananas as much as those Italy folks can't be all bad.'"[28]

Nevertheless, increasingly the young Bunche encountered hints of prejudice as well as acts of discrimination. The Bunches were evicted from a coach on a journey to Knoxville, Tennessee. Things got even worse when the family moved to Albuquerque, New Mexico, where the American Indians and the defeated Mexicans bore the brunt of white hostility and prejudice. Through all this travail, Nana and her clan survived, and the young boy did well in school. The family's migration to Los Angeles in 1917 would have been undoubtedly disastrous had not his redoubtable Nana, profiting from her light skin, secured housing for the family. Here Bunche began to experience the contradictions and complexities posed by his color and aspirations. He felt himself relegated to the role of interlocutor when members of his family sang Negro spirituals and the like. He also reported "some inner feeling of resentment about not being 'Negro' enough, compared to my negro chums."[29] He found it difficult to behave like his peers, and in some ways wanted to be like them.[30] But here again Nana came to his rescue. She tirelessly monitored his education at the predominantly white Thirtieth Street Intermediate School (now John Adams Junior High School) during his attendance from 1917 to 1919. And when she noted his failing grades, she discovered that he was being tracked into vocational classes (shorthand, commercial arithmetic, etc.), rather than the academic ones. Nana visited the principal and declared, "This boy is going to college and he must be ready for it."[31] She was not going to let him be socialized as a second-class person.

Ralph went on to Jefferson High School, and though he led his class, racism intervened. To the chagrin of some of his white teachers, he was excluded from the Ephebian Society, the citywide student honor society, and wanted to quit. But again he was pulled up short when he remembered his mother telling him, "Don't let anything take away your hope, faith, and dreams." Despite these pressures, Bunche excelled at basketball and enjoyed all types of literature. Meanwhile, in order to help his family economically, he "worked as a delivery boy for the Los Angeles *Times* and later on got a job in the paper's printing plant, . . . as a 'pig boy,' whose function was to carry lead bricks to the linotype machines."[32] Despite these trials and tribulations, Ralph finished first in his class.

The young Bunche faced discrimination at UCLA as well as at Stanford, the Bruins' chief competitor. But his brilliance impressed his professors, and although attracted to philosophy, he decided to study political science so that he could use his ideas and ideals to improve the condition of his people. Meanwhile, he enjoyed exchanging ideas and debating relevant issues. And while racism kept him out of the official college debating society, he and friends formed their own. Here Ralph and his colleagues debated such themes as racial identity and world peace, and he sought to come to grips with the contours of his life. He was a light-skinned Negro, but still faced color prejudice. He recognized racial discrimination in the swimming pool in Los Angeles, and recalled with displeasure the willingness of some of his peers to use the sporting facility in his neighborhood under such humiliating conditions. He felt that Negroes should compete equally with other people and not be, as he felt others perceived them, "kings of the alibi."[33]

Meanwhile Ralph Bunche's academic brilliance made it clear that he would not accept any alibi and was prepared to use his intelligence for the good of all. At the end of one speech he encouraged a group of primarily adult Negroes to support their youth: "We have *youth,* we have *racial pride,* and we have *indomitable will* and boundless optimism for the future. . . . We'll make you all *proud* of the young Negro."[34] Yet, he decided that "racial chauvinism" was not the answer, and later fought any belief in either black or white supremacy. One of his maxims was drawn from the prophet Isaiah: "They shall beat their swords into plough-shares; and their spears into pruning hooks; nation shall not lift up sword against nation, neither shall they learn war anymore."[35] But what would be long remembered at UCLA was Bunche's valedictory address in 1927, during which he declared, "Humanity's problem today is how to be saved from itself.... It did not require the Great War to convince us of this sobering fact.... Prejudices, antipathies, hatreds still disrupt with their sinister influences the equilibrium of the world. [The war] has, however, contributed its 'jot of good'—it set mankind in a universal quest of a panacea for its suffering."[36] Thus we note that at the end of Bunche's undergraduate education, his major concerns were racial harmony and world justice.

Nana supported Bunche's desire to go east to Harvard to seek higher education, and he received help from a black women's club, which raised funds for his travel and education. Seeking a job in New York, he contacted DuBois, then famous in the National Association for the Advancement of Colored People. Had the great man imagined that a star was on the horizon, he would have found room in that particular manger. Nevertheless, Bunche proceeded to Cambridge, where he found and did so well working at a bookstore close to Harvard Yard. To his chagrin, the owner confessed that it was only the accident of failing eyes and Bunche's light skin that got him in the door. Bunche was also lucky to find at Harvard a cohort of brilliant black students with whom he kept a good relationship throughout his life.

The curriculum at Harvard must have seemed to Bunche a veritable smorgasbord of academic riches, but like students who arrive at graduate school, the choice of study is often mysterious. Nevertheless, at that time his interest in "race relations" must have directed his reading in the echoes of the history and travail of African peoples in the world and especially in the United States. Most Americans, both black and white, accepted the reality of racial discrimination and its echoes. Booker T. Washington still had supporters of his concept of "separate but equal," and Garvey's followers, who believed in "Africa for Africans at home and abroad," still mourned his deportation. DuBois still continued with his Pan-African Congress, and Bunche must have heard about the advocates of the Harlem Renaissance, who lauded the arrival of the "New Negro" who had notions about Black Manhattan and "hibiscus in the snow" and played jazz and sang the blues. What was Bunche's reaction?

The late Nathan Huggins of Harvard wrote that Bunche found no "Africanists" at Harvard, except possibly Rupert Emerson. Yet Bunche must have known about the Peabody series on Africa, and must have heard about professors such as Leslie Buell, whose scathing two-volume study *The Native Problem in Africa* had raised a firestorm.[37] As a faithful reader of the NAACP *Crisis* magazine, Bunche must have followed the so-called Black Scandal in Liberia, involving Buell, Firestone's rubber plantations, the African American community, the U.S. State Department, the League of Nations, and some European nations still eager to seize the troubled "Black Republic." But regardless of what Bunche knew or did not know about Africa because of the lack of a sustained interest in that continent during his early education at Harvard, he was brilliant enough to win the prestigious Thayer Fellowship for his master's thesis in 1928. Then a combination of factors, which included a black academic network identifying him as a "comer," the state of the economy (which may have conditioned if and where he could find an academic job), and an invitation for him to teach at Howard University in Washington, D.C., proved providential, and he declined the Thayer Fellowship.

The constellation of brilliant black scholars at Howard when Bunche arrived there still dazzles scholars. Consider philosopher Alain Locke, the first African American Rhodes Scholar, who had seminal ideas about the cultural orientation of the New Negro with the potential to revolutionize the world. While still at Oxford, Locke met and had advised brilliant Africans to go to the United States to meet important black Americans, including the ailing Booker T. Washington and the radical W. E. B. DuBois. At least one student, Pixley ka Seme, sought, through the good offices of Booker T. Washington, to study anthropology with Franz Boas at Columbia University, from the placement he secured at Teachers College–Columbia. Later he was one of the founders of the South African Native National Congress, which would become the African National Congress, famous for liberating South Africa from white domination. At Howard, Bunche also met Abram Harris Jr., a brilliant economist whose Marxist orientation insisted that control of the means of production largely determined how human societies functioned. Also at Howard at that time was the brilliant sociologist E. Franklin Frazier, who also discussed with Bunche and Abram the economic factors affecting black families and social classes. Historians Charles Wesley and Rayford Logan were busily studying and teaching about the progress and plight of blacks in the United States. One is almost certain Bunche must have heard conversations between

Logan and black scholars and activists visiting Howard about how the bright but bigoted president Woodrow Wilson spurned the recommendations of such persons as DuBois to encourage the emerging League of Nations to institute a mandate to deal with the plight of the ex-Axis countries in Africa under the direction of the intelligentsia of the black world, aided by that continent's traditional rulers. One is not sure how Bunche dealt with Leo Hansberry's *Africa gloriana* (in praise of ancient Egypt), but he did serve as diplomatic consultant for Hansberry's Ethiopian Research Council, dedicated to protecting the Queen of Sheba's children from the claws of Mussolini. Providentially it was during this time at Howard that Bunche met Melville Herskovits, an anthropologist from Columbia University, then studying the changing characteristics of peoples of Negro descent, and who would later influence his study of Africa. It would have been surprising if he did not also encounter Zora Neale Hurston at Howard.

The atmosphere at Howard University in this period was full of radical thought and activities. It is understandable why a politically inclined Bunche would not only try to understand the world around him but also attempt to change it. He had learned about the theories of the classic English and American philosophers while at Harvard, and probably through Abe Harris's Marxism must have heard how the American anthropologist Lewis Henry Morgan influenced Frederic Engels, who in turn played an important role in Karl Marx's theory about communism. True, Bunche would later challenge certain aspects of "praxis," especially when these appeared to contradict or misunderstand specific historical factors such as the future of Negroes in the United States, especially the Leninist notion of the possibility of a Negro republic in the United States. Bunche was no more successful with the views of the Negro National Congress about how to change the political conditions of contemporary blacks in the United States. For him, theory was one thing, but existence trumped essence thus amplifying his commitment to black Americans as organic members of American society. He was increasingly interested in understanding how peoples of African origin had to deal with the real world in which they lived. The alternative was going to Harvard to study how the real Leviathan dealt with the imponderables of human lives.

Much is known about how Bunche also protected and defended campus radicals such as Kenneth Clark, angry at a racist world. Overseeing this variegated population, and attempting to keep the academy alive was Mordecai Johnson, a theologian-cum-politician. His goal was to save Howard from the wrath of mainly Southern white congressmen who hated what Black Reconstruction sought to achieve. Johnson was so annoyed with Bunche's activities and his growing interest in African peoples in the world arena that at a faculty meeting he ridiculed Bunche for wishing to go abroad to deal with the "Negro problem," when that could be done in the United States. But Bunche sensed that blacks in America were then better placed than elsewhere in the world to deal effectively with the global problem of African peoples in all aspects. Getting funds was always important in order to study these matters, but in the early 1930s a black scholar could expect to get funding only from such sources as the Rosenwald Fund, the General Education Fund, and the Phelps-Stokes Association. There is some indication that Bunche considered comparing race relations in Brazil with those in the United States but was steered away from those in foundations who thought that "U.S. Negroes might get 'dangerous ideas' in Brazil."[38] Finally he was encouraged to apply for and subsequently accepted a Rosenwald Fellowship to compare French colonial administration in Dahomey and Togo, the French administered mandate from the League of Nations.

It is not clear why Bunche chose this subject; a hypothesis as good as any other is to believe that his choice may have grown out of his encounter with Rayford Logan and DuBois, who had earlier dreamt of a mandate system for the German colonies in Africa. This idea was bruited about at the Paris Peace Conference in 1919. The possibility also exists that Bunche may have heard about or even seen a reported study by Alain Locke that had been commissioned by the State Department on study the situation in West Africa.

Bunche finally went to Europe in June 1932, spending four months in France collecting data from the French colonial office and later on from the League of Nations offices in Geneva. Several questions about this trip are relevant here. For example, did he meet Maurice Delafosse, who headed L'Ecole Coloniale in Paris and who had done seminal studies of the French Soudan (modern Mali). Did he see the early studies of Louis Tauxier on West Africa? And how about the early work of Leo Frobenius, *African Genesis,* which was later to have such an impact on the early generations of Africans in Paris—a group that would challenge European views about Africa with their own "anti-racist racism"? The pragmatic Anglo-Saxonsim of Bunche may not have appreciated the romanticism of the French, but was it not possible that the student from Dahomey, whose apartment he inhabited while in Paris, could have introduced him to the young radicals in the city? Then when Bunche was joined by his family in Paris, in January 1933, and took them to see Josephine Baker in Montmartre, he must have recognized this talk of the town. Her skirt of bananas was famous in the cafes where a small cadre of African and Caribbean students were enamored of *le jazz hot* from the United States and were developing revolutionary ideas about African culture. Hints of this surface in Bunche's dissertation on West Africa when he contrasted this "gaulliste" philosophizing about the "African" with the rigid notion of the "Anglo-Saxons" about the fixity of race and culture.[39]

Bunche spent what to anthropologists would have been too short a time, slightly more than three months during the winter of 1932–33, in West Africa, studying French administration in its own colony of Dahomey and in the League of Nations mandate of Togoland. The alleged difference was that while Dahomey could be subjected to a "civilization mission," and treated as any other colony of France, Togoland was a ward of the League. That difference invited comparison since even though Dahomey was a colony in the French West Africa system, its neighbor, Togoland, had been a German colony until the Versailles Treaty and the League of Nations placed it as a mandate territory under French administration. Bunche's study, then, permitted a comparison between the European administration of African peoples not only under conventional colonial rule but also under the mandate system of the League of Nations. Since Togoland and Dahomey were neighboring territories of comparable circumstances and administered by the same European power, a comparison between them might be all the more trenchant with regard to the effect of international involvement in colonial administration.

In principle, while mandate territories were under the protection of the League and the mandate commission had the right to oversee their administration, Leslie Buell had previously found only slight differences in France's administrations of the two territories.[40] Bunche was also to discover that the reality of the "colonial situation"—one of "total domination" instructed by the white man's burden and his "civilizing mission"—would be true for all European-controlled territories in Africa regardless of the various orientations of the whites. Specifically, he was appalled to see only slight differences "in the treatment and status of the natives under the Togo mandate, and that of their neighbors in the colony of Dahomey."[41] Bunche was particularly disturbed by the similarities in the taxation system in both Togoland and Dahomey, which invariably led to large differences between the revenue paid by European colonials and Africans. Moreover, the practice of using traditional leaders to collect the taxes destroyed local political systems. Equally disturbing for him was the emergence in Togoland of a wealthy African bourgeoisie whose extravagant behavior created schisms between them and the ordinary people. Finally, Bunche saw how the practice of forced labor for infrastructural development led some local Togolese to flee to the British Gold Coast. Thus, the determination of all Europeans to exploit the Africans made a mockery of the differences between mandates and outright colonies and contradicted the whole notion that African studies could be limited to colonial studies.

It was the educational programs of the francophone and anglophone areas that especially troubled Bunche because it was here that the future of the two territories lay. He noted philosophical differences between the French and British in their expectations of the Africans: assimilation by the French and accommodation by the British. Yet he felt that racism and cultural chauvinism often militated against the different approaches, and he doubted their efficacy. He was especially critical of glorification of the noble savage as an excuse of some Europeans not to influence African traditional cultures, but I suspect that the French penchant for philosophical nuances that would later result in a concept of negritude among its subjects escaped him. Bunche felt that the problem was not whether the Africans should be educated, but what could be accomplished. Would assimilation lead to peace or to conflict? And what would be controlled and to what objectives should it be directed? Bunche saw the possibilities of training a few leaders, educating the masses to become useful citizens, and collaborating with the colonizers to achieve eventual self-rule. Unfortunately, Bunche could not discover any evidence that either the French or British had viable educational plans elsewhere in Africa.

Bunche was especially hostile to Dr. Thomas Jesse Jones, of the Phelps-Stokes Fund, who championed applying to Africa a model similar to Booker T. Washington's Tuskegee model. Washington's model advocated industrial and agricultural training, considered to be the type of education most suitable for Africans—thus, Jones's ideas rested on the non sequitur that what was good for black Americans would be good for Africans in European colonies. Bunche also believed that educated Africans rejected the Washington model since it was not used universally. Lastly, he was concerned about the status of African languages and about what aspects of traditional African culture should be transmitted. He concluded that French educational policy and administration were similar in both Togo and Dahomey: suppress African languages and the reluctance of missionary schools to support African culture. This to me was to misunderstand the French missionaries' determination not to lose their catechists to better jobs in the French administration.[42] He concluded that the bottom line was to create class divisions and to exalt French culture. The paradox created for him was that the French did not really believe that Africans could readily assimilate French culture. Bunche found a similar paradox in the judicial systems used in Dahomey and Togoland. In the final analysis Bunche found the mandate system was at best a mixed bag, with few significant differences between African life under colonial rule and that under mandate control.[43]

What Bunche found especially disturbing was the stimulation of new needs among the Africans that could be met only by forced labor. The result was that the African cultural systems in colonized areas were being systematically destroyed by a global, expanding industrial revolution that facilitated "detribalization" and that, in South Africa, brought native trade unionism. According to Bunche, such conditions resulted in a forced labor problem not greatly different from early industrialization in the West.

Bunche's dissertation indicates that he had started to view colonialism and race in larger terms. He wrote in its preface that his study was "stimulated by a deep interest in the development of subject peoples and the hopes which the future holds for them."[44] Perhaps it was his subsequent experiences at Howard, the political work that he did with the Negro National Congress, and his troubling feeling about the theoretical and questionable solutions to these that he detected in Marxist formulations that led him to accept both similarities and differences among the issues facing African peoples both in the colonial world and in the United States. Yet he was apparently not prepared to accept the notion that theories alone would change those realities. Bunche was convinced that the self-determination of the Africans was "morally right and ultimately possible." He apparently had questions about whether African cultures and institutions were sufficient bases on which to build modern nation-states. The domination of the world by whites was a reality Bunche adjudged a dominant factor to be viewed without questionable ideologies. My suspicion is that Bunche's stay at Howard before he went off to the field had a greater impact on his theory about Dahomey and Togoland than normally recognized and that it instructed his feeling about how and why African studies should best be decolonized.

While Harvard felt that Bunche's dissertation in political science merited the Toppan Prize, some scholars lamented that he did not deem that this "thoughtful, well-written analysis of colonial administration, and ... one of the earliest serious works on this subject"[45] warranted developing into a book. Perhaps Nathan Huggins was correct in his feeling that Bunche's training as a political scientist had not prepared him to deal adequately with African cultures and their institutions.[46] But this experience apparently whetted his appetite for anthropology, and he apparently continued to read in that subject, traveling regularly to Northwestern University, where he took courses with Melville Herskovits, whose increasing interest in Africa and its diaspora had led to an increasing interest in "acculturation" or culture change. Meanwhile, the world was moving rapidly to Nazism and Bunche had to be prepared to help. Thus, while his thesis raised very significant questions about the manner in which the emerging African elites were affected by a radically changing colonial situation, he faced the growing dilemma of a return to the reality of Howard University and all that meant for himself and his family.

Back at Howard, Bunche could not escape the tensions of living in a racist society that feared change; he increasingly felt badgered by economic depression, the fear of Russian-inspired communism, the militancy of young blacks, and especially the imperial designs of the Japanese in East Asia and the rise of fascism in Germany and Italy. Many persons of African descent in the United States, influenced by Marxism, were not only prepared to fight in Spain, but also mobilized as best they could to persuade their country to help an Ethiopia threatened by the Fascisti of Mussolini. As the United States felt the pressure of understanding the "world of race," the State Department sought to understand conditions in Africa and turned to Alain Locke, who must have sought the help of Bunche, who had actually studied the situation in West Africa. But it was Bunche's expertise as a political scientist and one who had intimate knowledge of race relations in the United States that led him to accept the opportunity to work with Gunnar Myrdal on what DuBois had long termed the American Dilemma. Fate and racial politics entered into this experience, which increased his appetite to consider the "race problem" from a global perspective. It was natural that he would start his study by journeying first to Africa.

Bunche's relationship with Herskovits came in handy for a person going first to the United Kingdom, known as the epicenter for anthropology of colonial areas, before his worldwide odyssey. Herskovits had become well known among anthropologists the world over, and while little specific information records the nature of his seminars at Northwestern, various philosophies infused the intellectual climate at that time. The Marxists were emphasizing that existence was essence, but the anthropologists, especially those at Columbia, were insisting that the past was very much part of the present—whether it is in cranial indices or family organization, the present could only be understood on the basis of the past. It is true that Herskovits, like Franz Boas before him, believed in science and objectivity. This made for a situation at Northwestern where Herskovits distrusted what some would later consider "a self-serving" conclusion regarding "the romanticism of Negroes to attribute to race and history" more than he deemed acceptable. It is probably this combination of hardheadedness and American pragmatism and willingness to deal with reality that facilitated the relationship between Bunche and Herskovits. The latter was instrumental in paving the way for Bunche to get the opportunity to take a seminar with Bronislaw Malinowski, at the London School of Economics, before undertaking a two-year field study of South Africa and Southeast Asia. Both Herskovits and Malinowski arranged for him to work with Isaac Schapera in South Africa.

Bunche's experiences in Britain were probably as important as his early encounter with black intellectuals at Howard. At that time, the second wave of students of African origin was studying at the major educational institutions in Britain. Eric Williams and others were studying capitalism and slavery at Oxford and were part of a group of Caribbean students that included C. L. R. James, who was interested in the Black Jacobins of Haiti, and George Padmore of Trinidad, who had been one of Bunche's students at Howard. Other black Americans Bunche met in England included Paul Robeson, then a concert and movie celebrity, and his wife, Eslanda, who also studied at the London

School of Economics and had also visited South and East Africa, and Jomo Kenyatta of Kenya, who studied with Malinowski. This cohort of students greatly enhanced Bunche's insight into the thinking of black intellectuals around the world. Bunche tried as best he could to mediate among all his fractious colleagues while dutifully learning all he could about English politics and how the Europeans were attempting to appease Hitler. It is possibly at that point that Bunche understood the efficacy of his nationality as an American. This was the most important constant in this inexplicable racial universe. Thus, it was no accident and possibly fortunate when on his application to travel to South Africa in the box designated for race he wrote American.

While at the LSE Bunche did profit from the functionalist approach of Malinowski, who insisted on recognizing the tight relationship between the institutions of each society in space and time. What Malinowski distrusted was the emphasis on the supposed dominance of any single institution in societies, and the dependency on history or even on our ability to understand the processes inherent in institutions held to account for cultural change. Malinowski's rigidity did not satisfy Bunche, who, after all, had read Lewis Henry Morgan's *Ancient Society,* in which economic factors were the engine of cultural growth and whose work had influenced Engels, who later influenced Marx. Moreover, Bunche had worked in West Africa, where he had witnessed the complexity and economic importance of cultural impact. Since Bunche possibly considered functionalism as rigid as Marxism and Christianity (as a Baptist he had experienced baptism by immersion but had been immune to religion), he was therefore not about to buy into Malinowski's functionalism.

Significantly, Malinowski's views about the complexity of understanding culture and change revealed themselves during Bunche's voyage to South Africa. For some on board the ship he was black, but a middle-class intellectual and also an American. When he arrived in Dakar, Senegal, he was described as an Egyptian, but except for the French passengers, whose subtle cultural racism puzzled him, his Negroness started to trump all other views about his identity. Perhaps because Bunche had already been to Dahomey and Togoland, his arrival in Africa from Europe did not seem to have been marked by an epiphany of encountering the landscape of Africa, as was the case of many diasporic Africans who touched African soil for the first time. What he did remark on were the various reactions of different types of white South Africans he encountered on board. Each person's reaction to him reflected his or her own particular status in South Africa.

Except for having to post bond for a return passage if not permitted to disembark in Cape Town, Isaac Schapera easily facilitated Bunche's entry into South Africa. Yet, he could never escape the warning he received from the South African consular officials in London that, willfully or not, African Americans were natural subversives in South Africa. Bunche was often forcibly reminded that black Americans were role models, whether they liked it or not. He may or may not have been aware of a letter that Bishop Levi Jenkins Coppin wrote to his congregation in America. It read in part:

> Pity them, pity them, Christians at home. It is not at all likely that any more will be done for this class of natives by the Europeans than is being done.... Once they owned all the land by inheritance, and now they are not permitted to domicile on it, or, only upon such portions of it as may be allotted to them out of pity. When we are told that a man in America is denied civil and political rights on account of being a descendant of Africa, we are content to call it unjust, ungodly; but when we are told that an African in Africa is denied civil privileges because he is an African, we feel that besides being unrighteous and unworthy [of] our Christian civilization, it is ridiculous in the extreme.[47]

Thus from the very beginning of his sojourn in South Africa, Bunche quickly understood that he was structurally subversive. Therefore he understood also that Schapera, a Jew, had to be careful how he permitted him to interact with the locals. Bunche was a polite guest, careful not to rock the boat, but always a keen observer.

Bunche was fascinated but deeply troubled by the situation in Cape Town. Here were street scenes that reminded him of Harlem, populated with persons of all hues of dark and pale, with only Malay and Indian strains accounting for the more frequently observed straight black hair. He possessed an uncanny anthropological ability to enter a room or place and to later describe the behavior and interaction of all the people there. He was also embarrassed by the "tomfoolery" of the people he saw, especially an episode in which one colored man capered for a crowd by walking and dancing on his hands as a woman sang a little song. Bunche was not amused when one drunken white man encouraged the crowd to pose for him, not conscious that his hand was covering his camera's lens. Yet, Bunche could not help being amused by the false camaraderie of the entire crowd and was amazed by the relative lack of color segregation on public transport.

One of the most important lessons Bunche learned in Cape Town was the agony of color contrasted with the efficacy of culture: minor variation in tint structured the lives of colored people. Mothers valued lighter pigmentation in their offspring as indices of mobility and possibly a better life, but as Bunche indicated, this often resulted in babies born out of wedlock. Sex, race, and culture were categories that came through consistently in his description of the people in Cape Town, where his own complexion, which identified him as colored, exposed him to the radical differences between the Malays and Indians and the Africans. Here pigmentation reigned supreme, with the hues ranging all the way from white to almost black. The black people in the town ranged from those who were traditionally Africans, such as Zulu, to educated Africans, such as Jabavu and Seme, who attempted to pattern themselves after the American Negro. Bunche himself, while designated by the South African whites as colored, witnessed so many contradictions among the coloreds that one has the feeling that he became convinced that the black American, while providing a very important model for Africans, was very different from them. Did these experiences of Bunche contribute to his pivotal role in looking at the studies of Africa and Africans outside the narrow boundaries of the colonial situation?

Bunche increasingly noticed signs of protest among the South Africans, beginning in Cape Town, that signaled the colonial world was ending. He was especially intrigued by a black man, an apparent "Garveyite," who harangued crowds of coloreds and blacks during a parade. This man wore a UNIA (United Negro Improvement Association) button on his lapel, carried copies of the *Pittsburgh Courier*, *The Bantu World*, and *The Black Man*, and spoke fairly good English. The political scientist in Bunche could not help noting the manner in which this Garveyite exemplified how the various "worlds of race" were coming together. Increasingly Bunche grew troubled by the character of South African black politics. He knew a great deal about the evolution of political protests in the region. He recounted how at the beginning there were a collection of "tribal organizations, burial societies," and so on. Bunche knew how the South African Native

National Congress was organized in 1912, and he was deeply troubled about the role being played in that country by Dr. Pixley ka Seme, who though from Swaziland, had studied in Britain and the United States. Bunche sought to put into perspective the early meetings of the organization, its activities on the eve of the Natives' Land Act of 1913, and how it sent delegations to England to protest the development of unbridled white supremacy. He attempted to put into perspective the agitation by some of the politically active young Africans, the role of the first pass-burning demonstration, of mine workers being shot, and how the white government frustrated a congress increasingly riddled with graft and corruption. Bunche was embarrassed by the lack of strong African leadership at meetings he attended. This left him with some troublesome questions about black politics in South Africa. More important were serious queries such as how this handful of whites could keep millions of blacks down. The blacks couldn't be so dumb—they were too adept at handling the white man's contraptions: bicycles, cars, carpentry, forges, football, cricket, European languages. Most surprising for Bunche was the reluctance of many university-trained Africans to recognize the efficacy of African institutions, even though in hindsight we know that people like Nelson Mandela, who were youths while Bunche was in South Africa, did not hesitate to use traditional models effectively when tackling contemporary and future problems. Thus African studies seemed less and less like colonial studies than studies of an emerging African people in the contemporary world.

Bunche's departure from South Africa and his trip through Mozambique on his way to Kenya marked a significant political transformation in how he saw the role of anthropology in African studies. It increasingly seemed that Bunche, like many persons of African origin, remained suspicious of anthropology. On the one hand, many ethnic Africans learned enough anthropology to glimpse what whites saw in African anthropology, but they did not fully trust it. The accents and stresses were always different. During his subsequent visit to Kenya, Bunche would have liked to have mixed anthropological techniques of observation and analysis of "tribal and cultural life," but another reality kept intruding. His reception by the Kikuyu was quite revealing: they welcomed him as a *karioki,* a relative who had gone away and returned. Thus he was fully inclined to use his anthropological insights to understand many aspects of Kikuyu culture, especially the male and female circumcision ceremonies, which could only be understood against the backdrop of traditional culture, then under attack by Europeans, but which had taken on meanings that were now defiantly alien to their original sense. Bunche's reaction to the manner in which the Kikuyu used their cultural traditions was instructive. He must have known that Kenyatta was circumcised, but one can never forget the terrible altercation that Bunche witnessed in Malinowski's office between Kenyatta and a white student about aspects of African culture. Bunche understood why the circumcision ritual had different meanings to himself as an anthropologist, to the Kikuyu, and to the Europeans. Yet, his anthropological understanding did not prevent him from being, as he said, horrified by this aspect of Kikuyu culture. He had seen Africans in ways that "the other" could not see them, and the issue of "double-consciousness" kept intruding. On the one hand, his discussion of circumcision rites in Kenya yielded important "anthropological" insights,[48] but on the other hand, the theoretical insights of the political scientist always intruded. Some contemporary African intellectuals apparently felt that Bunche's reaction to such aspects of traditional African culture indicated that he had accepted some Kiplingesque ideas, such as the white man's burden and the civilizing mission of the Europeans.[49] He was clearly not at ease when he witnessed the male circumcision ceremonies of the Kikuyu leading to *kugimara* status (becoming an adult), even though he attempted to understand it both "anthropologically" and "politically"—a classic disagreement about what was being perceived.[50]

Bunche's trip to Mozambique, then to Dutch-ruled Indonesia, to the Philippines, to Macao, Hong Kong, and other parts of China sharpened his growing anthropological insights to deal with the cultural differences he encountered. Bunche was anxious to go to his family reunion in Los Angeles, and while this helped him to place his life in perspective, one can well understand why he was increasingly convinced that the narrow academic environment at Howard and the now more objectionable sociocultural atmosphere of Washington, D.C., would stifle him.

Bunche's work with Gunnar Myrdal on *The American Dilemma,* his service to the United States as an Africanist in World War II and the founding of the United Nations, and his subsequent fame as a UN mediator in the Arab-Israeli conflict in Palestine made it understandable why he would have been chosen to help the United Nations deal with what was feared as a possible disaster in decolonizing the Congo.

In contrast to his previous experience with the problems of trusteeship and outright colonialism in Africa and his subsequent experiences in South Africa and Kenya, the Congo would represent a major challenge to Ralph Bunche. He was not quite prepared for the social, cultural, and political realities he would face there. Basic contradictions marked his view of the cultural reality in the Congo, how the Congolese viewed their own plight, and how the rest of the world saw it. Here elements of culture, race, nationality, and the cold war were ready made for disaster. First of all, the Congolese did not fully understand the political implication of modern statehood that was being suggested to them, nor in fact did anyone else understand the oxymoronic notion of a colonial state to which they had been subjected under the rule of the Belgians. Not only did Joseph Kasavubu and Patrice Lumumba misunderstand whether a president or a premier was really in charge of the emerging state, but matters became worse when Lumumba misunderstood the limitations that faced the representatives of the United Nations in his embattled country. The arrogance of the Belgian officers and the panic of whites in the face of Congolese fear and distrust of all whites made life itself dangerous for Bunche. He was almost killed when mistaken for a white man, and the situation did not improve when Lumumba objected to having the United Nations represented by "ce nègre américain." It was unfortunate (and possibly because he was from the eastern Congo) that Patrice Lumumba did not know more about "les Américains noirs." Many black Americans who visited Léopoldville (now Kinshasa) were Garveyites, deeply mistrusted by the Belgians for selling the "Negro World" and preaching "Africa for the Africans at home and abroad." Unfortunately for Bunche, the same thing was not true of Thomas Kanza, the first of few college graduates in Congo, and later Lumumba's ambassador to the UN. Kanza sought to mediate between Bunche and Lumumba, but the cold war and the conflict between nation-states determined to foster neocolonialism in Africa proved disastrous to all.

Reflections

In retrospect it might seem that Bunche never fully adopted negritude because it might have threatened his American Dream. I'm struck by Bunche's reaction to the changing concept of the Negro. We know that many persons of Bunche's generation never referred to themselves as anything but Negro, and we are aware of DuBois's dream that if Negroes were to achieve anything in the world, they had to do it by themselves. This came to mean that over time Negroes, with their own black hands, would be in charge of their own salvation. The Black Power movement left many Negroes speechless because in a very interesting way they could not deal with being both black and American. I have not been able to find references to Bunche ever calling himself an African American. Indeed in his last speech he constantly referred to himself as a black American, but to be a black American to many of the younger generation was not enough. They had to go beyond Bunche and become an African American. In other words, to be an African American is to finally place the American in context. Many whites balk at the notion that they are European Americans rather than simply Americans. In a very interesting way, African Americans contradict but add a great deal to what America meant. The early people who called themselves Americans felt that only people of European origin could be Americans. But today we know that there are many kinds of Americans. If the African American or the black American has done anything, it has been to help free persons of African origin of any racial or cultural complexes. This is what DuBois meant when he said he would not want to "Africanize America, for America has too much to teach the world and Africa."[51]

The problem for persons such as Bunche, and for DuBois, for that matter, was that the rhetoric of "race" loyalty, or what later became known as Africanity, had to deal with a pressing reality, that is, to rid the world of colonialism, which meant the domination of the world by persons of European descent. Again, we know that DuBois sensed the dilemma of black people during his lifetime, and we are familiar with the angst he felt when confronted with the reality of the twentieth century, an epoch whose major characteristic was the "problem of the color-line, the relation of the darker to the lighter races of men in Asia and Africa, in America and the islands of the sea."[52] DuBois wondered, somewhat rhetorically, "how far differences of race, which show themselves chiefly in the color of the skin and the texture of the hair, are going to be made, hereafter, the basis of denying to over half the world the right of sharing to their utmost ability the opportunities and privileges of modern mankind."[53]

What Bunche's generation did was to help destroy the colonial situation and instead of relegating African studies to the realm of colonized peoples, to destroy the notion of the white man's burden. Bunche's generation emphasized that the study of humankind is universal, that it covers all our species throughout space and time. Taking Bunche's cue, we assert that the proper study of human beings, black or white, is the human condition in all its cultural, social, and political contexts.

Notes

1. Ralph J. Bunche, "French Administration in Togoland and Dahomey" (PhD diss., Harvard University, 1934).
2. Nobel Foundation, "Ralph Bunche, Biography," http://nobelprize.org/peace/laureates/1950/bunche-bio.html (accessed October 29, 2004).
3. Alfred A. Moss, *The American Negro Academy: Voice of the Talented Tenth* (Baton Rouge: Louisiana State University Press, 1981).
4. W. E. B. DuBois, *The Souls of Black Folk* (1903; repr., Nashville: Fisk University Press, 1979).
5. Ibid.
6. Ibid., 3.
7. Henry Luce, "The American Century" (1941; repr. in *The Ambiguous Legacy: U.S. Foreign Relations in the American Century,* ed. M. J. Hogan [Cambridge: Cambridge University Press, 1999]).
8. DuBois, *Souls,* 11.
9. Brian Urquhart, *Ralph Bunche: An American Life* (New York: Norton, 1993).
10. Georgia Writers Project, Savannah Unit, *Drums and Shadows: Survival Studies among the Georgia Coastal Negroes* (Athens: University of Georgia Press, 1986).
11. Excerpted from W. E. B. DuBois, "Of Our Spiritual Strivings," in *Souls.*
12. Ralph Bunche, *A World View of Race,* Bronze Booklet Series (Washington, DC: Associates in Negro Folk Education, 1936). In this ninety-eight-page booklet Bunche argues that race was a social rather than a scientific construct and that conflict frequently identified as racial was in reality based on social, political, and economic causes.
13. Philip D. Curtin, ed., *The Image of Africa: British Ideas and Action, 1780–1850* (Madison: University of Wisconsin Press, 1964), 36–37.
14. Ibid., 42.
15. Eric Williams, *Capitalism and Slavery* (Chapel Hill: University of North Carolina Press, 1970), 208.
16. This notion dies hard; it was held by many European colonials in Africa, from Cecil Rhodes to Ian Smith.
17. In an early draft of the Declaration of Independence, Thomas Jefferson castigated George III for transporting Africans to America against their will, subjecting them to slavery, and encouraging them to murder the slaveholders. Other slaveholders who, like Jefferson, profited from the labor of these slaves, felt that he had been carried away by his rhetoric and excised the African charge from the document.
18. Thomas Jefferson, "Notes on the State of Virginia," Electronic Text Center, University of Virginia Library, http://etext.lib.virginia.edu/toc/modeng/public/JefVirg.html (accessed October 29, 2004).

19. Thomas A. Bailey, *The Man in the Street: The Impact of American Public Opinion on Foreign Policy* (New York: Macmillan, 1948), 16.

20. James C. Thomson, Peter W. Stanley, and John C. Perry, *Sentimental Imperialists: The American Experience in East Asia* (New York: Harper and Row, 1981), 14.

21. David J. Burton, *Theodore Roosevelt: Confident Imperialist* (Philadelphia: University of Pennsylvania Press, 1968), 132ff.

22. A few years ago, the African Studies Association in the USA castigated Philip Curtain for suggesting that "part-historians" and some of their white counterparts were prejudicial to African studies.

23. Thomas Jefferson, *Notes on the State of Virginia: With Related Documents,* ed. David Waldstreicher (Notre Dame, IN: Palgrave Macmillan, 2002).

24. Clinton Caldwell Boone, *Liberia As I Know It* (Westport, CN: Negro Universities Press, 1929), 27.

25. Adelaide Cromwell Hill and Martin Kilson, eds., *Apropos of Africa: Sentiments of Negro American Leaders on Africa from 1800 to the 1950s* (London: Frank Cass, 1969), 94–97.

26. Elliott P. Skinner, *African Americans and U.S. Policy toward Africa, 1850–1924: In Defense of Black Nationality* (Washington, DC: Howard University Press, 1992), 110n47. Smyth goes on to say, "I hope it may be found in consonance with the foreign policy of our Government to aid Liberia in a retention of her self respect unimpaired, her control of her territory, her prestige which is the consequence of her control."

27. Burton, *Theodore Roosevelt,* ch. 2.

28. Urquhart, *Ralph Bunche.*

29. Ibid., 34. "Bunche's group on Central Avenue consisted of George Duncan, Charles (Sandy) Saunders, Wilalyn Stovall, Melvin Thistle, and Erskin and Charlie Ragland. Their theme song was, 'There'll Be Some Changes Made.'" Ibid., 34n15.

30. Richard Wright, *Black Power: A Record of Reactions in a Land of Pathos* (New York: Harper, 1954). Intriguingly, this was the plight of Richard Wright when confronted with the swaying bodies in an African backyard in Kwame Nkrumah's Ghana.

31. Urquhart, *Ralph Bunche,* 33.

32. Significantly, on Saturday nights and in a manner comparable to Ralph Ellison's experience in *Invisible Man,* the pig boys had to fight each other to amuse the whites.

33. Herschelle Challenor, "The Contribution of Ralph Bunch to Trusteeship and Colonization," in Benjamin Rivlin, ed., *Ralph Bunche, the Man and His Times* (New York: Holmes and Meier, 1990).

34. Urquhart, *Ralph Bunche,* 41; emphasis in original.

35. Ibid., 39.

36. Bunche, "The Fourth Dimension of Personality," commencement address, UCLA, June 1927; http://content.cdlib.org/ark:/13030/hb0489n7nw/.

37. Raymond Leslie Buell, *The Native Problem in Africa* (London: Frank Cass, 1965). Martin Kilson told me personally that Bunche was aware of Buell's lectures and activities at Harvard during this period.

38. Urquhart, *Ralph Bunche,* 51.

39. Bunche, "French Administration." See his comments about the strange French view on cultural specificity.

40. Buell, *Native Problem.*

41. Ibid.

42. Elliott P. Skinner, *The Mossi of Upper Volta: The Political Development of a Sudanese People* (Stanford: Stanford University Press, 1964).

43. Bunche wrote in his PhD dissertation, "It is not so important that the territories under mandate be better administered than the colonies of the world, but it is important

that the mandate principle assure to these territories an unselfish, helpful administration, which will afford them an opportunity to properly prepare themselves for the eventual day when they will stand alone in the world. The African is no longer to be considered a barbarian, nor even a child, but only an adult retarded in terms of Western civilization." Bunche, "French Administration."

44. Ibid.

45. Rivlin, *Ralph Bunche,* 78.

46. Nathan Irvin Huggins, "Ralph Bunche the Africanist," in Rivlin, *Ralph Bunche,* 79.

47. Bishop Levi Jenkins Coppin, *Letters from South Africa* (Philadelphia: A.M.E. Books Concern, 1901), 210ff., quoted in Hill and Kilson, *Apropos of Africa,* 245ff.; see also "American Negro's Religion for the African Negro's Soul," *Independent* 54 (March 27, 1902): 748–58; Coppin, *Observations of Persons and Things in South Africa, 1900–1904* (Philadelphia: A.M.E. Book Concern, n.d.), 205.

48. Elliott P. Skinner, "Female Circumcision in Africa: The Dialectics of Equality," in *Dialectics and Gender Anthropological Approaches,* ed. Richard Randolph, David Schneider, and May N. Diaz (Boulder: Westview, 1988).

49. W. Ofuatey-Kodjoe, "Ralph Bunche: An African Perspective," in Rivlin, *Ralph Bunche,* 98.

50. Ibid.

51. DuBois, *Souls,* 3.

52. Ibid., 11.

53. Alexander Walters, *My Life and Work* (New York: Fleming H. Revell, 1917), 257.

CHAPTER FIVE

Ralph Bunche the Africanist
Revisiting Paradigms Lost

PEARL T. ROBINSON

ON MAY 11, 1927, the young Ralph Bunche sent a letter to W. E. B. DuBois, the preeminent African American intellectual of his time. Bunche was about to receive his AB degree in political science from UCLA (then the University of California, Southern Branch). He would deliver the valedictory address at the 1927 commencement exercises and had accepted a scholarship for graduate studies at Harvard University. Connecting with DuBois seemed the next logical step toward fulfilling his ambitions for a future of service to "the cause of human fellowship."[1]

The two men had met briefly on several occasions when DuBois visited Los Angeles, and Bunche's academic achievements would soon receive recognition in the pages of *The Crisis*, a magazine edited by DuBois.[2] Nevertheless, with studied modesty, Bunche indicated that he did not expect the senior scholar to remember him. Then he proceeded to reintroduce himself:

> Since I have been sufficiently old to think rationally and to appreciate that there was a "race problem" in America, . . . I have set as the goal of my ambition service to my group. . . . I am even now fulfilling that ambition. . . .
>
> But I have long felt the need of coming in closer contact with the leaders of our Race, so that I may better learn their methods of approach, their psychology and benefit in my own development by their influence.[3]

In short, Ralph Bunche reintroduced himself to W. E. B. DuBois as one of the Talented Tenth. DuBois's now-classic essay "The Talented Tenth" was first published in 1903 as the second chapter in a book entitled *The Negro Problem*.[4] The piece was DuBois's response to the widespread embrace of Booker T. Washington's advocacy of industrial education as the best means to improve the lot of black Americans—then barely a generation removed from slavery. DuBois countered, presenting the case for liberal education of a critical segment of African Americans who would then be equipped to provide the leadership necessary for racial progress. Stating that "the Negro race, like all other races, is going to be saved by its exceptional men," he argued that roughly a tenth of the black population in the United States should receive a liberal arts education that emphasizes "intelligence, broad sympathy, knowledge of the world that was and is, and of the relation of men to it."[5]

DuBois defined the Talented Tenth largely, though not entirely, by its educational training.[6] Some, like abolitionist Fredrick Douglass, were well educated but self-trained. And Sojourner Truth, the abolitionist and women's rights crusader, never learned to read. Indeed, central to DuBois's notion of the Talented Tenth was the special mission of racial uplift. As he put it, "The Talented Tenth of the Negro Race must be made leaders of thought and missionaries of culture among their people."[7] Keen to prepare himself well for that role, the young Ralph asked DuBois for an opportunity to spend his summer before entering Harvard working in the Eastern or Southern United States, either connected with the National Association for the Advancement of Colored People or as a teacher. DuBois acknowledged the letter but had nothing to offer.[8]

Beyond the drama of a polite rebuff, Bunche's letter is particularly striking for the clarity with which it reveals his internalization, at an early age, of the duty to work for racial uplift. Virtually all who comment on Bunche's character, intellectual brilliance, and professional accomplishments make the link with the Talented Tenth. It is often noted that he imported this prescription for group uplift into his academic research and policy prescriptions for Africa.[9] Emboldened by the rigorous methods and new paradigms of modern social science, Bunche made "the status of subject peoples" and the training of their Talented Tenth one of the central organizing ideas that guided his research agenda, framed his policy outlook, and gave a larger purpose to his scholarly interest in Africa.[10] Far less appreciated, however, is the fact that his intellectual agenda as an Africanist encompassed a much broader nexus of issues.[11]

Bunche's empirically grounded work on Africa is dispersed in a wide variety of relatively obscure sites: his Harvard dissertation; articles and book reviews published largely in Negro journals; thousands of photographs shot during episodes of field research in Dahomey, Togoland, South Africa, Kenya, and on safari through Uganda, Congo, Tanganyika, and Kenya; travel notes chronicling his research in Kenya and South Africa; ethnographic film footage;[12] the unpublished bibliography that soured his years in U.S. government service; as well as the formal documentation of interest articulation by "subject peoples" in the mandated Territories collected under his directorship of the United Nations Trusteeship Council. Taken together, these materials constitute the elements of the paradigm that informed Bunche's Africanist scholarship. That paradigm—grounded in economic determinism—emphasized the problems posed by colonial policies, imperialism, and the changing status of the contemporary African population.[13] For Bunche, these were the defining issues of late-colonial Africa. And with the conviction of a man who *knows* that he is right, he insisted that these matters should constitute the central terrain of modern African studies.

As used here, the term Africanist refers to someone who engages in the production and validation of knowledge about Africa on the basis of primary-source data and empirically grounded field research.[14] An inventory of the diverse elements and scattered artifacts of Bunche's production of knowledge about Africa sheds new light on the intellectual agenda that was to shape his life's work. More than a discussion of the range of techniques and methodological rigor Bunche used in data collection, this chapter aims to understand how Bunche the Africanist deployed his rich data sets to challenge the accepted wisdom of recognized authorities and offer his own policy prescriptions. Close scrutiny reveals both the tenacity of his beliefs and the real-world consequences of his conviction that intellectuals skilled in the tools of modern social science are equipped to play a directive role in restructuring society. This belief connects Bunche's Africanist scholarship with trajectories forged and followed during his career at the United Nations.

Bunche Goes to Africa to Find a Problem

Ralph Bunche joined Howard University's faculty in 1928,[15] immediately after completing his Harvard master's thesis on the seventeenth-century English political philosopher Robert Filmer.[16] A brilliant student,

Bunche nevertheless declined Harvard's offer of a doctoral fellowship in order to accept the Howard job. Within three years Bunche had set up a political science department, become department head, and assumed additional duties as assistant to Howard's president, Mordecai Johnson. For four years his time would be split between Harvard and Howard; Bunch spent a year's leave and summers in Cambridge doing coursework toward a doctorate. He shifted his academic focus to American government and international affairs. Staunchly independent, Bunche did not base his dissertation on the scholarship or expertise of his Harvard professors. Instead, he settled on a topic that was a product of his Howard experience and the environment crafted by its remarkable president.[17]

Mordecai Johnson's thirty-four-year tenure at Howard began in 1926. He was the thirteenth president and first African American to head the institution. A Baptist minister and skilled orator, with degrees from the University of Chicago and Harvard Divinity School, his goal was to modernize the university and secure its reputation as the foremost black university in the nation. Working closely with Alain Locke, the first black Rhodes Scholar, he recruited the best and the brightest of a new generation of black academics trained at top research universities. The politically savvy Johnson was an effective fundraiser and was *connected*—to official Washington as well as to private foundations.[18]

Bunche arrived at Howard as an intellectually ambitious young instructor on the fast track. His niche was the social sciences, and he contributed toward building the reputation of the university's new Division of Social Sciences as a unit that produced well-trained researchers, teachers, and policy experts.[19] Together with economist Abram Harris and sociologist E. Franklin Frazier, Bunche formed part of a young cohort of progressive academics known for their intellectual independence and political boldness, as well as for their commitment to bringing the latest theories to bear on problems affecting black Americans.[20] Bunche was the junior partner in this threesome.

Harris, who was writing his dissertation when he joined the Howard faculty in 1928, completed his doctorate in economics at Columbia two years later. He had previously worked for the National Urban League in New York and Minnesota and had already published an analysis of black life in Minnesota.[21] Frazier arrived at Howard a full professor with a steady record of publications going back to 1922. A protégé of Robert Park at the University of Chicago, he had a productive career as an applied social scientist before becoming a full-time academic sociologist. Harris and Frazier both taught at historically black colleges before taking up their positions at Howard, and each published a major book during the 1930s that was to become a classic in their respective disciplines.[22] In short, both scholars had gravitas. Their academic success set the benchmarks of expectation for the young Ralph Bunche, whose early career was characterized by its meteoric rise.

While Howard had much to offer, relationships in the university community could at times be petty and vindictive. Bunche would experience the harsher side during his final years on the faculty. What pulled the positive elements together and made them work especially well for the young Bunche during his early years was the guiding hand of Alain Locke, in whom Bunche found a mentor and lifelong friend.[23] The two men shared interests in political philosophy and international affairs. In subtle and occasionally career-shaping ways, Locke encouraged Bunche to cultivate the latter discipline.[24] This influence became especially critical as the choice of a dissertation topic became imminent.

Howard's preeminence in the world of black higher education led Bunche to spend a good deal of time addressing issues of American politics and race relations. In fact, his earliest political science publication examined the role of the Negro in Chicago politics.[25] He might therefore have been expected to develop a dissertation proposal with a focus on some aspect of the U.S. domestic situation. Instead, he stuck with his interest in international organizations. Yet picking a topic took him several years—and was not easy.

Bunche initially considered examining the role of the League of Nations in the suppression of slavery. He later flirted with the idea of doing a comparative study of racial mixing by contrasting racial assimilation in Brazil with the practice of continued segregation in the United States. When the prospect of a dissertation fellowship from the Rosenwald Fund materialized, he received advice from Edwin Embree, the fund's president. Embree suggested a study of West Virginia politics. Bunche bristled. In a letter to Arthur Holcombe, his dissertation adviser, he explained, "I am fully persuaded that the Negro of all scholars must first develop a broad international background if his contribution to the solution of our own domestic problems are [sic] to make much impress."[26]

Bunche ultimately settled on a topic that would take him to Paris, London, Geneva, and West Africa. Shortly after he left on research leave, Mordecai Johnson announced at a faculty meeting, "Bunche is going all the way to Africa to find a problem."[27] Though this quip can be read as a sign of disapproval, doing research abroad was not out of step with the prevailing faculty norm. In fact, Howard in the 1930s was an atypically cosmopolitan place, and a number of its leading academics sought overseas research opportunities. Locke had studied at Oxford and in Germany, made frequent trips to Europe throughout his career, and relished initiating younger colleagues into life "on the other side [of the Atlantic]."[28] Frazier researched folk high schools and the cooperative movement in Denmark; Abe Harris did a post-doc at Oxford; Mercer Cook, a professor of Romance languages at Howard, studied the *négritude* movement in Paris; and political science instructor Emmet Dorsey got a firsthand look at the consolidation of communism in the Soviet Union. Biologist Ernest Just, head of Howard's Department of Zoology, worked at labs in Italy, France, and Germany. And the Paris literary salon run by Paulette and Jane Nardal, two Howard graduates originally from Martinique, regularly hosted faculty who visited the City of Light.[29]

Also, Howard's location, in the nation's capital, made it a black mecca of sorts for international visitors. Public figures from Liberia, Ethiopia, South Africa, the Caribbean, and elsewhere were no strangers to the campus. Students from British West Africa and the Caribbean had a definite influence on the curriculum; they connected campus intellectual and political life with the emerging tide of anticolonial nationalism.[30] Indeed, speakers from many parts of the world such as Europe, India, and China found a welcome platform on the Hill, as the Howard campus was called.

White scholars with a serious interest in the black world were also part of this mix. Some taught at Howard. Others spent time on the campus, interacted with students, and actively engaged the intellectual currents that animated the university's unique brand of internationalism. Two who had a decisive impact on Bunche's formal training and career as an Africanist were Raymond Leslie Buell and Melville J. Herskovits.

Buell authored the monumental two-volume work *The Native Problem in Africa*, published in 1928.[31] A specialist in international relations and comparative politics, he had been an assistant professor of government at Harvard before leaving in 1927 to become research director (and later president) of the Foreign Policy Association (FPA) in New York. It was Buell who suggested Bunche's dissertation topic.[32] Herskovits spent 1925 at Howard as a lecturer in anthropology. A recent Columbia University PhD at the time, he was a student of Franz Boas and had already done fieldwork in Dutch Guiana, Haiti, and Trinidad. While at Howard he held a National Research Council fellowship and was doing research on racial mixing. Herskovits moved to Northwestern University in 1927, where he established the program in African studies and rose quickly to become acknowledged as the leading American Africanist.[33] It was he who secured Bunche's 1937 award of a two-year postdoc sponsored by the Social Science Research Council for anthropological study and fieldwork in Africa.

Alain Locke was Bunche's bridge into the world of African studies. As a member of the London-based International Institute of African Languages and Cultures, his Africanist credentials carried weight in U.S. academic and policy circles. Buell had sought and received Locke's assistance during the research phase of *The Native Problem,* and Locke wrote one of the book's first published reviews. In 1927 the FPA sent Locke to Geneva to study the work of the League of Nations in African reconstruction and asked that he focus on administration of the African mandates. Buell subsequently tried to persuade Locke to do a more in-depth study of the mandate system in Africa. But Locke's interest in Africa centered on the arts and humanities. When Buell indicated that he wanted to see "an American Negro take a thorough study of the situation in Africa,"[34] Locke was not shy about promoting his young colleague.

By the summer of 1931, Bunche had warmed to Buell's suggestion of a dissertation on French colonial administration in Africa. While attending the Williamstown Institute of Politics he was able to meet Charles Le Neveu, president of the Paris-based Union Coloniale Française. Le Neveu provided Bunche with a pamphlet, "The Methods of Administration and of Government in the French and English Colonies," and would later become a key contact for gaining access to documents in the French colonial office.[35] Meanwhile Buell, who had authored a book on postwar French politics, loaned Bunche materials from his personal library, including copies of French budget reports. Beyond facilitating development of a strong dissertation proposal, Buell pressed Bunche on three methodological points: the superior value of knowledge derived from empirical data and hypothesis testing, the analytical leverage gained by addressing the interracial situation as a world problem,[36] and the critical importance of fieldwork for the validation of knowledge about Africa.[37] These points became the touchstones of Bunche's Africanist scholarship.

The matter of fieldwork was a sticky problem for a black scholar doing African studies in the 1930s. The example of Leo Hansberry at Howard was a stark reminder of the prevailing attitudes and constraints. Hansberry taught courses on Negro civilizations of ancient Africa in the history department. When he completed his MA in archeology from Harvard, in 1932, he sought advice on whether, as a black American, he might have difficulty joining a British archeological expedition to Egypt. A letter from Dows Dunham of Boston's Museum of Fine Arts confirmed his apprehension: "To be perfectly frank with you, if I were in charge of such an expedition, I should hesitate long before taking an American Negro on my staff. . . . I should fear that the mere fact of your being a member of the staff would seriously affect the prestige of the other members and the respect which the native employees would have for them."[38]

This advice most likely had a chilling effect on Hansberry. Unable to join an archeological expedition, he oriented his career around library and archival research, and was a devoted teacher. Popular with students, he also organized symposia and lectured widely to audiences outside the university. It was not until 1953, with the award of a Fulbright Fellowship, that Hansberry finally went to Egypt, Ethiopia, and Sudan for field research.[39]

The example of historian Rayford Logan, a Harvard-trained PhD who joined the Howard faculty in 1938, shows how a black scholar could accommodate the fieldwork problem. Logan was an internationalist but not an Africanist. In 1928 he published "The Operation of the Mandate System in Africa" in the *Journal of Negro History*.[40] Based on primary research done at the League of Nations headquarters in Geneva, this densely empirical article incorporates material from the minutes of the League's Permanent Mandates Commission as well as documentation compiled in *Statistical Information Concerning Territories under Mandate*, also available in Geneva. For facts about the situation in Africa, Logan acknowledges his debt to Buell's "encyclopedic" *Native Problem in Africa*. Perhaps the utility of this approach explains why, a month after Bunche arrived in Paris with fellowship stipends from the Rosenwald Fund and Howard University, Locke advised him, "If you don't get as far as Africa, . . . [t]he study could be done out of Geneva."[41]

Once Bunche committed to a dissertation on colonial administration, it was understood that fieldwork in Africa would be the union card for the kind of academic career he envisaged. Aware that access to the field was controlled by the colonial powers, he acquired a stack of letters of introduction from high-level academic and political gatekeepers in the United States. Bunche saw these letters as "a form of protection in the colonies against any undue suspicion which might arise."[42] He asked each referee to state the exact nature of his mission and its purely scholarly objectives. Buell gave Bunche an extra push and advised him to get a letter of introduction from the French Colonial Ministry to the governor of the colonies. Acquiring such a letter necessitated the involvement of the U.S. State Department and the U.S. ambassador in France.[43] Bunche successfully worked these channels. He managed to obtain official introductions to the governor general of French West Africa as well as to his lieutenant governors in Senegal, Dahomey, Ivory Coast, Niger, and Mauritania. Moreover, in a letter written from Blaise Diagne, the Senegalese politician who at the time was France's sole black member of Parliament, he had, in writing, a letter of introduction to the president of the French Republic.[44] Direct access to the colonial records in all these French territories meant that Bunche would be in a position to test hypotheses and even challenge the arguments and policy prescriptions advanced by Buell.

In June 1932, Bunche set sail for Paris on the SS *Europa*. This was his first trip abroad and he had prepared meticulously to assure its success. His research design combined comparative political analysis, economic determinism, and hypothesis testing to investigate whether the type of colonial administration made a difference in the life of the native. Fieldwork enabled him to gather data on the internal dynamics of French colonial administration in the two settings. Finding little difference between the two, he then marshaled evidence to argue that French economic interests shaped colonialism in both Dahomey and Togoland. For this groundbreaking study, Bunche won Harvard's Toppan Prize for the year's best dissertation in the field of government. In recognition of the pioneering nature of this work, Harvard's government department created a new field called International Relations with Special Attention to the Government of Dependencies.[45]

Bunche and Buell: The Native Problem in Africa

Bunche the social scientist was empirically driven, partial to analyses designed for hypothesis testing, and imbued with a technocratic faith in objectivity.⁴⁶ He engaged the world of big ideas and in so doing sought to effect change. Bunche the Africanist was an iterative thinker. He identified fault lines in works of high repute, and then using his own Africa data (*always* generated by field studies), he challenged prevailing certainties with the subtle phrasing of a skillful draftsman. In his dissertation, journal articles, and book reviews—tacking back and forth between his own and a counterpart's data—Bunche sketched out the elements of a new paradigm for African studies. His first step in this direction appears in his Harvard dissertation, "French Administration in Togoland and Dahomey."

In writing the dissertation, Bunche used Buell's *Native Problem* as a template for the scholarly analysis and a foil for his own hard-hitting political critique of the colonial situation in Africa and its lessons for black-white race relations in the United States. He took no issue with the social Darwinist assumptions explicit in Buell's statement of the problem. Indeed, he shared Buell's Enlightenment view of the perfectibility of humankind. The similarity in their language on this score is striking:

> BUELL: The purpose of this report is to set forth the problems which have arisen out of the impact of primitive peoples with an industrial civilization, and to show how and to what extent these problems are being solved by the governments concerned.⁴⁷
>
> BUNCHE: The basic problem has a two-fold aspect, viz.: (a) the immediate effect of the impact of a capitalistic, industrial civilization upon the primitive African, and (b) the specific objectives of the native policy and the native welfare measures applied by the colonizing power.⁴⁸

Continuing along this line, Bunche echoed Buell's assertion that Africa was the one continent in the world where social engineering could most readily make inroads and rectify a host of problems. Again, they appear to be emphasizing the same points:

> BUELL: Africa is the one continent of the world where by the application of intelligence, knowledge and good will, it is not too late to adopt policies which will prevent the development of the acute racial difficulties which have elsewhere risen, and the evils of which have been recognized only after they have come into existence.⁴⁹

BUNCHE: Here is one place in a troubled world where mistakes previously committed may be corrected; where, indeed, a new and better civilization may be cultivated, through the deliberate application of human intelligence and understanding.[50]

Buell argued that in the French mandates of Togoland and Cameroun, the military, educational, and native policies were better than in the French colonies. Bunche, however, did not share his mentor's largely positive assessment of the League's mandate system. M. Rappard, director of the mandates section of the League's secretariat, explained the arrangement as "a kind of compromise" between "the advocates of annexation" and "those who wanted to entrust the colonial territories to international administration."[51] Bunche pressed the point in his dissertation by translating Buell's conclusions about the difference between mandate and colonial administration policy and organization into concrete measures that affected the social, political, and economic welfare of native populations. A case in point is the question of whether mandate administration was preferable to colonial administration—from the perspective of the African. To support his argument Buell provided comparative statistics on taxes, conscription, and social services in the French mandates of Togoland and Cameroun, then cited the views of a few Togolese elites who compared their situation with that of relatives in the neighboring French colony of Dahomey. Bunche, who did fieldwork in both Togoland and Dahomey, collected data in these same areas of colonial activity.[52] Then, holding the domestic arena constant, he sought to determine whether ordinary Togolese perceived a difference in their situation following the change in Togoland's status from a German colony to a French mandate. Conclusions drawn from these two methods of analysis reveal dueling perspectives:

BUELL: French military policy in the mandates differs vitally from French policy in the colonies proper. This difference is appreciated by the most pro-French natives in Lome, the capital of Togo, who declare that they would not live in the neighboring colony of Dahomey because of the military obligations to which their relatives there must submit.[53]

BUNCHE: To the Togolese, the French in Togo are merely some more colonial administrators with a new and strange language and a knack for collecting taxes. In truth, this new status means little to them now and will continue so for many years.[54]

Bunche was certainly no apologist for French colonialism. He observed that the assimilated francophone elites showed little concern for the plight of their fellow Africans and attributed this attitude at least in part to the educational system. Still, when he weighed in on the relative merits of different colonial philosophies, the French fared better than most, in his judgment. This was especially the case after the French reformulated their long-standing policy of assimilation to articulate a new doctrine of association, which recognized "the separate cultures and institutions of African peoples," and relied on African elites knowledgeable about both French and African culture to function as "translators."[55] Buell, on the other hand, maintained that the British practice of indirect rule took the African perspective into account and, as such, amounted to a form of self-determination. Here again, he and Bunche disagreed:

> BUELL: [Indirect rule] is a system which, differing vitally from the system followed in the Transkei, Kenya, and the French colonies, rests upon the doctrine of self-determination and the philosophy of free-will.[56]
>
> BUNCHE: If the French are really willing to put the fundamentals of their excellent doctrine of association into effect, their ability to win the hearts of their black subjects should open to them a more successful future in their African colonial ventures than their Anglo-Saxon neighbors.[57]

In the preface to his dissertation, Bunche explained that his study was "stimulated by a deep interest in the development of subject peoples and the hopes which the future holds for them."[58] While unsure about where that future might lead,[59] he sought to contribute toward an understanding of alternative trajectories and policy choices. He therefore honed his arguments to produce a work that would mirror the academic and policy relevance of Buell's *Native Problem*. This was indeed an ambitious goal.

Propositions advanced in *The Native Problem* would frame the agenda for debates about colonial policies in Africa for decades to follow. Buell used his authoritative analyses of the diverse types of colonial experiments in French, British, and Belgian territory and Liberia to recommend policy on major issues affecting U.S. involvement in Africa[60] and to advance a set of conclusions about "best practices" for colonial rule. He generally favored British colonizing methods and maintained that the British policy of indirect rule was a form of governance that took African interests into account because it allowed Africans to retain their own culture and traditions. Bunche took issue with this line of reasoning:

> BUELL: The framework upon which the edifice [of indirect rule] is reared is traditional, and not artificial. It is a framework developed in a native and not a European milieu.[61]
> BUNCHE: It [indirect rule] often takes little account of the new economic, social, and political influences at work in the country.[62]
> BUELL: While the British government naturally prefers educated to illiterate chiefs, an educated commoner can not, under this system, become a chief.[63]
> BUNCHE: The British policy of maintaining hereditary chiefs in power, even though they may be illiterate, has often proven irksome to the educated commoner. The members of the native intelligentsia of the British colonies thus find themselves "lost souls."[64]

Bunche further insisted that the chief objective of indirect rule was to prevent the African from becoming too Westernized by containing the African population within a realm of "indigenous development under native chiefs subject to British guidance and control."[65]

In his "application of intelligence" and "knowledge" to the race problem, Buell turned to South Africa as a laboratory for testing different theories about how to construct a political system that would avoid exacerbating racial tensions. He identified three principles said to inform hotly debated policy alternatives: compulsory segregation, assimilation, and differentiation. Segregation and assimilation have long been bedrock staples in the tool kit of deeply divided societies. In Buell's analysis, differentiation was advanced as something new—a third way. Its South African advocates asserted "a fundamental distinction between a European, with a civilized background, centuries in duration, and a native only a few years removed from primitive conditions." They therefore insisted that the welfare of "the native" could best be promoted by "developing the native group as a whole, upon its own, and not upon European lines." Accordingly, the theory of differentiation indicated that giving "the natives" a part of South Africa to "build, with European assistance a political system of their own and also live a self-sufficing economic existence" was the best way to avoid a race war.[66] Buell supported this rationalization.

With a half million whites living alongside five and a half million blacks, Buell concluded that pure segregation was untenable. On the grounds that a steadily increasing number of assimilated blacks would eventually pose a threat to the political power and security of South Africa's white population, he also dismissed assimilation as a credible strategy for avoiding racial conflict. Then, shifting from theory to facts on the ground, he found much to commend in the native policy introduced in 1926 by the government of Prime Minster J. B. M. Hertzog, an Afrikaner nationalist. The Hertzog program began the abolition of the Cape Coloured franchise,[67] provided for European representation of blacks in a separate native council, and ratcheted up the restrictions against blacks living outside designated native "reserves." Buell explained that the theory of differentiation provided the rationale for these changes. Taking pains to chide "the so-called 'liberals' in both Europe and America" for being "addicted" to the theory of assimilation, he argued that the principles articulated in the Hertzog program might prove useful in addressing the potential for racial conflict elsewhere in Africa. Bunche considered this proposition flat-out wrong:

> BUELL: As the Natal Native Affairs Commission said, " ... [the natives] will not die out or succumb to ordinary adversity, and as we can neither assimilate nor destroy them, political forethought and common sense alike call for a settlement of the question on a broad, enlightened, and permanent basis."
>
> The principles sanctioned by the Hertzog Government are an important contribution to this settlement ... These principles may serve as a guide to other colonies, such as Kenya and Rhodesia, the white settlement of which has, comparatively speaking, only begun and where, consequently, the application of these measures should be easier to achieve than in South Africa. ...[68]
>
> BUNCHE: The policy of segregation assumes a variety of forms. ... To the extent that it limits [the native's] contact with the forces that are at work in the transformation of his country, it is an obstacle to his progress. Moreover, it is a policy that stirs up natural resentment on the part of the native populations subject to it.[69]

Bunche learned well from Buell the utility of looking at race from a global perspective. The many references in his dissertation to the situation of U.S. blacks serve as data for testing hypotheses about the consequences of comparable educational policies and patterns of race relations in Africa. At the same time, some of the comments are not-too-veiled references to DuBois's advocacy of a segregated "Negro nation within the nation" structured around racialized economic cooperatives.

> BUELL: This theory presupposes legislation designed to protect white communities against black penetration and black communities against white penetration.[70]
>
> BUNCHE: The American Negro has also learned that differentiation because of race, without equality, too often perpetuates inferiority.[71]

By 1933, DuBois had come to believe that short-term segregation was the necessary price for achieving racial equality in the long run. Abandoning his staunch support for integration, he began openly discussing "self-segregation" as a strategy for securing a better quality of life in a racially hostile society.[72] This anticipated solution to the scourge of racial conflict accommodated the principle of differentiation and thus came full circle to connect with Buell's solution for the native problem in South Africa. Bunche would have none of it. While still a junior scholar, he took on two academic giants whose expertise spanned his own fields of concentration in international relations, African studies, and the intersection of race relations and politics, and he dared to argue the fallacy of policies embraced by both. The result was a prize-winning dissertation that opened up fissures in the relationships established with his Talented Tenth role model and an academic mentor. In 1935, DuBois published "A Negro Nation within the Nation" in *Current History*.[73] Buell was elated.[74] Bunche the young Turk held his ground, wasting little time establishing his intellectual independence.[75] In fact, Bunche omitted Buell's name from the list of acknowledgments in his dissertation—an astonishing exclusion in light of Buell's centrality to the project's origins and execution.[76] Then, in a 1935 review of DuBois's book *Black Reconstruction in America*, Bunche demonstrated his capacity for balanced analysis by praising the senior scholar for unloosening "his brilliant and bitter eloquence" on "the falsifiers of Reconstruction history," and then denouncing his advocacy of black economic cooperatives as "a policy of Negro chauvinism" that amounted to little more than "an economic escape for the race."[77]

Paradigm Lost

According to Bunche biographer Charles Henry, "One senses a tension between Bunche the idealist or leftist and Bunche the pragmatist or social scientist."[78] That tension is particularly evident in the dissertation, which is written in two registers—an upper (dominant) register that tests the mandates-versus-colonial-administration hypothesis, and a lower (muted) register that treats the broader context of imperialism and argues that economic determinism is the driver of observed outcomes of both systems of administration. In what was to become a pattern in his Africanist scholarship, Bunche elaborated the full implications of his paradigm for the study of maturing colonialism in texts written for popular audiences, which included book reviews, articles published without footnotes, and his booklet *A World View of Race,* which was part of a series issued by the Associates in Negro Folk Education.[79]

For example, to read Bunche's candid thoughts on the League of Nations' mandate to oversee the interests and development of subject peoples as "a sacred trust of civilization,"[80] one could turn to the pages of the National Urban League's journal, *Opportunity*. Here, reviewing *Liberia in World Politics,* a book by the young Nigerian nationalist Nnamdi Azikiwe,[81] Bunche pronounced the author "naïve" for his "surprising faith in the sincerity of the League and its potential ability to protect weak states." Then, to explain why the League could not be counted on to uphold this sacred trust, he addressed the broader context and elaborated on "the forces at work in an international capitalist society which breed such horrors as imperialism, which create such institutions as the League of Nations as mere empty gestures and which make the application of principles of 'high morality' to defenseless states like Liberia utterly impossible."[82]

Bunche doubtless knew that such language would not earn him a doctorate from Harvard.[83] It may be for this reason that he articulated the broad outlines of the paradigm in the dissertation but located the hard-hitting critiques with rhetorical flourishes offsite. Interestingly, while writing the thesis he discussed drafts with Buell and apparently used that feedback to further sharpen some of the arguments related to their points of disagreement.[84] This behavior sheds light on Bunche's state of mind and self-assurance as the work finally drew to a close.

Before the dissertation was completed, he planned for its publication with the expectation that his adviser, Arthur Holcombe, would help. He must therefore have been sadly disappointed when, barely a few weeks after the successful thesis defense, a letter arrived from Holcombe suggesting "a short book . . . dealing with your observations and impressions in Africa." The letter further instructed that the scholarly material should be used as "the foundation of separate articles for the learned periodicals" rather than as the basis of a book. Bunche plucked what he could from Holcombe's advice and within a month published "French Educational Policy in Togo and Dahomey" in the *Journal of Negro Education*.[85] Then he began the work on turning his 492-page thesis into a small book for a general audience. Holcombe, an expert in public administration, might have been unaware of the full scope of his student's scholarly ambitions. This could explain why he concluded, "The thesis has served your purpose."[86]

Others thought differently. Rupert Emerson, then a young assistant professor of government and the junior member of Bunche's Harvard committee, encouraged publication of the dissertation and expressed preference for a scholarly book. Emerson was interested in the politics of anticolonial nationalism and would eventually become a leading scholar in that field.[87] He expressed concern that Bunche was having such difficulty trying to rewrite the text for a general audience and told him, "It does not seem to me that it needs much popularizing—unless no one will publish it otherwise."[88] A year later Charles Johnson, head of Fisk University's Department of Social Sciences, offered help with finding a publisher. Johnson had a copy of the thesis, which he considered "valuable and useful" and thought should be available in published form.[89] However, nothing came of this initiative. A second article drawn from the thesis appeared in *The Journal of Negro History* in 1936, but this was a largely rhetorical discussion of British and French imperialism in West Africa written without any scholarly references.[90] The shell of Bunche's critique of imperialism remains, but gone are the elements of social scientific thinking so brilliantly on display in the doctoral thesis. Bunche eventually moved on to new projects. The dissertation would never be published.

PEARL T. ROBINSON

The Talented Tenth Redux

Bunche began his career as an Africanist by articulating a paradigm for the study of the colonial situation that problematized the nexus of issues posed by colonial policies, imperialism, and the changing status of contemporary African populations. Ironically, what now remains as the strongest piece of published scholarship derived from his prize-winning dissertation in government is an article on educational policy in francophone West Africa. This highly informative analysis of British and French colonial educational policy is part ethnography and includes 107 footnotes citing scores of official documents as well as secondary sources. But the great debates that were animating colonial policy, and that put Bunche and Buell at loggerheads over some of the big issues, are not joined.

In this article, education holds the key to the African's future. The lesson is simple and localized. The policy prescription, well-suited to the temperament of the small-scale social engineer, points the way for Africans to transcend the local conditions of native life:

> To the African, education is as significant as magic. In large measure the education which is permitted him by the Western world dominating him holds the key to his economic, political, and social future.[91]
>
> The native is entitled to an introduction to that realm of literary, historical, religious, and scientific ideas which, having no immediate practical value, will nevertheless enable him to raise himself above the drudgery of his hum-drum life of daily toil. Only in this way can the African be expected to cultivate that spirit and articulateness necessary to the development of a national and racial soul, which alone will justify his ultimate right of self-control in his own country.[92]

Bunche collapsed a much broader set of issues into an analysis based on DuBois's paradigm of the Talented Tenth and narrowed his focus to the implications of the process of elite formation. Perhaps he thought that this was a more appropriate framework for an article appearing in a journal of education. Whatever the case, his overarching paradigm for the study of international relations with special attention to the government of dependencies—arguably a potentially major contribution to scholarship—was lost. Bunche would later rekindle that passion for global analysis when he left the academy for a career as an international public servant.

Notes
Abbreviations

RBP Ralph Bunche Papers, UCLA
SCR Bunche Papers, Schomburg Center for Research in Black Culture, New York

1. Ralph J. Bunche, "The Fourth Dimension of Personality," UCLA Commencement address, June 1927, made available by Mrs. Ralph Bunche and reprinted with her permission in Benjamin Rivlin, ed., *Ralph Bunche: The Man and His Times*, 224 (New York: Holmes and Meier, 1990).

2. "The College Negro American, 1927," *Crisis—A Record of the Darker Races* 32, no. 4 (August 1927): 187, 206.

3. Ralph Bunche, "Letter to Dr. William E. B. DuBois," repr. in Rivlin, *Ralph Bunche*, 218.

4. W. E. B. DuBois, "The Talented Tenth," in *The Negro Problem: A Collection of Articles by Representative African Americans of Today* (New York: James Pott and Company, 1903), 33–75.

5. DuBois, "Talented Tenth."

6. As he grew older, DuBois became increasingly elitist in his articulation of the requisite education and special mission of the Talented Tenth.

7. DuBois, "Talented Tenth."

8. Brian Urquhart, *Ralph Bunche: An American Life* (New York: Norton, 1993), 42.

9. Charles P. Henry, *Ralph Bunche: Model Negro or American Other?* (New York: New York University Press, 1999), 87; Jonathan Scott Holloway, *Confronting the Veil: Abram Harris Jr., E. Franklin Frazier, and Ralph Bunche, 1919–1941* (Chapel Hill: University of North Carolina Press, 2002).

10. An introduction to Bunche's Africanist training and scholarship is provided by Nathan Irvin Huggins, "Ralph Bunche the Africanist," in Rivlin, *Ralph Bunche*, 69–82.

11. Pearl T. Robinson, "Ralph Bunche and African Studies: Reflections on the Politics of Knowledge," *African Studies Review* 51, no. 1 (April 2008): 4–6. See also the chapters by David Anthony, Robert Edgar, and Elliott Skinner in this volume.

12. In 1938 Bunche returned from his SSRC fieldwork with fourteen thousand feet of movie film and twelve thousand still photos. Ralph Bunche to Melville Herskovits, October 5, 1938, box 1, folder 12, RBP.

13. Ralph Bunche to Miss Anna Kosslow, October 25, 1938, box 1, folder 12, RBP.

14. In Rivlin, *Ralph Bunche*, the following chapters are especially instructive on Bunche's career as an Africanist scholar: Lawrence S. Finkelstein, "Bunche and the Colonial World: From Trusteeship to Decolonization," 110–13; Nathan Irvin Huggins, "Ralph Bunche the Africanist, 69–82; and Martin Kilson, "Ralph Bunche's Analytical Perspective on African Development," 83–95.

15. Ralph Bunche taught at Howard University from 1928 to 1941. Technically, he remained on Howard's faculty until submitting a formal resignation on May 5, 1950.

16. Robert Filmer was a royalist and theorist of patriarchy who believed that democracy was the worst form of government. Bunche examined Filmore's theory on the origin of political authority. He was particularly interested in understanding justifications for existing powers premised on inequality. "Filmer's Conception on the Origin of Political Authority," typescript, box 12, folder 4, SCR.

17. Holloway, *Confronting the Veil*, 65–66.

18. Under Mordecai Johnson's administration, Howard's faculty tripled, salaries doubled, and congressional appropriations increased to $6 million annually. www.aaregistry.com/detail.php?id+23.

19. Holloway, *Confronting the Veil,* 16.
20. Ibid., introd.
21. Abram Harris Jr., *The Negro Population in Minneapolis: A Study of Race Relations* (Minneapolis: Urban League/Phyllis Wheatley Settlement House, 1926).
22. Sterling D. Spero and Abram L. Harris, *The Black Worker: The Negro and the Labor Movement* (1931. repr., Port Washington, NY: Kennikat Press, 1966); E. Franklin Frazier, *The Negro Family in Chicago* (Chicago: University of Chicago Press, 1932); Frazier, *The Negro Family in the United States* (Chicago: University of Chicago Press, 1939), which won the Anisfeld Award for best book on contemporary race relations.
23. Locke shared his feelings about Howard in a letter written to Bunche while he was doing dissertation research in Europe. He lamented, "I find some of our 'best' almost intolerable [in] their narrowness, crude provincialism and dirt-mindedness is really nauseating. What is it? Neither Harvard, Yale or Williams seem to be able to take it out of them." Alain Locke to Ralph Bunche, July 12, 1932, box 10b, folder 1, SCR.
24. For instance, in July 1931, Locke nominated Ralph Bunche for membership in the London-based International Institute of African Languages and Cultures and asked that he be allowed to attend an upcoming Paris conference in his stead. Himself a member, Locke described Bunche as "our young professor of government" who would be a valuable asset to the institute "from the point of view of the American Negro's interest in Africa Affairs." Alain Locke to Miss Brackett, July 25, 1931, box 10b, folder 10, SCR.
25. Ralph Bunche, "The Negro in Chicago Politics," *National Municipal Review* 18 (May 1928); repr. by the Boston *Transcript.*
26. Ralph Bunche to Arthur Holcombe, cited by Charles Henry, *Ralph Bunche,* 66.
27. Henry, *Ralph Bunche,* 65.
28. Alain Locke to Ralph Bunche, box 1, folder 3, November 13, 1929, RBP.
29. Bennetta Jules-Rosette, *Black Paris: The African Writer's Landscape* (Urbana: University of Illinois Press, 1998), 59–60.
30. Bunche taught courses on imperialism and colonialism in Africa and attracted international scholars to conferences such as the one he helped organize at Howard in 1936, "The Crisis of Modern Imperialism in Africa and the Far East." Henry, *Ralph Bunche,* 75.
31. Raymond Leslie Buell, *The Native Problem in Africa* (New York: Macmillan, 1928).
32. Henry, *Ralph Bunche,* 66.
33. Jane I. Guyer, *African Studies in the United States: A Perspective* (Atlanta: African Studies Association Press, 1996); Pearl T. Robinson, "Area Studies in Search of Africa," in *The Politics of Knowledge: Area Studies and the Disciplines,* ed. David Szanton, 119–83 (Berkeley: University of California Press, 2004). See also Jerry Gershenhorn, *Melville J. Herskovits and the Racial Politics of Knowledge* (Lincoln: University of Nebraska Press, 2004).
34. Raymond Buell to Alain Locke, October 2, 1928, box 164-18, folder 2, Alain Locke papers, Manuscript Division, Moorland-Spingarn Research Center, Howard University.
35. Ralph Bunche to M. Le Neveu, April 12, 1932, box 62, folder 1, RBP.
36. Raymond Buell to Ralph Bunche, April 25, 1932, box 1, folder 6, RBP.
37. Buell, *Native Problem,* preface, v.
38. Dows Dunham, quoted in William Leo Hansberry, *Pillars in Ethiopian History: The William Leo Hansberry African History Notebook,* ed. Joseph E. Harris (Washington, DC: Howard University, 1974), 13.
39. Hansberry, *Pillars,* 16.
40. Rayford Logan, "The Operation of the Mandate System in Africa," *Journal of Negro History* 13 (October 1928); repr. in Rayford W. Logan, *The Operation of the Mandate System in Africa, 1919–1927,* Washington, DC: Foundation Publishers, 1942), 1–50.

41. Alain Locke to Ralph Bunche, July 25, 1932, box 1, folder 6, RBP.
42. Ralph Bunche to Mr. George Arthur, March 24, 1932, box 62, folder 1, RPB.
43. This intervention was significant because the letters of introduction to the governor general and his lieutenants enabled Bunche to replicate the methodology Buell used to collect data for *The Native Problem in Africa*. Buell explained the situation to the U.S. assistant secretary of state: "It was my experience when visiting Africa in 1925 that a letter to the governor of the colonies was almost essential and that such letters could be obtained from the French Ministry of Colonies only through the good offices of the American Ambassador in Paris." Raymond Buell to James Grafton Rogers, May 12, 1932, box 62, folder 1, RBP. By contrast, Melville Herskovits advised Bunche against soliciting State Department help because it could cause suspicion that he was collecting information for government use. Melville Herskovits to Ralph Bunche, May 24, 1932, box 62, folder 1, RBP. Bunche opted to follow Buell's advice over that of Herskovits.
44. Blaise Daigne to President of the French Republic, October 25, 1932, box 62, folder 3, RBP.
45. Harvard University, Department of Government, to Ralph Bunche, October 6, 1933, box 62, folder 1, RBP.
46. Holloway, *Confronting the Veil*, 16–17; Robinson, "Ralph Bunche," 7.
47. Buell, *Native Problem*, 1:v.
48. Bunche, "French Administration," 3.
49. Buell, *Native Problem*, 1:v.
50. Bunche, "French Administration," 1.
51. Minutes of the Permanent Mandates Commission, first session, p. 4, in Logan, *Operation of the Mandate System*, 6; and in Bunche, "French Administration," 134.
52. Bunche, "French Administration," 217–418.
53. Buell, *Native Problem*, 2:283.
54. Bunche, "French Administration," 138; Robinson, "Ralph Bunche," 7–9.
55. Patrick Manning, *Francophone Sub-Saharan Africa, 1880–1985* (Cambridge: Cambridge University Press, 1988), 15, 61, 93.
56. Buell, *Native Problem*, 1:717.
57. Bunche, "French Administration," 134.
58. Ibid., ii.
59. Ralph Bunche to Robert Weaver, December 1, 1932, box 1, folder 6, RBP.
60. Buell was a harsh critic of U.S. intervention in Liberia in support of the Firestone Company's arrangements with the Liberian Labor Bureau. Working with local chiefs, the bureau procured forced labor for its rubber plantations. See Ibrahim Sundiata, *Brothers and Strangers: Black Zion, Black Slavery, 1914–1940* (Durham: Duke University Press, 2003), 117–26.
61. Buell, *Native Problem*, 1:717.
62. Bunche, "French Administration," 111.
63. Buell, *Native Problem*, 1:717.
64. Bunche, "French Administration," 113.
65. Ibid., 112.
66. Foreign Policy Association, "The Race Problem in South Africa," *Information Service* 4, no. 13. Gen. Jan C. Smuts details this position and its rationale in his 1929 Rhodes memorial lecture, "Native Policy in Africa," in *Africa and Some World Problems* (Oxford: Clarendon Press, 1930), 73–103.
67. For proponents of differentiation, South Africa's mixed-race Coloured population posed an intractable problem. Coloureds had been granted the franchise on an equal basis with whites and were allowed to vote along with whites for representatives in Parliament.

Robert Edgar, ed., *An African American in South Africa: The Travel Notes of Ralph J. Bunche, 28 September 1937–1 January 1938* (Athens: Ohio University Press, 1992), 29–31; Anthony W. Marx, *Making Race and Nation: A Comparison of the United States, South Africa, and Brazil* (Cambridge: Cambridge University Press, 1998), 84–119.

68. Buell, *Native Problem*, 1:151.

69. Bunche, "French Administration," 117–18.

70. Buell, *Native Problem*, 1:136.

71. Bunche, "French Administration," 317.

72. Holloway, *Confronting the Veil*, 91–94.

73. W. E. B. DuBois, "A Negro Nation within the Nation," *Current History* 42 (June 1935): 265–70.

74. Raymond Buell to Rayford Logan, May 21, 1935, box 166-8, folder 23, Rayford Logan Papers, Howard University, Moorland-Spingarn Research Center, Howard University.

75. Holloway refers to Ralph Bunche, Abram Harris, and E. Franklin Frazier as young Turks who marked a new generation in the genealogy of black intellectuals who gained visibility as a result of the Second Amenia Conference, sponsored by the NAACP in August 1933. DuBois had previously used this term. Holloway, *Confronting the Veil*, 4–16.

76. In the preface to his dissertation Bunche acknowledged his debt to "a great many people whose sympathetic encouragement, kindly interest and helpful advice were invaluable aids." Then he specifically named Professor Arthur N. Holcombe, Assistant Professor Rupert Emerson, and Dr. George Benson of Harvard University; M. C. A. Le Neveu, director of the Union Coloniale Française; and M. Rappard of the Permanent Mandates Commission.

77. Ralph J. Bunche, "Reconstruction Reinterpreted," *Journal of Negro Education* 4, no. 4 (October 1935): 568.

78. Henry, *Ralph Bunche*, 73.

79. Ralph J. Bunche, *A World View of Race*, Bronze Booklet 4 (Washington, DC: Associates in Negro Folk Education, 1936).

80. Article 32 of the League of Nations' covenant, cited in Logan, "Operation of the Mandate System," 6.

81. Nnamdi Azikiwe was Bunche's student at Howard and would eventually become Nigeria's first president.

82. Ralph Bunche, "Firestone's Africa," *Opportunity* 15, no. 1 (January 1937): 26.

83. Charles Henry, comment in the documentary film *Ralph Bunche: An American Odyssey* produced by 2001.

84. Buell to Bunche, May 31, 1933; Bunche to Buell, June 13, 1933, box 1 folder 7, RBP.

85. Ralph J. Bunche, "French Educational Policy in Togo and Dahomey," *Journal of Negro Education* 3, no. 1 (January 1934): 69–97.

86. Arthur Holcombe to Ralph Bunche, February 10, 1934, box 62, folder1, RBP.

87. Rupert Emerson, *From Empire to Nation: The Rise to Self-Assertion of Asian and African Peoples* (Boston: Beacon Press, 1960) would become a classic text.

88. Rupert Emerson to Ralph Bunche, November 19, 1934, box 1, folder 8, RPB.

89. Charles S. Johnson to Ralph Bunche, December 10, 1935, box 1, folder 9, RBP.

90. Ralph J. Bunche, "French and British Imperialism in West Africa," *Journal of Negro History* 21, no. 1 (January 1936): 31–46

91. Ibid., 69.

92. Ibid., 91–92.

PART TWO

Bunche the Statesman for Africa

CHAPTER SIX

Decolonization through Trusteeship
The Legacy of Ralph Bunche

NETA C. CRAWFORD

RALPH BUNCHE was born in 1904, the same year that the Germans began their genocide of the Herero and Nama people of South-West Africa, now Namibia. In that episode, for which Germany apologized in 2004, the Germans articulated and enacted what they then called an extermination policy. The policy was remarkably successful—they shot, drove into the desert, and starved thousands, 50 to 75 percent of the Herero and Nama peoples. Germany had entered the imperial game and the Scramble for Africa late but was not unusual in any other respect in its tactics, and few outsiders took notice at the time of the genocide. It is a remarkable change in world politics that such a policy—brutal colonial occupation accompanied by genocidal killing—is today abhorred and outlawed. Ralph Bunche was an important actor in the long process that brought about that shift in beliefs and policy.

In 1947, Bunche, perhaps optimistically, told a scholarly audience, "The international conscience has gradually recognized the essential anomaly in the profession of democratic principles as the basis for world order and the ruling of one people by another."[1] Bunche was a pioneering scholar of trusteeship and, unusual for an academic political scientist, an equally important policymaker and administrator. However, Bunche's contributions to diplomacy have overshadowed his perceptive doctoral dissertation on colonial administration and mandates and his later work administering the United Nations trusteeship program. Bunche's analysis of the tensions of foreign rule—even in the context of trusteeship intended as benevolent administration—points to the perils and pitfalls of trusteeship arrangements as well as their possible amelioration. Indeed, even as the paradox Bunche articulated—the "essential anomaly" of the rhetoric of freedom and the reality of subjection—was apparently resolved by the end of formal colonialism, new tensions emerged.

Just as the last of the former UN trust territories were achieving full independence in the early 1990s, as the UN Trusteeship Council was finishing its work and closing its doors, and as the first of several proposals to eliminate the council were made at the UN, a call for the return to trusteeship arose in respected policy journals and newspapers across the political spectrum.[2] In *Foreign Policy*, Gerald Helman and Steven Ratner wrote about saving failed states by reinstituting trusteeship.[3] The historian Paul Johnson argued for the return of international trusteeship managed by the "civilized" nations: "The Security Council could commit a territory where authority has irretrievably broken down to one or more trustees ... empowered to not merely impose order by force but to assume political functions." The trusteeship, according to Johnson, would "usually be of limited duration—5, 10, 20 years ... but a mandate may last 50 years, or 100."[4] Former U.S. ambassador to Israel Martin Indyk proposed trusteeship for Palestine, arguing that the "concept of trusteeship has been used to good effect in other places—such as East Timor and Kosovo—where the collapse of order and the descent into chaos have necessitated outside action."[5] And even more to the point for those who live in postconflict states, the United Nations has played an increasingly active role in transitional administrations. Richard Caplan examines the new UN transitional administrations in the post–cold war era in an Adelphi Paper, "A New Trusteeship," and a new book, *International Governance of War-Torn Territories*.[6] Caplan argues that despite the practical difficulties of these forms of administration, they generally do good. Others are less sanguine and fear that the new practice is a return to colonialism.

Thus, despite the invocation of trusteeship as a worthy model for rebuilding contemporary failed states, trusteeship remains an ambiguous institution; under trusteeship a people is not fully self-determining, but nor are they a colony. The history of trusteeship embodies that tension; begun as an adjunct of imperialism, trusteeship evolved into a route out of colonialism and toward full independence. In the contemporary era, trusteeship has reemerged in the form of international administration as, simultaneously, the paradigm of responsible Western humanitarianism and, as seen by some in the South, renascent paternalism. Thus, even as General Assembly members at their world summit in 2005 endorsed a proposal by then secretary general Kofi Annan to eliminate the Trusteeship Council, the oversight provided by just such a body might be all the more necessary.[7]

At the United Nations, Ralph Bunche had a great deal to do with the end of colonialism, with the organization's evolution from mandates to trusteeship, and with the operation of the UN's Trusteeship Division. Indeed, Bunche, as one of the principal authors of the chapters in the UN charter on non-self-determining territories and trusteeship, and later, as head of the Trusteeship Division of the UN, was a key architect of the institution of trusteeship. But well before arriving at the UN, Bunche had written a doctoral dissertation comparing the administration of a League of Nations mandate with that of a colony. Bunche was thus keenly aware of the tensions and contradictions inherent in the discourse and practice of trusteeship. An examination of Bunche's scholarship and his role in the development and institutionalization of trusteeship provides insight not only into the complexities of the man himself but into the institution he helped create.

An evaluation of Bunche's work in the context of renewed interest among policymakers and scholars in trusteeship as a model for postconflict governance raises several questions. What kind of institution was and is trusteeship? In other words, when there were United Nations trust territories and relationships of trusteeship, how did trusteeship work? What did it mean to be "under" trusteeship? What were the obligations of trust powers? Was trusteeship a progressive development, one that led to the emancipation of colonized individuals? Or was trusteeship a regressive and repressive institution, merely emphasizing the paternalistic side of colonialism rather than its exploitative aspect? Given its early-twentieth-century origins in colonial and anticolonial discourse and institutions, is trusteeship an appropriate model for the troubled, weak, or failed states of the twenty-first century? How might trusteeship be conducted today so as to overcome the stigma that has, rightly or wrongly, become attached to it? Why would any group of self-respecting peoples with aspirations of autonomy submit to trusteeship? Should the institution of trusteeship be considered a backward step? What roles should various actors—the UN, the administering authorities, nongovernmental organizations (NGOs), and the affected population—play in structuring and administering trusteeships?

Trusteeship Then

Trusteeship was a core element of colonial discourse before it became part of the discourse of decolonization.[8] Conquerors had long talked of a sacred trust and a duty or mission to civilize the natives. This was David Livingstone's call to spread Christianity, Commerce, and Civilization to the Africans, and the notion expressed in the Berlin West Africa Conference, in 1885, that the mission of colonization was the well being of the so-called native races. The core idea of trusteeship was simply that someone should watch over the incompetent and (temporarily) infirm. Guidance was necessary. The subject of trusteeship could, with careful tutelage, be made suitable for self-governance; the metaphor was of a child who needs a firm hand, support, and education until the child reaches maturity. But perhaps the child would always need help from a more able and mature older brother. As Bunche wrote, "Frequently, in recent years, the world has been deluded and often dazzled by the intricacies of imperialist diplomacy, the amazing statistics of colonial resources and trade, periodical expressions of broad but vague humanitarian principles and the development of popular sentimental slogans such as 'white man's burden,' 'trusteeship,' 'mandates,' '*mission civilisatrice,*' and others."[9] The key transition in meaning, then, occurs in the early twentieth century, when the idea of trusteeship shifts from a notion of permanent or perpetual tutelage to the view that outsiders could act to help peoples and nations become self-determining. Trusteeship could thus be a relatively short-term, transitional form of administration; it was not to be associated with blatant and rapacious exploitation.

The other key innovation in the idea of trusteeship came with the institution of the League of Nations mandates system, which grew out of the settlement of World War I. The defeated powers—Germany and Ottoman Turkey—lost their colonies to their opponents during the war. Both during and after the war, the question arose of what to do with those territories. It was decided after lengthy debate among the victorious allies that the captured territories would not simply be transferred to the victors, as they would have been in the past. Rather, at the Paris Peace Conference, the creators of the League of Nations devised a system whereby territories that were judged "inhabited by peoples not yet able to stand by themselves under the strenuous conditions of the modern world" should be governed by "the principle that the well being and development of such peoples form a sacred trust of civilization."[10] Of course, as Bunche observed, "The idea of 'sacred trust' is not a new one." Rather, he noted, what was "distinctive" about the mandate system was "the accountability of each mandate power to an impartial and international body for the fulfillment of the obligations assumed."[11]

The charter of the League of Nations created three classes of mandates according to perceived differences in those territories' "development" and "civilization." Class A mandates were thought to have reached a "stage of development" where, with some assistance, they might soon be "able to stand alone." The class B mandates were "at such a stage, that the Mandatory must be responsible for the administration of the territory under conditions which will guarantee freedom of conscience and religion, subject only to the maintenance of public order and morals, the prohibition of abuses such as the slave trade, the arms traffic and the liquor traffic." The class C mandate territories were those that, "owing to the sparseness of their population, or their small size, or their remoteness from the centre of civilisation ... can

Table 6.1. League of Nations Mandates

Class	Territory	Administrative Power
A	Iraq	Great Britain
	Palestine and Transjordan	Great Britain
	Syria and Lebanon	France
B	Togoland	France
	Togoland	Great Britain
	Cameroons	France
	Cameroons	Great Britain
	Tanganyika	Great Britain
	Ruanda-Urundi	Belgium
C	South-West Africa	South Africa
	New Guinea	Australia
	Nauru	Great Britain/Australia
	Samoa	New Zealand
	Pacific Islands (Carolines, Marianas, Marshalls)	Japan

be best administered under the laws of the Mandatory as integral portions of its territory, subject to the safeguards above mentioned in the interests of the indigenous population."[12] The nominal aim was the betterment of the inhabitants' lives, with a view toward their gradual assumption of self-determination or self-rule.

The general template of mandatory administration was similar in each mandate. The mandatory power administered the mandate, essentially as it saw fit, and the League of Nations oversaw that administration, using three levels of oversight and accountability. First, the mandate agreements between the League and the mandatory power specified conditions of governance, to which the mandatory could be held to account. Second, there was oversight by the League's Permanent Mandates Commission (PMC), which required annual written reports on conditions in the mandates by the manadatory power as administrator. Specifically, through the use of increasingly comprehensive questionnaires, the mandatory powers were closely questioned about progress in the mandates on areas such as labor conditions, health, education, and the rule of law. In addition, representatives of the mandatory powers appeared before the commission in Geneva to answer questions about their reports. The PMC had little authority, however, beyond what its members called the power of publicity; the proceedings of the League were made public, allowing journalists and activists to use that information to challenge conditions and the practices of mandate administrators.

Of course the central question of the day was whether the inhabitants of mandates were better off than those inhabiting simple colonies. There was some debate, but most observers argued that those in the mandates were better off. For example, the American international-relations scholar Quincy Wright wrote, "The system has already resulted in wider recognition of the principle of trusteeship, that dependencies should be administered in the interests of their inhabitants; in the principle of tutelage, that the cultivation of the capacity for self-government is such an interest; of the principle of international mandate, that states are responsible to the international community for the exercise of power over backward peoples even if that responsibility is not fully organized."[13] But, to answer the question of which was better required systematic comparison between a mandate and a colony.

Ralph Bunche's doctoral dissertation made such a comparison.[14] Completed in 1934, Bunche's thesis compared French rule in one colony,

Dahomey, with a class B mandate, Togoland, administered by France. Dahomey (now Benin) and Togoland (now Togo) were contiguous territories in West Africa. In August 1914, in the first Allied victory of World War I, British and French forces had captured Togoland from the Germans. In 1922 the League of Nations divided the region into two mandates, one French and the other British, and in 1946 the mandates became trust territories of the United Nations.[15] French Togoland became independent in 1960 as the Republic of Togo. Dahomey also became independent in 1960.

Bunche found that the French administration of Togoland as a League mandate was better in important respects than the French rule of Dahomey as a colony. Bunche was careful to note that exploitation had not disappeared in the mandate—indeed in the conclusion of his analysis, he describes a "slight difference in the treatment and status of the natives" in the mandate versus the colony.[16] Nevertheless, Bunche's analysis shows that conditions of forced labor, taxation, representation, education, and the rule of law were better in the mandate and that "on the whole the mandates administration pursues a more liberal native policy" (426). Specifically, the French required forced labor of the natives of both Togoland and Dahomey, but the terms of *prestation* were lighter in Togoland, where natives were required to work only four days per year, versus ten in Dahomey. Similarly, the tax burden was lighter in Togoland, there was greater representation of the natives in the Togoland administration, and better education was more widely available for its people. Also significant, natives in French colonies lacked basic legal rights, whereas in Togoland, there was an explicit penal code and a right to appeal all court decisions.

Bunche attributed the difference in the administration and outcome of French administration in the two territories to Togoland's status as a League mandate: "This is perhaps influenced by the necessity of making annual reports to the Mandates Commission. The sharpness with which members of the Mandates Commission have occasionally questioned the French delegates to the Commission at Geneva on certain aspects of administrative policy and practice in Togo, has undoubtedly acted as a deterrent of no little significance" (426). And more generally, Bunche argued, "It is more than probable that the mandate principle has operated generally to liberalize and humanize the policies of the colonial powers toward their native subjects throughout the world" (428).

Nevertheless, Bunche thought the mandate system was flawed in several respects. Specifically, he noted that the mandate system still failed to include the voice of the native subject and lacked a means for natives to directly appeal to the League. Bunche also noted that while mandatory powers were required to report annually to the Permanent Mandates Commission, the mandate system lacked the means for the PMC to verify the statements of the mandatory powers in their reports (140). Bunche said more than once in his dissertation that the annual reports were misleading. "To read the glowing accounts of the recently established *Conseils des Notables* in French Togo is one thing, and to see the same in action is another" (140). "The annual reports do not constitute an adequate basis for consideration of the effects of French administration in the mandate by the Commission, however. They are often guilty of misleading errors of omission, if not of commission. The tendency is strong to paint pictures of roseate hue which do not represent the actual conditions" (426–27). Perhaps most important, Bunche noted that there was "no machinery to issue positive orders for the improvement of native welfare." Nor was there a mechanism to issue "injunctions to restrain unjust practices" (139). Instead, Bunche noted, "In the Mandate's Commission itself, it is rarely that any vital or energetic attacks are made on the administration of these areas. Rather, the tendency is to deal softly with those complaints which reach the ears of the members" (139).

Bunche proposed that the mandate system could be improved. Specifically, he argued for increasing accountability and oversight by the PMC, for instance, by including natives more directly in the process of government. "If these native peoples are actually progressing under the tutelage of the Mandatories, the time should come when they could be permitted to send an official and representative 'voice' to the international body which is ultimately responsible for their welfare" (141). Further, Bunche argued for allowing the representatives of the PMC access to the territory each year. "It would seem that no just objections could be raised against such proposals by the Mandatories, since they have willingly accepted the principle of trusteeship. It can scarcely be maintained that the trustee is a law unto himself and subject to no scrutiny but his own" (142).

Despite his criticisms of the mandate system and his desire to improve it, Bunche saw it as a progressive institution, moving toward the fulfillment of the "sacred trust mission" articulated in the League's charter. "It is certain that the mandate system will exert an influence far beyond that affecting those areas presently subjected to its provisions. The inexorable force of public opinion will compel, as it has to an extent already, the extension of identical principles to retarded peoples throughout the world, whether they dwell in areas held as colonies and possessions or not. A steady exosmose is carrying these ideas beyond artificial boundaries which originally contained them, and they are having a revolutionary effect on the colonizing nations, great and small" (143).

During the period of mandate administration, self-determination grew, and some class A mandates even achieved independence. There was, overall, a decrease in the amount of forced labor required in mandates as compared to colonies. For instance, the period of forced labor required in the Belgian mandate territory of Ruanda declined in the late 1920s and early 1930s, from twenty-nine to thirteen days per year, while forced-labor requirements remained high in Belgium's other African territory, the Congo, reaching 120 days in World War II. Indeed, compulsory labor grew in some nonmandate territories: forced labor went from seven to twelve days per year in French West and East Africa during the interwar period, and in the Portuguese colonies in Africa forced labor was officially six months per year for men from fourteen to sixty years old. There was also, overall, greater attention to social welfare and legal rights in mandates and a greater likelihood of the investigation of public abuse by mandatory powers. And in cases of gross abuse, such as the 1922 massacre of four hundred Bondelswarts in South-West Africa by South Africa, the PMC issued a stern report that appears to have caused the South Africans to exercise greater, albeit still inadequate, restraint. Like Bunche, H. Duncan Hall attributed the power of the mandate system to the process of public accountability:

> The more complete the annual reports became, and the longer and more closely the Commission and the accredited representatives worked together, the more committed the governments were to carrying out the principles of the mandates. The more complete the background statistics given by the mandatory powers and the longer the period of years over which the information stretched, the more they were committed to telling the truth and nothing but the truth. It became part of the wisdom of the Geneva experience that a government which gave statistics committed its future. For once

it had begun to give ordered data, nothing was more likely to come quickly to light than a serious inaccuracy. To the trained eye of an international body—and its secretariat—... a serious inaccuracy, or even the variant fact, stood out as red lights on the page and invited immediate question and comment.[17]

The mandate system ended when the League of Nations died, during World War II. The founders of the UN decided to replace the League's mandate system with the United Nations trusteeship system. Bunche, having left academia during the war, was working in the U.S. State Department when he was enlisted to participate in the foundation of the United Nations and the drafting of the UN charter.[18] He participated in drafting the chapters in the charter having to do with colonial issues and specifically the Declaration Regarding Non-Self-Governing Territories (chapter 11) and the chapters on trusteeship (12, 13). To read the text of the chapters Bunche participated in drafting is to see his hand. In the final paragraph of his dissertation, Bunche argues that the mandate system has "only begun" to fulfill its promise. "To continue the good work radical modifications in the spirit and operation of the system must be made. It is not so important that the territories under mandate be better administered than the colonies of the world, but it is important that the mandate principle assure to these territories an unselfish, helpful administration which will afford them an opportunity to properly prepare themselves for the eventual day when they will stand alone in the world."[19] The trusteeship system incorporated many of the ideas for improving the mandate system Bunche had articulated more than a decade earlier. Where the mandate system had been an innovation in international oversight, Bunche's reformulation allowed the trusteeship system to fulfill the original mission of "sacred trust," paving the way for more gradual and peaceful decolonization.[20]

The key institutional innovations were in the areas of oversight, participation, and accountability. Bunche had essentially argued that the League's Permanent Mandates Commission needed more power and that the subjects of mandatory administration needed a voice. Those aims were accomplished when the trusteeship system required explicit agreements between the UN and trust powers, when more detailed questionnaires were developed to assess trusteeship administration and those reports became mandatory. More important, the

Trusteeship Council was empowered to make periodic visits to trust territories and to hear petitions directly from the inhabitants of the trust territory without having those petitions first screened by the trusteeship power. In a 1947 speech Bunche, then director of the Trusteeship Division of the United Nations, described the system:

> The Trusteeship System, like the Mandates System recognizes the international responsibility involved in the administration of the dependent territory placed under it. But the Trusteeship System goes considerably beyond the Mandates System in the implementation of this responsibility. The Trusteeship provisions in the Charter deal more positively with the promotion of the welfare of the inhabitants of the territories concerned than did the Mandates system. It calls specifically for the promotion of the advancement of the inhabitants, their development toward self-government or independence, and for the encouragement of respect for human rights and freedom without discrimination. Specific provision is made for the right of petition, oral as well as written, and such petitions may come from any source whether in or outside the Trust Territories. Moreover, they may be submitted directly to the United Nations and need not be conveyed through the administering authorities. The new system also provides for periodic visits by the United Nations to the Trust Territories for purposes of on-the-spot inspection.[21]

Most of the territories in the new trusteeship system were previously mandate territories (see table 6.2). Indeed, all the mandate powers, except South Africa, announced their intention to transfer their mandates that had not already achieved independence, to the trusteeship system. More than the mandate system, the aim of the trusteeship system was explicitly self-determination, self-government, and autonomy.

The key distinction between mandates and trusteeship was greater oversight of the sort Bunche described in his dissertation as desirable. The trusteeship system helped keep the trustee power accountable and administration relatively transparent by institutionalizing third-party accountability. As Bunche argued in 1947, "The principle of Trusteeship involved in the new system is that of third party or international responsibility—not the customary conception of the colonial power itself unilaterally recognizing a moral trusteeship on behalf of its colonial subjects."[22] With the addition of Bunche's critical mechanisms

Table 6.2. United Nations Trust Territories

Trust Territory	Administering Power	Previous Status	Date of Independence
British Cameroons	Great Britain	League mandate	1961 (Northern Cameroons incorporated into Nigeria; Southern Cameroons into present-day Cameroon)
French Cameroons	France	League mandate	1960 (as Cameroon)
New Guinea	Australia	League mandate	1975
Ruanda-Urundi	Belgium	League mandate	1962 (became two states: Rwanda and Burundi)
Nauru	Australia	League mandate	1968
Pacific Islands (Carolines, Marianas, Marshalls)	U.S.	League mandate (under Japan)	(Palau became independent in 1994; Marshall Islands in 1991; Marianas and Federated States of Micronesia, including Carolines, became self-governing U.S. territories in 1975 and 1979, respectively)
Somaliland	Italy	Italian colony	1960 (as Somalia)
Tanganyika	Great Britain	League mandate	1961 (as Tanzania)
British Togoland	Great Britain	League mandate	1957 (incorporated into Ghana by plebiscite)
French Togoland	France	League mandate	1960 (as Togo)
Western Samoa	New Zealand	League mandate	1962

for oversight, participation, and accountability, the trusteeship system operated much as the mandate system did. It provided for annual reports by the trustee powers, and for oversight by the Trusteeship Council. The new institution helped trust territories to independence and often their first elections. The twin practices of development assistance alongside international assistance in the transition to independent self-government became a model for increasing autonomy in other non-self-governing territories. Its mission essentially accomplished, the Trusteeship Council voted on November 1, 1994, to suspend its operations after Palau achieved independence.

Decolonization through Trusteeship: The Legacy of Ralph Bunche

Between Trusteeship and Transitional Administration

As I have discussed elsewhere, even as formal colonialism and the innovation of trusteeship were concluding, the United Nations undertook a series of increasingly complex missions—from administering elections and plebiscites to long-term peacekeeping—that gradually evolved into a form of governance, what is now called transitional administration.[23] In other words, just as the idea of trusteeship should have been retired, it achieved a new, more controversial—and less institutionalized—form. Bunche's legacy is marked here as well. Bunche had been intimately involved with the conceptualization and structuring of the UN's first peace observation mission in Palestine in 1948 and its first peacekeeping forces in Egypt in 1956.[24] Over the decades, as peacekeeping became more assertive and comprehensive, becoming peace building, the practice merged with the notion of trusteeship to become transitional administration.

The key case in this respect is probably the increasing role the UN took with respect to South-West Africa (now Namibia), a former mandate territory. As noted above, only South Africa, which had occupied South-West Africa since 1914, refused to designate the territory as a trusteeship. In 1949, South Africa said that its obligations as a mandatory power were over. Even as the South Africa government argued that it had fulfilled its terms as the administrator of a mandate, South Africa brutally suppressed the independence movement in South-West Africa, extracted strategic minerals from the land and tried to extend South African–style apartheid to the territory. South Africa's refusal to administer South-West Africa as a trusteeship started a long battle with the UN General Assembly and in the International Court of Justice and prompted the increased internationalization of the problem.

By increasing its involvement in the struggle for Namibian independence, the UN in effect backed into the role of transitional administration, merging a trusteeship role with that of peacekeeping, peace building, and development assistance. In other words, because South Africa refused to treat the territory it occupied as a sacred trust, the UN moved to help the people of South-West Africa directly. Between the 1960s and late 1980s, even as South Africa continued to rule South-West Africa with brutality, the United Nations gave assistance to the exiled South-West Africa People's Organization liberation movement and essentially formed a shadow international government for the territory. In 1967 the United Nations Council for Namibia, and in 1976 the UN Security Council, authorized the UN Transition Assistance Group (UNTAG) to plan for UN-supervised postindependence elections. For over a decade the UN helped devise plans for the transition to majority rule in South-West Africa, and ultimately, when agreement was finally reached that South Africa would exit the territory, UNTAG facilitated demobilization, helped organize the first democratic elections in November 1989, and finally helped write a constitution and guarantee independence in 1990.

Following Namibia, the UN and other ad hoc coalitions of nations established nine other transitional administrations, of varying degrees of comprehensiveness, in postconflict situations. A different sort of transitional administration, described below as a hybrid form, was created by the U.S.-led Coalition Provisional Authority in Iraq in 2003. In these cases, the UN went beyond the more limited peacekeeping, electoral assistance, and development aid roles it had taken during the cold war. There was a tendency during the 1990s to call this gradual broadening of the UN's role mission creep, but it was more than that.

The emergence of a rationale for greater intervention is evident in a chronological reading of key UN reports written during the 1990s on peacekeeping and peace building where the extension of the UN's mission from limited to comprehensive intervention was driven by an analysis of the causes of war as defective states or even total state failure. The UN secretary general's *Agenda for Peace, Supplement to* An Agenda for Peace, and the "Report of the Panel on United Nations Peace Operations" ultimately argue that the only way to bring lasting peace is to repair the defects of the state that had led to war and collapse in the first place.[25] Each report articulates a rationale for more complex intervention by the UN to provide and preserve the peace. The logic of ever-greater involvement was compelling, resting on the idea that war would likely resume in these postconflict settings if peace building was unsuccessful. And peace building was to be comprehensive—specifically, the development of robust political institutions, a strong civil society, and a more fully "developed" economy. Peacekeeping missions thus evolved into peace enforcement and peace-building missions and then to state-building and liberal market democracy–building exercises, in the belief that this was the route to stability.[26] Further, the period of transitional administration is often associated with transitional justice—war crimes tribunals and truth commissions—on the assumption that peace and good governance are more likely if the wounds of the past are recognized and hopefully healed through a judicial process or a comprehensive reckoning with the past. Table 6.3 describes the transitional administrations undertaken from 1990 through 2006.

Table 6.3. Transitional Administrations

Territory	Administration	Legal Authority
Namibia, 1989–90	UN Transitional Assistance Group (UNTAG)	UN Security Council resolution 632, February 1989
Western Sahara, 1991–	UN Mission for the Referendum in Western Sahara (MINURSO)	UN Security Council res. 690, April 1991
Cambodia, 1992–93	UN Transitional Authority in Cambodia (UNTAC)	UN Security Council res. 718, October 1991
Eastern Slavonia (Croatia), 1996–98	UN Transitional Administration for Eastern Slavonia (UNTAES)	UN Security Council res. 1037, January 1996
Bosnia and Herzegovina, 1995–	Office of the High Representative (OHR)	1995 Dayton Accords, ad hoc Peace Implementation Council (PIC)
Kosovo, 1999–	UN Interim Administration Mission in Kosovo (UNMIK)	UN Security Council res. 1244, June 1999
East Timor, 1999–2002	UN Transitional Administration in East Timor (UNTAET)	UN Security Council res. 1272, October 1999
Sierra Leone, 1999–2005, 2006	UN Mission in Sierra Leone (UNAMSIL); UN Integrated Office for Sierra Leone (UNIOSIL)	UN Security Council res. 1270; Economic Community of West Africa States (ECOWAS); UN Security Council res. 1620, August 2005
Afghanistan, 2002–	UN Assistance Mission in Afghanistan (UNAMA)	U.S. invasion and occupation, 2001; UN Security Council res. 1401, March 2002; Bonn Agreement, December 2002
Liberia, 2003–	UN Mission in Liberia (UNMIL)	UN Security Council res. 1508; ECOWAS
Iraq, 2003–4	Coalition Provisional Authority (CPA)	U.S. invasion, occupation recognized by UN Security Council resolutions

A discussion of the specific crises and wars that prompted each transitional administration, and the operation of each, is beyond the scope of this chapter. Such cases have all followed armed conflicts. What is most notable is that since 1990 the scope of activities has tended to increase, so that the transitional administrations are increasingly comprehensive and come to function more and more like trusteeships. In some cases, as in Kosovo, the transitional administration performs nearly all the functions of a national government; in other cases, the transitional administration operates almost in parallel, as a support to the national government. For instance, the responsibilities of the United Nations Integrated Office for Sierra Leone, created in 2005 to replace the apparatus of the previous transitional administration, parallel those of the national government of Sierra Leone. Set to operate for one year, beginning on January 1, 2006, the responsibilities the UN are at once comprehensive and shared among other institutions. Specifically, according to UN Security Council resolution 1620, UNIOSIL is:

> (a) to assist the Government of Sierra Leone in:
>
> > (i) building the capacity of State institutions to address further the root causes of the conflict, provide basic services and accelerate progress towards the Millennium Development Goals through poverty reduction and sustainable economic growth, including through the creation of an enabling framework for private investment and systematic efforts to address HIV/AIDS;
> >
> > (ii) developing a national action plan for human rights and establishing the national human rights commission;
> >
> > (iii) building the capacity of the National Electoral Commission to conduct a free, fair and credible electoral process in 2007;
> >
> > (iv) enhancing good governance, transparency and accountability of public institutions, including through anti-corruption measures and improved fiscal management;
> >
> > (v) strengthening the rule of law, including by developing the independence and capacity of the justice system and the capacity of the police and corrections system;
> >
> > (vi) strengthening the Sierra Leonean security sector, in cooperation with the International Military Advisory and Training Team and other partners;

(vii) promoting a culture of peace, dialogue, and participation in critical national issues through a strategic approach to public information and communication, including through building an independent and capable public radio capacity;

(viii) developing initiatives for the protection and well-being of youth, women and children;

(b) to liaise with the Sierra Leonean security sector and other partners, to report on the security situation and make recommendations concerning external and internal security threats;

(c) to coordinate with United Nations missions and offices and regional organizations in West Africa in dealing with cross-border challenges such as the illicit movement of small arms, human trafficking and smuggling and illegal trade in natural resources;

(d) to coordinate with the Special Court for Sierra Leone.[27]

But contemporary transitional administrations are not simply the reincarnation of UN trusteeship, and the character and practice of transitional administration is evolving. While the core idea of trusteeship—the benevolent governance of the incapable by the capable outsider—is present in the contemporary institution of transitional administration, some of the safeguards associated with idea of trusteeship are absent. Specifically, while contemporary transitional administrations share features with traditional trusteeship arrangements, they differ in important respects. For example, these transitional administrations are a new hybrid because they are essentially ad hoc, characterized by a patchwork of oversight by various UN organizations, individual states, or "coalitions of the willing." Further, accountability by the transitional administrators to either the subjects of administration or to the United Nations is less institutionalized than was characteristic of formal trusteeship or mandate arrangements. And while international media and NGOs may have greater access to these post-conflict states, the ability of either insiders or outsiders to influence the governance of these territories may be minimal.

The new hybrid transitional administrations, such as the Coalition Provisional Authority in Iraq, have sought neither accountability to the United Nations nor to the citizens of the occupied territory. In the Iraq case, the idea of trusteeship as including accountability to an international body was essentially eliminated. Rather, the UN assumed a rather different function with respect to the CPA, which had little to do with overseeing the justice or benevolence of CPA administration, even as the United States used the trusteeship and state-building discourse. "A senior American official said the United Nations was playing the role of 'trusted adviser' in getting Iraqis to agree on a plan among themselves [for the composition and structure of Iraq's interim government in 2004]. Others described the United Nations as more than that, a mediator brokering an accord that was beyond the power of the United States to bring about."[28] But mediation or advice is a far cry from the role of oversight that the Trusteeship Council had. Indeed there is perhaps less oversight and accountability to an international body than was characteristic of the mandate system.

Yet even as the list of tasks for UN peace building expanded to encompass many of the typical duties of a well-functioning government, as Simon Chesterman notes, there was little willingness to explicitly link transitional administration with the idea of trusteeship: "One of the many ironies in the recent history of transitional administration of territory by international actors is that the practice is regarded as novel." Thus, Chesterman notes, "Attempts to draw analogies either with trusteeships and decolonization on the one hand, or the post-war occupation of Germany and Japan on the other are seen as invitations to charges that the United Nations or the United States is engaging in neocolonialism or imperialism respectively. Within the United Nations in particular, such comparisons are politically impossible."[29] During the early days of the U.S. occupation of Iraq, many observers and top U.S. officials made analogies to the postwar occupations of Japan and Germany, but those comparisons were dropped as the occupation of Iraq proved much more difficult and bloody than many anticipated.

Despite what may be a reluctance in some quarters to compare transitional administration and trusteeship, it is instructive to compare the two institutions. The idea of trusteeship as employed in the mid-twentieth century, and as shaped in large part by Ralph Bunche and his contemporaries, had three core elements: third-party legal accountability mechanisms for the trustee power, meaning they report to someone besides themselves; a duty to improve the conditions of the subjects of trusteeship; and respect for the ability of the subjects of trusteeship to shape their own lives.

Contemporary observers of transitional administrations, and some UN administrators, worry that the core elements of trusteeship have not been retained in the new practice of transitional administration. UN official Edward Mortimer has argued that without proper accountability, transitional administrations have a potential for abuse. Mortimer thus suggests that may do to "revive and reform the Trusteeship Council, using it as a mechanism through which the community of nations could effectively exercise its tutelage and responsibility for the interests of those unfortunate peoples who may from time to time find themselves in need of international protection." Mortimer suggests that such a move would be consistent with the UN charter. "That it smacks of imperialism should not be a decisive objection." Mortimer argues for a bit of self-reflective and historical honesty when he suggests that "international administration has imperialistic features whether one likes it or not. It is adopted not as an ideal, but as expedient and seems unlikely to disappear any time soon. The wise course would be to limit the evil by facing up to its true nature and making dispositions accordingly."[30]

But there are two evils here that must be avoided and an essential tension that may be inescapable. There is the sin of commission and evasion, where outsiders either permit or are complicit in human rights abuses. In its most extreme form, the sin of inaction may result in a situation like Rwanda in 1994—where outsiders literally abandoned a promise to protect the weak from abuse and genocide occurred. In this case, abusers are allowed to hide behind the shield of legal sovereignty while those charged with protection left the scene. Then there is the sin of too much "help." This is the evil of paternalism, that in its extreme form becomes an element in the crime of colonialism. The essential tension is how to thread the needle between these two extremes: how does an institution help those who need it, but both acknowledge and foster their own agency?

To the extent that they are ad hoc arrangements, lacking mechanisms for systematic oversight and accountability, contemporary transitional administrations are at once both too weak and too strong. As Richard Caplan argues about the transitional administrations that were established in the 1990s, "All international territorial administrations lack accountability mechanisms that ensure meaningful independent review and that allow also for significant local input into the review process."[31] Similarly, Jarat Chopra, a former official in the UN administration of East Timor, argues that transitional administration "will be merely another form of authoritarianism unless the transitional administrators themselves submit to a judicious separation of powers and to genuine accountability to the local people whom they serve."[32] The emotional legacy of trusteeship has hampered clear discussion of the institution of transitional administration.

> Arguments used in the past to justify imperialism—that it spreads "civilization," provides stability, protects minorities, "builds nations," or prepares people for self-government—are all now regarded with skepticism. Do they become more acceptable when deployed to justify rule by an international organization or coalition rather than a single state? If so, it is not obvious why. Undoubtedly, it is this discomfort that explains the general reluctance to codify or institutionalize arrangements for international administration.[33]

These arguments acknowledge and employ the emotional legacy of the idea of trusteeship. By emphasizing the lack of accountability in contemporary transitional administration, and linking transitional administrations with colonial attitudes, the work of William Bain, Caplan, Chesterman, Chopra, and Mortimer suggests that by all contemporary standards of sovereignty and democratic principles, contemporary transitional administrations are a step backward. Indeed, it is likely that Bunche, if he were in the UN today, would work to formalize the mechanisms of accountability and participation that made the trusteeship system a step forward from the mandate system.

If we put the institution of trusteeship in historical context, it is neither as terrible as its detractors assert nor as beneficent and benign as its proponents argue. The League's mandates and UN trusteeship were founded on the twin discourses of paternalism and self-determination. On the one hand, these institutions infantilized inhabitants and pushed them into a European-derived model of a secular, rational, bureaucratic state. Bunche saw this clearly in Togoland, as it was administered as a French mandate. In this sense, Bunche did not make a strong distinction, in attitude or practice, between colonial and mandate government. "The French do not find it possible to let the native forget that his progress is measured in terms of absorption of French culture."[34] Rather, although Bunche believed that the natives would someday become powerful voices and actors, he saw little evidence of that in either mandate or colony. "The French determine the broad outlines of policy as well as the smallest detail of regulation. There is no check other than the weak consultative voice of a pitiful little group of hand-picked members of the elite, who are 'honored' by their presence on advisory councils dominated by Europeans. The role of the native mass is to follow blindly the French lead, in policy, and to obey commands in practice."[35]

On the other hand, at their best the institutional arrangements of oversight and accountability in mandates and trusteeship acknowledged the reality of occupation and served as a check on the occupying power. When made accountable, trusteeship not only limits the power of the occupied and externally governed subject, but it binds the hands of the occupier and bounds the scope of the occupier's activities. As designed by Bunche and others, under UN trusteeship, the occupying trust power is accountable to the United Nations, it is committed to improve the lot of the occupied, and trusteeship gives the people in the trust territory someone to appeal to besides the occupier. Further, because the aim was self-determination and eventually sovereignty, trusteeship limited the duration of outside occupation. It was a route to improving conditions and to sovereignty, albeit not always or even usually a roadmap to democracy.

There is sometimes a tendency to want to enlist great thinkers and powerful actors to bolster one's arguments. I am tempted to do so with Ralph Bunche and the contemporary practices of transitional administration, whether practiced by ad hoc coalitions of the willing dominated by the Great Powers or by the United Nations. I suspect that Bunche would be a harsh, if diplomatic, critic of the current practices of transitional administration. I suspect he would advocate for both the recognition of historical injustice and the obligations of former colonizers and exploiters to help repair what was harmed by colonialism and cold war intervention. Bunche would likely see a pattern emerging—of occasional humanitarian intervention followed by ad hoc transitional administration—and he would probably urge that scholars and practitioners acknowledge the paternalism that affects both. But Bunche would likely do more. He would work to institutionalize greater third-party oversight and accountability for transitional administration.

Notes

I thank the editors of this volume for their generosity and patience, and the participants in the UCLA conference "Trustee for the Human Community: Ralph J. Bunche and the Decolonization of Africa" (June 3, 2004) for their stimulating questions and comments.

1. Ralph J. Bunche, "The United Nations and the Colonial Problem," in *Imperialism, Ancient and Modern*, Marshall Woods Lectures, Brown University, October–November 1947, 59.

2. In 1992, Morton Halperin wrote a study of trusteeship for the Carnegie Endowment. Halperin and David Scheffer, with Patricia Small, *Self-Determination in the New World Order* (Washington, DC: Carnegie Endowment for International Peace, 1992). See also Ralph Wilde, "Trusteeship Council," in *The Oxford Handbook on the United Nations*, ed. Thomas G. Weiss and Sam Daws (Oxford: Oxford University Press, 2007), 149–59.

3. Gerald B. Helman and Steven R. Ratner, "Saving Failed States," *Foreign Policy* 89 (Winter 1992–93): 3–20.

4. Paul Johnson, "Colonialism's Back—And Not a Moment Too Soon," *New York Times Magazine*, April 18, 1993, 44.

5. Martin Indyk, "A Trusteeship for Palestine?" *Foreign Affairs* 82, no. 3 (May–June 2003): 54; also see 65. Also see William Bain, *Between Anarchy and Society: Trusteeship and the Obligations of Power* (Oxford: Oxford University Press, 2003); Mats Berdal and Richard Caplan, eds., "The Politics of International Administration: A Special Issue," *Global Governance* 10, no. 1 (January–March 2004).

6. Richard Caplan, "A New Trusteeship? The International Administration of War-Torn Territories," Adelphi Paper 341, International Institute for Strategic Studies, 2002; Caplan, *International Governance of War-Torn Territories: Rule and Reconstruction* (New York: Oxford University Press, 2005).

7. Annan suggested eliminating the Trusteeship Council in his report *In Larger Freedom: Towards Development, Security and Human Rights for All, Report of the Secretary General*, UN document A/59/2005, March 21, 2005, para. 114.

8. For an excellent genealogy of trusteeship, see Bain, *Between Anarchy and Society*. In Neta C. Crawford, *Argument and Change in World Politics: Ethics, Decolonization, and Humanitarian Intervention* (Cambridge: Cambridge University Press, 2002), I put the institutions of mandates and trusteeship in the larger context of decolonization.

9. Ralph J. Bunche, "French Administration of Togoland and Dahomey" (PhD diss., Harvard University, 1934), 2.

10. League of Nations, Covenant, art. 22, para. 1.

11. Bunche, "French Administration," 135.

12. League of Nations, Covenant, art. 22.

13. Quincy Wright, *Mandates under the League of Nations* (Chicago: University of Chicago Press 1930), 588.

14. The dissertation was probably innovative for Bunche's time in several respects—notably his systematic use of the comparative case approach, his extensive field research, and his careful explication of precolonial and colonial history.

15. France administered Togoland and Dahomey together from 1934 to 1937.

16. Bunche, "French Administration," 425. Subsequent references in this section to this source are cited in text by page number.

17. H. Duncan Hall, *Mandates, Dependencies and Trusteeship* (Washington, DC: Carnegie Endowment for International Peace, 1948), 188.

18. On these years of Bunche's life and his role in the writing of the UN charter, see Brian Urquhart, *Ralph Bunche: An American Life* (New York: Norton, 1993).

19. Bunche, "French Administration," 429.

20. This is not to suggest that decolonization was always peaceful. See Crawford, *Argument and Change*.

21. Bunche, "United Nations and Colonial Problem," 59.

22. Ibid., 58.

23. Neta C. Crawford, "How Previous Ideas Affect Later Ideas," in *The Oxford Handbook of Contextual Political Analysis*, ed. Robert E. Goodin and Charles Tilly (Oxford: Oxford University Press, 2005), 266–83.

24. According to Urquhart, in 1956 Bunche was tasked by UN secretary general Dag Hammarskjöld to "go and get me a force" to keep the peace in Egypt, creating the conditions for British and French withdrawal after the Suez invasion. Hammarskjöld, quoted in Urquhart, *Ralph Bunche*, 267.

25. Boutros Boutros-Ghali, *An Agenda for Peace: Preventive Diplomacy, Peacemaking and Peace-Keeping* (New York: United Nations, 1992); Boutros-Ghali, *Supplement to* An Agenda for Peace (New York: United Nations, 1995); Panel on UN Peace Operations, "Report of the Panel on United Nations Peace Operations," UN Document A/55/405-S/2000/809 (New York: United Nations, 2000).

26. See Roland Paris, *At War's End: Building Peace after Civil Conflict* (Cambridge: Cambridge University Press, 2004).

27. United Nations, Security Council, resolution 1620, August 31, 2005.

28. Steven R. Weisman and Warren Hoge, "U.S. Expected to Ask United Nations to Keep Trying for an Agreement," *New York Times*, February 21, 2004, A7.

29. Simon Chesterman, *You, the People: The United Nations, Transitional Administration, and State-Building* (Oxford: Oxford University Press, 2004) 11.

30. Edward Mortimer, "International Administration of War-Torn Societies," *Global Governance* 10, no. 1 (2004): 13–14.

31. Caplan, "New Trusteeship," 62.

32. Jarat Chopra, "The UN's Kingdom of East Timor," *Survival* 42, no. 3 (2000): 27.

33. Mortimer, "International Administration," 12.

34. Bunche, "French Administration," 419.

35. Ibid., 420.

CHAPTER SEVEN

An Unexpected Challenge
Ralph Bunche as Field Commander in the Congo, 1960

JOHN OLVER

BY EARLY 1960, Ralph Bunche was entitled to feel that his hectic, multifaceted life might be reaching a less tumultuous stage. Although he was still under sixty years of age, his character, energy, and knowledge had propelled him into such demanding and highly pressurized assignments that his health and normal buoyancy showed signs of stress. Diabetes was becoming a matter of enough concern so that he reluctantly agreed to follow a treatment program, with some positive results, but that and other ailments remained of much anxiety to family and friends.

The Suez crisis in 1956 and related Middle East issues had occupied him constantly for a lengthy period, and the equally driven UN secretary general, Dag Hammarskjöld, had discovered, to Bunche's disadvantage, the full extent of his expertise in the dominant issues of peacekeeping and decolonization. Just as important, a smooth working relationship as well as a personal friendship had grown between the two men in a manner that made possible successful actions such as the creation of the first UN peacekeeping force designed to separate Egyptian and Israeli forces. Bunche felt great satisfaction in his role in making such action possible; he wrote in a personal note, "It is, perhaps, my finest achievement, exceeding the armistice negotiations."

Decolonization, particularly in Africa, was coming more and more to the forefront of international affairs in the late 1950s, and Bunche had attended the independence ceremonies in Ghana in 1957 with the feeling that the tide was about to sweep across much of the continent. By 1960 the momentum was building, and Bunche joined Hammarskjöld in the last part of a lengthy tour of many African countries readying for a new future. Well aware that many problems lay ahead in Africa, it was nevertheless heartening for Bunche to accompany the optimistic and enthusiastic Hammarskjöld on a journey that symbolized the fruition of many years of hope, dreams, and hard work.

In spite of his overly optimistic attitude concerning the decolonization process in Africa, the secretary general foresaw potential trouble spots where specific assistance from the international community would be essential. The Belgian Congo—with its history of brutal colonial treatment; an indigenous population deprived of economic and social advancement; complete control of government, business, and industry; and military leadership in the hands of harsh Belgian masters—was clearly a fire awaiting any kind of match.

Hammarskjöld felt that the independence ceremonies, scheduled for the early date of June 30, 1960, could easily become at the very least a small flash point. He turned to Bunche, as both symbolic figure and master planner, to represent him at the ceremonies and to stay a few weeks to assist the new government in establishing itself and in securing the right kind of technical and other assistance to assure stability.

Accordingly, Bunche arrived on June 25 in Léopoldville (now Kinshasa) with a small staff consisting of a political officer, a development economist, the designated technical assistance representative for the Congo, and two bilingual secretaries. Establishing himself for both residential and office purposes in the Stanley Hotel in the center of the city (the United Nations had no offices in the Congo), Bunche began the task of finding his way on the already turbulent scene. His personal stature as a world leader and a friend of the downtrodden made him a central figure, but the already emerging rivalries between the new government's leaders preoccupied him.

Immediately the swirling currents in the Congo closed around him, highlighted by the fierce competitions for primacy in all aspects of governmental affairs between the future president, Joseph Kasavubu, and the future prime minister, Patrice Lumumba. Bunche saw quickly that this relationship and other aspects of governing linked to it would soon lead to rupture. Nevertheless, he maintained hope that the actual transfer of power from Belgium would have a calming effect and that the assumption of authority by the new officials would dissipate some of the intense rivalries that had blazed to greater heat in the months immediately preceding the independence ceremonies. It was not long before it became apparent that such hope could not be sustained in the face of the bitterness and rage that surfaced at the ceremonies and the disorder that quickly became a feature of the takeover of power.

Bunche was finding that each day after June 30 was bringing new evidence of inappropriate and often reckless behavior, and not just on the part of officials of the new government. His own compatriots were preoccupied by a fear that the cold war was about to find a new staging area in the Congo, while the Belgian officials and forces tended to behave as though Belgium continued to be in sole control.

Beginning on July 5, the bad situation worsened substantially when the Congolese army, newly transformed from the former colonial force but still lacking non-Belgian officers, mutinied at various bases, and Belgian citizens, including military and governmental officials, began to flee with their families. As the revolt spread to Léopoldville, Bunche himself was harassed and threatened by armed Congolese soldiers storming about the city in an uncontrolled manner.

By July 9 the situation had worsened, to the point that Hammarskjöld suggested that Bunche and his small staff might take refuge across the Congo River at Brazzaville. Typically, Bunche declined the offer on the grounds that his departure might encourage even more panic. He was also anxious to keep trying to help hold things together and to continue his discussions with the president of Katanga, Moise Tshombe, who was insistent on secession of the richest Congo province. His anxieties were constantly increased by the activities of Belgian army troops across the country and the breakdown of services and economic activity everywhere, a process hastened by the mass departures of Belgian specialists who had been counted on to serve the new government under the Treaty of Friendship.

By this time, it was apparent that the United Nations would be required to provide assistance in a massive way and immediately. This would include not only forces to maintain law and order but also specialists to strengthen the army for national defense. In addition, to replace the hundreds of fleeing Belgian specialists, technicians were desperately needed to keep the basic functions of government running. Bunche found that the new government's leaders, including Kasavubu, Lumumba, and the cabinet, had only the haziest ideas of the needs of government, but they realized clearly that the United Nations represented the best hope for getting rid of the aggressive Belgian troops and delivering the technical support services that were vanishing with the departing Belgian officials.

On July 12, Kasavubu and Lumumba requested (by commercial cable, for want of official linkage) that the secretary general provide military assistance as quickly as possible. Losing no time, since Bunche's reports reflected severe deterioration in security, Hammarskjöld took up the question with the Security Council, which authorized action on July 14. Hours later, Hammarskjöld succeeded in identifying the first elements for the operation, which became known as ONUC (Organisation des Nations Unies au Congo), and arranged for air transport in each case. By July 15 the first contingent arrived from Tunis, to be followed by others in the next couple of days, giving Bunche as interim commander some thirty-five hundred troops to begin the peacekeeping tasks. (At the same time, the first civilian staff leaders from UN headquarters arrived from New York, including Bunche's principal assistant, Brian Urquhart, and me, who had been assigned as chief administrative officer for the entire operation.)

It became apparent that Bunche's crowded, unsecured rooms at the Stanley Hotel were completely inappropriate as headquarters for the peacekeeping and technical activities of the rapidly expanding new mission. Alternative sites were far from easy to come by, since all military facilities were utilized by the Congolese army, which ONUC was anxious to assist, rather than displace, while a similar situation prevailed in government offices and other public facilities.

Bunche himself stolidly continued his round-the-clock directing efforts, regardless of the growing tumult surrounding him, but it was clear that a stand-alone building in Léopoldville, with at least some prospects for maintaining a degree of security combined with ready access for military and civilian staffs, was absolutely essential. Within a few days, Bunche and his directly associated staffs were moved to a multistory apartment building called the Residence Royale that had been largely deserted by its Belgian tenants. Key staff took up residence in the building, along with Bunche, who turned his salon into a busy work area and briefing center that quickly became known as the snakepit. Most apartments were converted to office use, and soon military and civilian staffs were vying with one another for use of highly inadequate elevators, furniture, and office supplies, and a motor pool run from the underground garage space. Through it all, Bunche continued his serene style of conferencing, interviewing, briefing, politicking, and writing.

A major distraction appeared in the form of a supreme military commander, selected by Hammarskjöld but quickly recognized in the

Congo as not up to the job of directing and inspiring the multinational force quickly emerging. Misadventures with General von Horn and his staff forced Bunche to continue in effect as force commander, overloaded as he was by the many demands for his energy, attention, and time from the Congolese officials, the stubbornly resisting Belgian commanders, the assignment and supervision of continually arriving civilian technicians, and above all the constant wrangles with new leaders, including especially the temperamental Lumumba and the mischief-making Tshombe.

Day after day, week after week, this remarkable and unsinkable leader carried on, surviving crises and eruptions that caused those trying to support him to become desperate in their efforts to sustain the new and highly vulnerable mission for peace. Bunche made no complaints, his only personal request being for an assured supply of Evian water to be kept in his refrigerator.

Bunche was so overburdened that it came as a surprise to his staff in the Royale when, only a little more than a month after the arrival of the first troops, he produced an explanatory document under his own signature as a guide to understanding by senior officers of the many delicate aspects of the unusual operation to which they were attached. This never-published document, called "Notes on Non-military Briefing for Senior Officers of the UN Force in the Congo," appears below to illustrate the comprehensive yet subtle manner in which Bunche sought to convey his thinking in regard to the dangerous and unprecedented operation just begun under his command.

On through the difficult and hazardous summer, Bunche continued his strenuous efforts, until Hammarskjöld was able to complete lengthy negotiations for a successor in the form of Rajeshwar Dayal, a distinguished and experienced Indian diplomat. As Bunche departed for New York in late August, still more than fully engaged as de facto force commander in addition to his many other responsibilities, he was exhausted and ill, but still determined. My own contribution to his well-being was to schedule a small aircraft to deliver him to Brazzaville, across the Congo River from the Royale, since the Léopoldville airport was still undergoing periods of disorder. He seemed to relax as he sank into his seat, and mentioned that he felt a great load lifting at last. Then his eyes closed, and he napped until touchdown across the river, happily completing the first short leg of the long voyage home.

Ralph Bunche as Field Commander in the Congo, 1960

Notes on Non-Military Briefing for Senior Officers of the UN Force in the Congo

The Republic of the Congo, formerly the Belgian Congo, was a colony of Belgium until it obtained its independence on 30 June 1960. It is not a sovereign, independent state. Soon after independence, disorder broke out in many parts of the country. Europeans, and especially Belgians, became objects of hostility and attack in many places and fear took firm grip on them. Conditions grew progressively worse, until finally the United Nations was appealed to for assistance, resulting in the UN Force in the Congo.

The United Nations Operation as a whole in the Congo (ONUC), is a combination of civilian and military activity. It is the largest single effort ever undertaken by the United Nations. It comprises the United Nations Force in the Congo; the Technical Assistance Program, covering assistance in many forms provided by the United Nations and the Specialized Agencies, which will involve eventually great numbers of experts and technicians; a large food appeal and distribution operation; and a special port clearance and river dredging project at Matadi.

The Special Representative of the Secretary-General, Mr. Ralph Bunche, on behalf of the Secretary-General, directs the overall operation. Major-General Carl von Horn is the Supreme Commander of the United Nations Force in the Congo. Mr. Sturo Linner, as Resident Representative, is in charge of all Technical Assistance and other non-military activities. Mr. Maurice Pate supervises the food distribution work. General Raymond A. Wheeler has responsibility for the port and river clearance project.

The United Nations Force in the Congo came into being as a result of a resolution adopted without opposition by the Security Council of the United Nations on 14 July 1960. This action was in response to *two appeals* made to the United Nations by the Government of the Republic of the Congo on 12 July 1960. The first appeal asked for general technical assistance in the formation of supervising personnel, and especially in aid to the Government in organizing and strengthening its national army toward ensuring national security and maintaining public order and respect for law. The second appeal asked for *military aid* and the sending urgently of *UN troops* to the Congo.

The first Security Council resolution appealed to the Government of Belgium to *withdraw* Belgian troops from the territory of the Republic of the Congo. It also authorized the Secretary-General to take the necessary steps, in consultation with the Government of the Republic of the Congo, to provide the Government with such military assistance as might be necessary until, through the efforts of the Congolese Government and with the technical assistance of the United Nations, the national security forces might be able, in the opinion of the Government, to meet fully their tasks. A second Security Council resolution was adopted unanimously on 22 July and called upon the Government of Belgium to "implement speedily" the Council's previous resolution on the withdrawal of their troops. It also requested all states to refrain from any action which "might undermine the territorial integrity and the political independence of the Republic of the Congo."

The UN Force, it should be emphasized, is in the Congo at the *invitation* of the Congo Government. It is in the Congo as a *friendly* force. It is a *peace* force, just as the United Nations Emergency Force (UNEF) has been a peace force, and most effectively, for four-and-a-half years along the line between Egypt and Israel.

The United Nations Force is armed, but its arms are to be used solely in legitimate *self-defence*. It has no fighting function. Rather, through its friendly presence, it seeks to give reassurance, to relax tension, to restore calm.

By "United Nations Force" is meant an *international* force. That is, a force composed of military contingents from a number of countries under the command of an officer designated internationally. In the case of the force in the Congo, Major-General Carl von Horn was designated Supreme Commander of the Force by the Secretary-General of the United Nations, Mr. Dag Hammarskjöld. The several national units together make up the Force. That Force and all the members of it, while on duty in the Congo, are under the exclusive command of the United Nations. The Force gets its orders from its Supreme Commander, who in turn receives all policy directives solely from the Secretary-General, either directly or through his Special Representative in the Congo. The Force, or any of its units or members, shall take *no* orders from any other source. This includes, of course, the national governments of the contingents and the government of the Republic of the Congo.

As indicated in the appeal of the Government of the Republic of the Congo to the United Nations, the United Nations Force is in the Congo to help the Government of the country maintain law and order. The Force will undertake patrolling, sentry, guard and other duties. It may have to take measures to protect certain groups or individuals from harm at the aroused hands of others. In any such case, there should be no firmness, but the methods employed should be as pacific as possible. Bear in mind that usually the mere *presence* of representatives of the UN Force will have a *quieting* effect. Every reasonable effort should be made to make the *UN presence* felt, but *never* in an aggressive way.

The United Nations Force in the Congo is *not* to participate in any way in any internal conflict. It must *never* intervene in domestic political disputes. All members of the Force should scrupulously avoid any involvement in the internal political affairs of the Congo Republic. They should also avoid any discussion of Congo Republic politics. In this regard, it is particularly emphasized that all members of the Force should refuse any statements or comments to the press except upon request of the UN Information Officers. It must be realized that a wrong statement to the press or a statement, misconstrued or misquoted, can cause harmful criticism of the UN Operation or even undermine it. Since the failure of this Operation could well mean the subsequent loss of very many lives, the importance of heeding this injunction is very clear.

There are many risks in this Operation. It takes place where little is known about the UN. The concept of nationhood itself is relatively new and only developing. Tribal and regional ties continue strong. Personalities often seem to attract more interest than issues. At the outset of the Operation, at any rate, the United Nations is largely lacking an important asset which it has enjoyed in its activities in many parts of the world: ready recognition by the population of its significance, its flag and its various other insignia of identification.

We hope to give meaning to the UN in the Congo, but it will take a little time and will depend almost entirely on the success of the UN Operation as a whole. Above all, the conduct of every member of the Force must be exemplary. An incident involving members of the Force, such as a conflict with Congolese civilians; or with members of the Force Publique; or with Belgians, civilian or military, could seriously jeopardize the Operation. In an action of the kind in which the UN Force is involved, the cultivation and maintenance of *friendly relations* with the people of the country is indispensable. It would seriously impede the task should the Congolese people generally or in any locality become hostile to ONUC because of bad or careless actions by members of the Force. Officers of contingents should impress upon their men the necessity for disciplined conduct and smart appearance. This UN Force can help very much just by being here and always making a good appearance in public. Every officer, non-commissioned and all the men should constantly bear in mind that they are all representing their countries as well as the UN.

Close to 14,000,000 people inhabit the vast territory of the Congo. They had been afforded very little preparation for the independence they achieved on 30 June of this year. They have had little political, parliamentary, executive or administrative experience. There are no Congolese doctors, engineers or professors. There are said to be less than twenty University graduates in the entire population. There are very few Congolese technicians. Because of the troubles besetting the country in the past two years or so, very many of the formerly more than 100,000 people of non-African origin have left. But there are still remaining an estimated 50,000 to 60,000 of the non-Africans, many of whom, however, are greatly fearful and feel insecure about the future. Many of these are said to be contemplating departure from the country, and the exodus may continue unless the UN Operation can succeed quickly in calming fear by providing reassurance about security.

There is great tension and fear in this country, among both African and European communities. It has relaxed somewhat, perhaps, since the arrival of the UN troops, but it is still very great. Rumours are as wild as they are constant. Moreover, they are widely believed. If the UN can eliminate much of the tension, fear and bitterness now pervading the Congo, it will make a vital contribution to the success of this country.

This condition of sharp differences dividing the people creates an obvious problem for the UN Operation in all of its aspects, and particularly as regards association or identification with Belgian activities. Under existing circumstances, prudence in this delicate matter of relationships is essential. Bear in mind always that the Force is against no one here, *friendly* to all.

The Congolese are sensitive and proud people. They have a sense of dignity and expect to be respected. Attitudes of paternalism or condescension toward them will be resented. For example, it could be *in*advisable to employ the widely used and familiar [French] "tu," because, owing to the recent background of racial attitudes here, it has today in the minds of some, at least, a demeaning connotation.

There is a special problem for the UN Force concerning the Force Publique, which is the national army of the Republic of the Congo. It is a very complex problem. There are some 25,000 men in that army, in camps throughout the country. It had a fine record in Libya and Ethiopia during World War II. But now it is largely demoralized and without an officer corps. It was the mutiny of this army on 6 July which set off the chain of reactions still bedevilling the country. There were probably many conditions which contributed to the uprising, which, in Leopoldvile [*sic*], at any rate, found the army in virtually unchallenged control for more than twenty-four hours. One of them, certainly, was the resentment of the men over the fact that independence had brought no change in their status. There were no Africans above the rank of non-coms. Their officers were all Belgian. They rejected their officers, in some instances violently, and took over. Since then, the "Africanization" of the Force has been imperative. They understandably desire to be led by African officers. The UN will do its best to help train Congolese officers—in a crash program, if possible. The UN should try to see to it, diplomatically and quietly, that the Force Publique in any locality shall not pose a threat to public order. Naturally, this is best achieved when the Force Publique is without arms and stays in its camps. Just as obviously, the UN cannot and must not try to accomplish this by any but friendly means. At the same time, the UN should assist the Force Publique in regaining its morale and discipline and in rebuilding itself into a bulwark of national and local security. This, undoubtedly, is the greatest challenge confronting the UN Force in the Congo.

The population has been little involved in recent disorders throughout so much of the country. That condition could quickly change, however, should a critical food shortage develop, or should there be any considerable inability to meet payrolls. In this latter regard, especially, the end of July could be a critical period and developments should be most carefully observed.

Administrative services for all aspects of ONUC are under the direction of the Chief Administrative Officer, John Olver, who is designated by and responsible to UN Headquarters; and, on the spot, to the Special Representative of the Secretary-General. For military men, it may seem rather strange to see the administrative responsibility of the Force in the hands of civilians. But these civilians are all members of the United Nations Secretariat. They are *international Civil Servants.* They are devoted to the UN and the causes it serves. They can be counted on to do everything possible to facilitate the work of the Force. They will loyally serve it.

Ralph Bunche as Field Commander in the Congo, 1960

In a statement in the Security Council on 21 July 1960, the Secretary-General of the UN, Mr. Hammarskjöld, in referring to the United Nations Operation in the Congo, said that in this effort "we are at a turn of the road where our attitude will be of decisive significance . . . not only for the future of this Organization, but also for the future of Africa, and Africa may well in present circumstances mean the world."

>Ralph J. Bunche
>
>Special Representative of the Secretary-General of the United Nations
>
>Léopoldville
>
>Republic of the Congo
>
>July 1960

Note

All emphasis in Bunche's briefing appears in the original.

CHAPTER EIGHT

Ralph Bunche and Patrice Lumumba
The Fatal Encounter

CRAWFORD YOUNG

THE PERVERSITIES of destiny drew into brief but fatal encounter in 1960 two extraordinary leaders, Ralph Bunche and Patrice Lumumba. Their paths crossed for only two intense months in the summer of the Congo crisis. In that abbreviated historical moment, a relationship that circumstance commanded to be collaborative and trusting degenerated, from initial cordiality into mutual contempt and animosity. This increasingly hostile interaction between two key actors in the Congo crisis was one of its many consequential subthemes.

Yet there might have been some basis for a more constructive outcome. The early Bunche was, like Lumumba in 1960, a radical critic of European colonialism and racial injustice. In his initial writings, Bunche articulates a radical, anti-imperial critique whose anticapitalist resonance bears comparison with the fiery Lumumba oratory of 1960 that led many in the cold war–obsessed West to suspect him of communist sympathies.[1] But their intellectual itineraries went in opposite directions. The radical certainties of the early Bunche became overwritten with the cautious, nuanced if principled judgments of the consummate diplomat Bunche became, first as an Africa specialist with the Office of Strategic Services and the Department of State during World War II, then as a top United Nations functionary after the war.

Lumumba, on the other hand, in his initial public role spoke the moderate language of the early generation of Congolese *évolués* (lit., evolved ones), whose message was better race relations and respectful treatment for educated Africans.[2] He came to the attention of Belgian colonial minister Auguste Buisseret in 1954, through whose good offices he had two extended personal meetings with King Baudouin during the royal visit in 1955.[3] His radicalization really began only in 1958, when he was able to escape the stifling isolation of the colonial Congo and make contact with the Belgian left at the 1958 Brussels World Exposition, and with radical Pan-African nationalism at the December 1958 Pan-African Conference in Accra. In the crucible of the Congo crisis, Lumumba's radicalization intensified.

By the time of their first meeting, in late June 1960, Bunche and Lumumba were already locked into totally different institutional matrices: the newly formed Congolese government on the one hand, and the UN Secretariat on the other. They observed unfolding events through utterly divergent prisms of interpretation. Indeed, the flow of information that shaped their understandings was so completely at odds that one might imagine that they were engaged in wholly separate settings.

My purpose here is to explain how these two gifted individuals came to such a disastrous parting of the ways. I will not retrace the chronology of the Congo crisis; any number of richly documented studies provide that background.[4] Nor is the aim to vindicate either protagonist. Rather, what became their mutual antagonism was a tragedy both for the Congo and for the UN. For Lumumba, the rupture with the UN was one factor leading to his overthrow and eventual assassination. For Bunche, many see the Congo episode as a rare blot on a long and often brilliant career as an international public servant.[5] The enormous pressures of the Congo role took a near-fatal physical toll on Bunche; his successor, Rajeshwar Dayal, records his shock at seeing Bunche on his return from the Congo assignment, "physically spent and looking much older."[6]

At the time of his dispatch to Kinshasa,[7] Bunche had unique qualifications for his assignment as special representative of the secretary general, then head of the Organisation des Nations Unies au Congo (ONUC). As a doctoral student at Harvard, he had written a prize-winning dissertation on French colonial policy in Dahomey and Togo. Though he had spent only three months' research time in these two countries, and had made only one trip up-country, he interviewed a large number of colonial officials and African elites in Paris and Africa during his overseas research in 1932 and 1933. The Social Science Research Council provided him an open-ended two-year fellowship (1936–38) to deepen his African knowledge by studying with such early anthropological luminaries as Melville Herskovits, Lucy Mair, Bronislaw Malinowski, and Isaac Schapera. While in London, he established close contacts with a generation of African and Caribbean intellectuals: Jomo Kenyatta, Peter Koinange, C. L. R. James, and George Padmore, among others. Bunche then made an extended study visit to South Africa and briefer visits to Kenya and Uganda.

After a couple of years as director of the research team for the massive Gunnar Myrdal study of the Negro condition in America, Bunche was recruited for the emergent Office of Strategic Services as the key Africa analyst. He closely followed continental affairs and wrote a valuable handbook on North Africa for the military. In 1943 he transferred to the State Department and began work on planning for the UN, especially for its Trusteeship Council, whose design and establishment bore the Bunche imprint.[8] More broadly, the provisions in chapters 11 and 12 of the UN charter were significant elements in creating a supportive international environment for African decolonization.

In 1946, Bunche transferred to UN service. In 1948 he drew the impossible assignment of mediating an armistice between Israel and its Arab neighbors, for which success he won the Nobel Prize in 1950. He used his acceptance speech to call for "an acceleration in the liquidation of colonialism."[9] Through the 1950s he was the primary architect of the principles and policies shaping UN peacekeeping. By 1956, Secretary General Dag Hammarskjöld had elevated Bunche to become his top aide, as undersecretary for special political affairs, a role that led him to one crisis area after another. When he was sent to the Congo on June 25, 1960, to represent the UN in the June 30 independence ceremonies and to help the new government establish UN membership and seek technical assistance, Bunche's credentials were impeccable.

Further, he enjoyed the complete confidence of Hammarskjöld, who gave him wide latitude to act on the spot. He shared the secretary general's vision that, in the words of a Hammarskjöld biographer, in 1960 Africa was a "continent launched on the road to cooperative success by new and able young leaders with the help and advice of the UN."[10] Hammarskjöld had met many of them during a whirlwind African tour at the beginning of 1960 and was convinced that the UN, unencumbered by any past in Africa, was uniquely qualified to play a leading role in African decolonization and development.

Bunche as well was entirely dedicated to the UN as an institution for advancing world peace. Through his role in its initial design, his central contribution to the definition of its peacekeeping role, and his prolonged role as key adviser to the secretary general, he had completely internalized its norms. Among these were the core value of its institutional preservation in the face of the many attacks it endured. Bunche also had attributes prefiguring the conflict with Lumumba. He had from his early years a visceral distaste for those he regarded as demagogues. Marcus Garvey, for Bunche, was an early prototype of the category.[11] Very quickly, the celebrated impromptu and impassioned Lumumba speech at the independence ceremonies appeared to confirm what Belgian officials and Western diplomats were whispering, warning of the demagogic tendencies of the new head of the Congolese government. A key Lumumba adviser and his UN ambassador, Thomas Kanza, notes that Lumumba's oratorical skills were one of his chief virtues, that he had "to the highest degree, the abilities needed to carry a crowd along with him: he could adapt what he said to suit his audience.... A demagogue yes, and not too scrupulous perhaps."[12] Bunche characterized Lumumba's oratory as electric and spellbinding, intoxicating even to Lumumba himself.[13]

Moreover, particularly once the crisis exploded into a cold war confrontation with the United States a major protagonist, American nationality was a handicap for Bunche. Throughout the Congo episode, his loyalty was entirely with the UN; he was in frequent conflict with American ambassador Clare Timberlake and utterly impatient with the "communist penetration" obsessions of the American embassy. However, at the onset of the crisis, before the UN had a real logistical presence, Bunche was compelled to use embassy communication and other facilities on occasion. And even behavior that impeccably followed international public servant norms cannot erase perceptions.

To some extent, early in the crisis, nationality suspicions were offset by the African connection of the diaspora. Kanza suggests that the racial bond initially earned Bunche a favorable predisposition among Congolese: "From the moment of his arrival, he had been received by the Congolese with the greatest sympathy and the most profound respect. He was one of the few coloured Americans to have earned an undisputed reputation on the international level, and in his dealings with the new government of the Congo, the fraternity of race played a part that must not be underestimated."

However, Kanza adds that Bunche "could never get away from the all-pervasive watchfulness of American agents," whether official or merely officious. For this reason, Congo officials were never completely frank with him, though he remained throughout "a most discreet diplomat, totally faithful to the instructions of his chief."[14]

Finally, and most surprising, Bunche was unable to communicate in French with Congolese officials. Given his research year in France and francophone West Africa, and a thesis topic that required use of French documents and presumably interviewing in French, not to mention his long service in the UN, where French is an important working language, this seems astonishing. But the sources are unanimous on this point and on the barriers to full mutual understanding that it posed. Urquhart, longtime assistant and intimate friend to Bunche, describes his French as rudimentary.[15] Jean-Claude Willame notes the problems this posed when Bunche would attend a Congo cabinet meeting.[16] Kanza suggests that the necessity to rely on Fou Chin-Liu, a UN diplomat from Taiwan, as his interpreter gave the impression that Fou to some extent dominated Bunche; in any event, Congo officials "finally came to deal directly with [Fou] whenever they wanted to have contact with Bunche."[17]

Turning to the Lumumba side of the Bunche-Lumumba equation, we need to first to distinguish between the historical symbol and the real human actor. The circumstances of his overthrow in September 1960, the revelation of CIA plots to assassinate him during that fall, and his eventual murder, in Katanga Province with Belgian involvement and doubtless CIA complicity, made him a martyr to African nationalism and Pan-African dreams. For much of Africa, the memory of Lumumba remains that of an unblemished hero of African independence, struck down by American, Belgian, and other Western forces determined to stifle radical anti-imperial nationalism.

The real Lumumba was more complex. As Kanza observes, truly outstanding men "always have exceptional qualities, which make them famous and set them apart, but they also have failings in proportion to these, which may destroy them, and will certainly make them hated, even sometimes by their closest friends."[18] The qualities that propelled Lumumba to the fore were indeed extraordinary: a prodigious energy; an exceptional intellectual curiosity, sustained by voracious reading; rhetorical gifts of the highest order; outstanding organizational skills.

He first began to attract notice in the early 1950s in Kisangani, where he became a leader in various évolué organizations. He experienced brief periods of imprisonment on charges undoubtedly at least partly politically motivated. By 1957 he had shifted his base of operations to Kinshasa, becoming a very successful sales promoter for a popular brewery. By 1958 he was emerging as an important political figure who stood out for the forcefulness of his advocacy of a unitary state in opposition to the federalism advocated by emergent political movements at both ends of the country, Lower Congo and Katanga.

The opportunity to attend the 1958 Pan-African Conference in Accra was a crucial occasion to acquire the sympathy and support of a number of other key African leaders, especially Kwame Nkrumah (president of Ghana, 1960–66) and Ahmed Sékou Touré (president of Guinea, 1958–84), both of whom came to view Lumumba as the indispensable key to enlisting his vast country in the Pan-African project. Lumumba came to share the Pan-African vision and in August 1960 signed a secret protocol with Nkrumah to form a Congo-Ghana union to enlarge the nebulous Ghana-Guinea tie as the embryo of a Pan-African state.[19]

When explicit nationalist claims first entered public discourse in 1956, the most intransigent voice was the Alliance des Bakongo, led by Joseph Kasavubu. Its demand for "immediate independence," as well as its dalliance with the notion of a reassembled Kongo kingdom with separatist overtones, made it anathema to the colonial administration, which until late 1959 saw it as a more dangerous adversary than parties committed to the preservation of colonial boundaries. With a proliferation of political parties by 1959, their primary means of differentiation was through the forcefulness of their critique of the colonial regime, the assertiveness of the claim for rapid independence, and for most, an appeal to their potential regional clientele. In this tumultuous environment, Lumumba's formidable oratorical and organizational skills catapulted his party, the Mouvement National Congolais–Lumumba (MNC-L), into a leading position. The sudden Belgian capitulation to the immediate independence demand in February 1960, with national elections to be organized from scratch by May, found the MNC-L positioned as the only national party of anticolonial persuasion whose message resonated throughout the country.

Lumumba's tireless campaigning necessarily had to exploit every available electoral advantage. The most important was the clarity of his commitment to a strong, united Congo with a vision, however undefined, of rapid development. This attracted support from a portion of the intelligentsia in all the urban centers. However, like all other politicians of the period, Lumumba built upon loyalties based on region and ethnicity as well. His initial base, Kisangani, and its rural hinterlands in Orientale Province provided a solid core of support; so also did his Tetela-Kusu ethnic community, and parts of the larger Mongo cultural universe to which it belongs.

Conversely, in a number of areas where Lumumba and his message were popular, a local regional or ethnic party preempted the electoral space.[20] Even though the 41 seats won by MNC-L and its direct allies were less than a third of the total of 137, in Congo and elsewhere Lumumba was regarded as the major winner, and the electoral achievement of the MNC-L in a crowded field of 250 electoral lists was seen as remarkable. The next largest contingent was from the Parti National du Progrès, with 15 seats, the only other movement to operate on a national basis, but largely discredited by its transparent backing from the colonial administration. To the dismay of the Belgians, Lumumba—now feared as the most aggressive nationalist voice—was an unavoidable candidate for leadership after an unsuccessful Belgian effort to have Kasavubu form a government. In the end, just three days before independence, the new government was installed, with Lumumba as prime minister and Kasavubu as president, an office modeled on the Belgian monarch.

Although the ascendant figure at the moment of independence, a number of critical weaknesses marked Lumumba's situation. He and his party won a sweeping psychological victory in the elections, but his actual parliamentary position was less secure. He stitched together a broad coalition of parties for his cabinet, but those chosen for ministerial rewards did not necessarily carry their parties with them. The parties represented in the cabinet should have assured a large majority, but on the confirmation ballot only 74 favorable votes were obtained, just 5 more than the minimum required; and no less than 57 were absent from the session, many of them disappointed office seekers boycotting the session. Already some of the personal traits that were the obverse of his extraordinary charisma and leadership talents were evident. In the words of Willame, "his impatience, his mercurial temperament, his difficulty in accepting tactical retreats, his inherent authoritarianism . . . his obstinate belief in a quasi-messianic role" put him on a collision course, first with Belgium, then subsequently with the United States and the West, and finally the UN—and Bunche.[21]

Another major handicap was the purely formal authority the new government enjoyed at the moment of independence. Virtually all the top bureaucratic posts, and the entirety of the army officer corps, remained Belgian. Kanza again recaptures the mood of the moment:

> The first meetings of our Council of Ministers were unforgettable. Our discussions were of the most desultory kind. All of us were happy, or at least cheerful and satisfied, at being ministers. . . . We argued about offices, about suitable and available sites for them, and how they should be shared among us. We discussed the allocation of ministerial cars; the choosing and allotting of ministerial residences; arrangements for our families and their travel. . . . Though we sat so comfortably in our sumptuous official cars, driven by uniformed military chauffeurs, and looked as though we were ruling this large and beautiful country, we were in fact ruling nothing and a prey to whatever might happen.[22]

Lastly, the struggle for power had lasted until the final moment before independence. The Lumumba government embarked on independence without any real program. Although Lumumba had some grasp of Pan-African politics, he had no exposure to the broader forces of the global political arena about to impinge on him. This rendered all but impossible an informed calculus as to their motives, worldviews, and resources. The inability to achieve a realistic reading of the larger international context into which the Congo was inserted was a fatal handicap.

To understand the rapid unraveling of the relationship between Bunche and Lumumba, one must also recall the psychological environment of independence. The sudden transition from total colonialism to full independence bewildered all of colonial society. For many, especially the younger generations, towering expectations were unleashed, reinforced by the often extravagant promises made on the campaign trail. Hitherto inconceivable social ascent and material well-being would come with independence. But jostling with these happy expectations were darker apprehensions: Who would really benefit? Might a rival group monopolize the fruits of independence? Might there be widespread disorder? Such fears were particularly uppermost in the minds of European residents, who saw their exorbitant privilege at risk.

There was ample cause for anxiety. Although Belgium by the beginning of 1960 had no other viable choice than acceding to immediate independence, the *pari congolais* was a remarkably risky gamble. The essence of the strategy was to concede independence first, then organize a transition. A Congolese political superstructure of ministers and parliamentarians would perch uneasily atop the ongoing apparatus of the colonial state, all of whose real levers of power would remain in European hands. Upon arrival five days before independence, Bunche was appalled at the lack of preparation and the patronizing attitude of many Belgian officials toward the Congolese leaders.[23]

The army was first to revolt against this fragile formula, mutinying five days after independence in protest against a policy assuring dramatic promotion to politicians, but none for soldiers. The army's act swiftly forced the ouster of the Belgian officer corps, and with armed mutineers on the loose, panic swept the Belgian community. Within a week of the mutiny, almost the entire cadre of Belgian bureaucrats had fled, except from Katanga, an exodus encouraged by a (subsequently withdrawn) promise by the Belgian government that all would be guaranteed incorporation into the Belgian public service. On July 11, Katanga seceded, followed not long after by the diamond production centers of Kasai Province. Thus the Lumumba government in less than two weeks found itself bereft of its security force, the top ranks of its bureaucracy, and its revenue. The Belgian army had intervened unilaterally in a number of cities, purportedly to protect the European population. The basic elements of the Congo crisis were now in place.

The eruption of the crisis placed both Bunche and Lumumba in desperate circumstances, under intense pressures. A hastily drafted resolution was passed by the UN Security Council on July 14, responding to a Congolese request for UN intervention, to preserve order, secure the withdrawal of Belgian troops, and provide emergency technical and food aid. Within a day, Bunche found himself organizing the arrival of a flow of UN military contingents and managing the largest and most complex peacekeeping operation in UN history. The logistics for this operation had to be improvised without the most basic facilities; the UN operated out of an apartment building abandoned by fleeing Belgians, lacking sufficient telephones, reliably functioning elevators, and basic office supplies. Insecurity was a constant threat; Bunche thought his last hour had come when he was taken at gunpoint and threatened with death by drunken soldiers. Controlling the multinational military force was a constant headache. The commander of the Ghanaian contingent, Gen. Henry Alexander, continuously agitated for an excessively risky disarming of the Congolese army. The Swede named to head the force, Gen. Carl von Horn, proved vain, headstrong, and altogether unsuited for that role, which meant that Bunche had to cling to ultimate command himself. The four-star general commanding the Guinean contingent announced his intention to march on Katanga and drive the whites into the sea.[24] The resolution authorizing the UN operation was vague on crucial points: the timetable for Belgian military withdrawal, the issue of territorial integrity, and the scope of UN military occupation. Bunche found the Belgians remarkably obtuse and foot-dragging on withdrawal.

Lumumba faced comparable pressures. The Katanga secession and the Belgian intervention in particular infuriated him. His administrative arrangements were as improvised as those of Bunche. A number of his ministers were of doubtful loyalty, and rumors of plots soon began to swirl. Some ethnic elements in the Kinshasa garrison, and in the population of that city, were increasingly hostile. The generalized insecurity and disorganization threatened one and all. Pervading all was the intense emotionality of the moment; for Lumumba, the very survival of his beloved country was at risk, a disaster that might be averted only by his own superhuman efforts.

Confronting the Congo crisis, Bunche and Lumumba were embedded in radically different institutional matrices. For Bunche, norms, practices, and unwritten codes of UN peacekeeping of which he was the principal author set fundamental parameters. Bunche was driven to set these precepts to paper on July 27 (a document included as an appendix to chapter 7 of this volume). The UN force was present at the invitation of the Congo government but was not subject to its orders. Its arms were to be used only in self-defense, and never in support of one or another party to a domestic Congolese dispute. All military assistance was to flow exclusively through the UN. At stake, for Bunche, was the integrity and institutional health of the UN and its Secretariat, whose preservation was an overriding imperative. Bunche and Hammarskjöld shared a vision of a UN at the service of the smaller powers of Africa and Asia to advance the process of decolonization and to support their developmental aspiration. They hoped for the solid support of an emergent Afro-Asian majority in the General Assembly for their vision. At the same time, they well appreciated the absolute necessity for retaining the support of the three veto-wielding Western powers—Great Britain, France, and above all the United States. Also desirable was retaining Soviet acceptance, or at least tacit toleration, for Secretariat actions. The constraints of the UN matrix became increasingly taxing as the summer wore on and the cold war divisions came to pervade policy debates. By mid-July Lumumba began threatening an appeal to the Soviet Union for direct aid, forcing Belgian withdrawal, and ending the Katanga secession by mid-July, a menace periodically repeated, and then withdrawn. Soviet criticism of the UN operation gradually intensified and metastasized by early fall after the Bunche departure; in addition, a limited intervention in belated support of Lumumba occurred in late August in the form of ten Ilyushin aircraft and a hundred trucks. Meanwhile, by late July much of the American policy establishment had concluded that Lumumba was under communist influence, and increased the pressures on Bunche, in Kinshasa, and the Secretariat, in New York, to focus their efforts on stymieing Soviet initiatives. Neither Bunche nor Hammarskjöld ever shared this phobia; Bunche, reflecting on his Congo role in 1964, described Lumumba as perhaps a leftist, but no stooge, not really ideological beyond his passionate commitment to Congolese unity.[25] However, Bunche and Hammarskjöld both regarded a direct Soviet intervention as a catastrophe that had to be averted, a position interpreted in radical Afro-Asian quarters as alignment with Western objectives.

The matrix that enclosed Lumumba was much less formed. The council of ministers never had a chance to congeal as a body. In any case, Lumumba's penchant for personal initiative, and his suspicions of others, often led him to act alone. His relations with Kasavubu were never close; they acted together only when compelled by circumstance and by August rarely met. In the formless tumult of the summer of 1960, the closest equivalent to an institutional matrix were those African leaders he trusted, especially Nkrumah and Touré, and the members of his entourage, characterized by Bunche as a cosmopolitan "riffraff."[26]

Meanwhile, Lumumba faced the succession of crises with frantic energy, while contending with antechambers overflowing with petitioners seeking favors, journalists itching for a headline, diplomats pushing their agendas, and occult counselors of diverse origins. Willame well captures the disorderly surroundings in which Lumumba struggled to save his country: "Utterly devoid of means, squeezed between a discredited Belgian technical assistance contingent . . . and the tutelary intentions of the UN Secretary General, the Lumumba government never had more than an embryonic functioning."[27] Crisis management, for Lumumba, was an exhausting daily round of improvisation.

Particularly in moments of crisis, any political leader requires a personal staff able to manage a flow of reliable information, provide a realistic analysis of alternative courses, and screen the flow of visitors to assure a rational deployment of the ruler's time. The Lumumba entourage fell well short of meeting those criteria. Indeed, Willame is persuasive in suggesting that there were multiple entourages. An inner circle consisted of political intimates of long standing, who shared the radical nationalist orientation but were not visible occupants of high office, with whom Lumumba met and relaxed late into the night; often important decisions were made in these settings. A second circle consisted of leading radical and nationalist political figures from various parties, mostly ministers aligned with Lumumba. An outer circle, especially visible to the diplomatic community, was a coterie of European leftists and radical African or Caribbean Pan-Africanists: Serge Michel, Frantz Fanon, Félix Moumié, Andrée Blouin, Maryse Hockers.[28] None of these circles really dominated Lumumba, who ultimately made his own decisions. But they did affect his external image; more important, they served as a critical filter through which often unreliable information selectively flowed.

Lacking to Lumumba was any institutional source of political information. Kinshasa swirled with rumors. What might be reported by the entourages, or gleaned from press and radio, was no substitute for carefully sifted and analyzed information that passed through a reliable staff. Lumumba faced his adversaries armed with only a very incomplete and often distorted image of the actual situation.[29]

As the Congo crisis unfolded, the political visions that shaped the policy choices of Bunche and Lumumba increasingly diverged. For Bunche, the UN operation in the Congo was always viewed in the larger context of international peacekeeping and the role that the world organization might play in aiding Third World development. Thus the operating principles of nonintervention, force only in self-defense, and UN command of all non-Congolese military units were paramount. The two core issues for Lumumba and the Congo government—Belgian military intervention and Katanga secession—had to be resolved through diplomacy, within the parameters of UN resolutions, and subject to continuing Security Council support. For Bunche and the UN in 1960, the Katanga secession fell under the category of internal disputes in which the international organization was not to intervene.

Lumumba found what he regarded as an unacceptably restricted understanding of the UN mission increasingly frustrating. From his perspective, the UN military mission had to include an immediate end to what he viewed as Belgian aggression and a restoration of the territorial integrity of the new nation. The subtleties of Hammarskjöld's juridical reasoning were incomprehensible and his noninterference principle a reprehensible complicity with the neocolonialist forces underpinning the Katanga secession.[30] If the UN refused to meet what Lumumba considered its obligations, then the Congo had a sovereign right to seek other external partners—radical African states or the Soviet Union—to secure the needed assistance.

The last straw in what by early August had become a tormented relationship between Bunche and Lumumba was the Katanga issue. Though Belgian troops had been withdrawn from other parts of the Congo by late July, they remained in Katanga as a protective cover for the secessionist regime of Moise Tshombe. Belgian prevarication on this issue had become increasingly frustrating for Bunche and Hammarskjöld. By this time Lumumba's threats to turn to direct Soviet intervention were increasing; Bunche decided to force the issue with a visit to Lubumbashi to negotiate immediate UN entry on August 4. Although he was received with civility by Tshombe and Belgian officials, they claimed that indigenous warriors would forcefully resist UN military detachments. This was a bluff since the Belgian detachments could not have confronted UN troops, and the organization of a Katanga gendarmery was still at a rudimentary stage, with its eventual mercenary encadrement not yet recruited. In what was the most widely criticized decision of his Congo tenure, Bunche felt sufficiently apprehensive about possible violent resistance to cancel the deployment plans. He believed that the Lubumbashi population was strongly hostile to Lumumba, and could easily be stirred up.

Hammarskjöld went back to the Security Council to secure a further mandate. On August 8 the council complied with a text delicately balanced for minimal acceptability to the Western powers, the Soviet Union, and Afro-Asian states. The clarified mandate demanded the "immediate" withdrawal of Belgian troops from Katanga, underlined the necessity of UN troop entry into the secessionist province, but declared that the force would not "in any way intervene in or be used to influence the outcome of any internal conflict, constitutional or otherwise."³¹

On the same day, August 8, Lumumba returned from a two-week trip that had taken him to the UN headquarters, Washington, Ottawa, and a number of African capitals, expecting that the new UN resolution meant that the secession would be crushed. On August 11, Hammarskjöld arrived in Kinshasa, determined to lead a contingent of Swedish troops into Katanga himself. He left Kinshasa the next day, without seeing Lumumba. The two companies of Swedes did land in Lubumbashi on August 12 in the company of Hammarskjöld, and the principle of a UN military presence in Katanga was established. However, it was also clear that at that stage force would not be used to end the secession.

Bunche and Lumumba had their final meeting on August 12. The session was prolonged and stormy, although it ended amicably. But the following day Lumumba was back on the offensive with a new set of impossible demands. When Hammarskjöld returned to Kinshasa on August 14, Lumumba abruptly canceled a planned meeting, then bombarded the UN staff with a series of violent letters. After the Hammarskjöld departure, Bunche sent a message to Lumumba with two UN security personnel, who were arrested and threatened with death. Bunche made a final effort to meet with Lumumba on August 18; the latter again refused to see him, and the rupture between the two was finally consummated.³²

The deepening despair felt by Bunche regarding the UN operation and his relations with Lumumba are eloquently expressed in his letters to his wife. En route to Katanga on his fateful August 4 journey, he wrote,

> What awaits us we do not know. There may be hostility, of course.... I'm dreadfully tired and sleepy as I got less than three hours sleep last night and even that was more than the night before. I cannot begin to tell you how complicated and maddeningly frustrating our operation out here is.... It is like trying to give first aid to a wounded rattlesnake. How much longer we can hang on here is anybody's guess. How long I can stand this physically is still another question.³³

On August 17, he wrote again, this time making clear his animosity toward Lumumba:

> That madman Lumumba is recklessly on the attack now—and most viciously—against Dag and the UN—and we will probably be in for a rough time since the public will be stirred up by the radio broadcasts. It is a tragedy, but it looks as though this greatest of international efforts will be destroyed by the insane fulminations of one reckless man. We may be washed up here in a few days.[34]

The depths of his feelings were made clear in another letter a few days later. "Lumumba gets worse and worse," he wrote. "He is the *lowest* man I have ever encountered. I despise [Vice Premier Antoine] Gizenga, but I hate Lumumba."[35]

Lumumba did not record his inner thoughts in writing, but one can hardly doubt that the feelings expressed by Bunche were mutual. By the time Bunche was setting his final thoughts regarding Lumumba to paper, the latter had given up on the UN and had decided to organize the assault on secessions with his own army, with Soviet logistical support. Even with the ten Ilyushins and the one hundred Soviet trucks, this mission was beyond the capacity of his ill-disciplined and irregularly paid troops. Their murderous rampage against civil populations in eastern Kasai in late August, before reaching Katanga, further isolated Lumumba.

The tides of fate leading to Lumumba's doom were now flowing rapidly. On August 18, CIA station chief Lawrence Devlin had sent his notorious cable asserting that "embassy and station believe Congo experiencing classic communist effort takeover government.... Whether or not Lumumba actually Commie or just playing Commie game to assist his solidifying power, anti-West forces rapidly increasing power Congo and there may be little time left in which take action avoid another Cuba." On August 26, CIA director Allen Dulles cabled Devlin that if Lumumba "continues to hold high office, the inevitable result will at best be chaos and at worst pave the way to Communist takeover of the Congo.... Consequently we concluded that his removal must be an urgent and prime objective and that under existing conditions this should be a high priority of our covert action."[36]

Bunche by this time knew that his usefulness in the Congo was at its end. In any case, he had been promised that his assignment would conclude no later than the end of August so that he could take his son on a college tour. According to Urquhart, Bunche saw the confrontation coming, but departed on August 30, six days before President

Kasavubu proclaimed the ouster of Lumumba. There is no evidence that Bunche was personally involved in the conspiracy leading to the Lumumba defenestration; the frequent Bunche conflicts with Ambassador Timberlake suggest the former would not have been trusted with such details, and in any case he surely would have refused to involve the UN in such planning.

After the announcement of the revocation, the UN did play a crucial role in permitting the consolidation of the Kasavubu coup. Bunche was replaced as interim head of the UN operation in the Congo by American Secretariat executive Andrew Cordier. Kasavubu apparently did not decide on his move against Lumumba until late August. On September 3 he consulted Cordier, who gave no advice and refused to commit the UN. On September 5, before the announcement of the Lumumba revocation, Cordier was again consulted, with the request that the UN at once assure Kasavubu's personal protection, that the radio stations be closed down, and that the airports be shut down to prevent pro-Lumumba troops being flown in from Kisangani on the Ilyushins.[37] These requests were fulfilled immediately following the revocation.

Ironically, Bunche's replacement as head of the UN operation in the Congo, Rajeshwar Dayal of India, arrived that same day, though he took over his functions only on September 8. He was astonished to learn from Cordier of the impending Kasavubu action. Dayal attests that "there had not been the faintest indication [of the possible Kasavubu action] in my talks with Hammarskjöld and Bunche. Information about the sudden turn of events had not reached New York before my departure, for it would have immediately been passed on to me."[38] Dayal lifted the measures and opened the radio and airports as soon as he could, but too late to undo the crucial advantage Kasavubu enjoyed as a consequence of these measures. Cordier and Hammarskjöld believed that article 22 of the Congolese Loi Fondamentale, which stipulates that the president "names and revokes the Prime Minister,"[39] gave clear authority for the presidential action. This view was not shared by Dayal, who along with many others believed that, in the European parliamentary tradition on which the Loi Fondamentale was based, the revocation of power could be exercised only if Parliament had withdrawn its support from the incumbent government by a vote of censure or of no confidence.[40] Even if the revocation power did exist, the constitutional situation following the Lumumba ouster was murky. The basic law was silent as to whether the existing government remained in office in a caretaker role pending confirmation of a new prime minister, or whether the president could rule on his own authority. Although Kasavubu nominated Joseph Ileo as new prime minister, he never proposed a cabinet for confirmation and soon parliament was prorogued. Thus, until the parliamentary confirmation of Cyrille Adoula, in August 1961, the UN operation functioned in a vacuum of clearly legitimate Congolese authority. However, Hammarskjöld concluded that the UN could only operate on the premise that President Kasavubu was the sole repository of constitutional authority, though he regretted the Cordier actions regarding the radio and airports.[41]

In any event, no Bunche role in these decisions is mentioned by his biographers or other sources; he may well have already left New York to vacation with his son when these crucial and controversial actions were taken. One can hardly doubt, however, that he welcomed the ouster of Lumumba. Retrospectively, the unhappiness in many quarters concerning these events cast their shadow over the image of Bunche's role. (Chapter 9 in this volume, "Ralph Bunche, Patrice Lumumba, and the First Congo Crisis" by Georges Nzongola-Ntalaja, is illustrative of this view).

Yet there was much to admire in the Bunche role in the Congo, operating under relentless pressures in exhausting conditions. Urquhart provides a generous appraisal:

> In setting up and running ONUC, the largest and most complex UN peacekeeping and civilian operation, Bunche had discharged an almost impossible task with extraordinary determination and compassion, under a barrage of criticism and second-guessing from many quarters. He had been working in a chaotic situation with an improvised organization and a completely inexperienced government. Those of us who worked closely with him in the Congo came away with greater respect and affection for him than ever.[42]

That a number of observers might dissent from this generous appraisal is one of the few shadows on the long and brilliant career of Ralph Bunche, in service to his race, his nation, and the world. I believe that throughout his Congo mission Bunche acted with wisdom and integrity, within the limits set by the matrix that defined his role. He cannot bear sole responsibility for the inability to sustain a cooperative relationship with Lumumba. Nor can the unhappy sequence of events that followed his departure be laid at Bunche's door. But one may fairly conclude that the Congo assignment constitutes a rare exception to an extraordinary roster of diplomatic accomplishments and missions successfully accomplished that mark his long career as an American diplomat and then international public servant.

Notes

1. See Bunche's 1929 paper "Marxism and the 'Negro Question,'" reprinted in Bunche, *Ralph J. Bunche: Selected Speeches and Writings*, ed. Charles P. Henry (Ann Arbor: University of Michigan Press, 1995), 35–45; and his brief book *A World View of Race* (1936), characterized by Henry as "a withering polemic on colonial policy in particular and White supremacy in general." Henry, "Ralph Bunche: American Diplomat," *Crisis*, July–August 2004, 21. This aspect of Bunche is ably delineated in the chapter by Martin Kilson in this volume, which was his keynote address to the June 2004 UCLA conference marking the centennial of Bunche, "The Young Ralph Bunche and Africa: Between Marxism and Pragmatism."

2. This was the theme of Lumumba's posthumously published volume, drafted in 1955. Patrice Lumumba, *Le Congo, terre d'avenir, est-il menacé?* (Brussels: Office de Publicité, 1961).

3. Jean-Claude Willame, *Patrice Lumumba: La crise congolaise revisitée* (Paris: Karthala, 1990). The Willame monograph is the most complete and reliable chronicle of Lumumba's brief but meteoric political career.

4. Of a vast literature, let me mention only two crucial sources: Jules Gérard-Libois and Benoit Verhaegen, *Congo 1960*, 2 vols. (Brussels: Centre de Recherches et d'Information Socio-Politiques, 1961); Madeleine G. Kalb, *The Congo Cables: The Cold War in Africa—From Eisenhower to Kennedy* (New York: Macmillan, 1982). The latter volume and Willame, *Patrice Lumumba*, both have extensive bibliographies.

5. There are several biographies of Bunche. By far the most important are Charles P. Henry, *Ralph Bunche: Model Negro or American Other?* (New York: New York University Press, 1999); Brian Urquhart, *Ralph Bunche: An American Life* (New York: Norton, 1993). I never met either Bunche or Lumumba; I was not in the Congo at this time, though I had begun the research for my dissertation on the country's decolonization.

6. Rajeshwar Dayal, *Mission for Hammarskjöld: The Congo Crisis* (Princeton: Princeton University Press, 1976), 13. Bunche had diabetes and a recurrent leg ulcer, both of which were exacerbated by the punishing hours and relentless pressures of the Congo labors.

7. For reasons of convenience, I use only current place names for Congolese cities and provinces, even though the purge of European designations occurred well after the Congo crisis.

8. In the bitter internal debates within the American administration over the concept of trusteeship and inclusion of the goal of independence for dependent territories in the UN charter, Bunche fought hard against War and Navy Department efforts to denature trusteeship to facilitate American annexation of the Pacific islands under Japanese-mandate territories in the Pacific. British pressure worked in the same direction. Though the Trusteeship Council itself was limited in the end to the League of Nations–mandated territories, chapter 12 of the charter, on non-self-governing territories, did include reference to independence, thanks in significant part to Bunche's efforts. See Lawrence

Finkelstein, "Bunche and the Colonial World: From Trusteeship to Decolonization," and Herschelle S. Challenor, "The Contribution of Ralph Bunche to Trusteeship and Decolonization," in *Ralph Bunche: The Man and His Times*, ed. Benjamin Rivlin (New York: Holmes and Meier, 1990), 109–57.

9. Challenor, "Contribution," 144.
10. Brian Urquhart, *Hammarskjöld* (New York: Knopf, 1972), 382.
11. Henry, *Ralph Bunche*, 112.
12. Thomas Kanza, *Conflict in the Congo: The Rise and Fall of Lumumba* (Harmondsworth, UK: Penguin, 1972), 31–32. This sensitive and self-reflective account remains one of the most revealing accounts of the Congo crisis through the eyes of an important participant. After many years of exile, Kanza reappeared in 1997 as a member of the first cabinet of President Laurent Kabila.
13. From a 1964 lecture on the UN operation in the Congo, repr. in Bunche, *Selected Speeches*, 189–204.
14. Kanza, *Conflict in the Congo*, 142.
15. Urquhart, *Ralph Bunche*, 312.
16. Willame, *Patrice Lumumba*, 318.
17. Kanza, *Conflict in the Congo*, 142.
18. Ibid., 8.
19. Kwame Nkumah, *Challenge of the Congo* (New York: International Publishers, 1967), reprinted in Kanza, *Conflict in the Congo*, 252.
20. Of the 33 MNC-L seats in the lower chamber of the national parliament, 31 are explicable by regional or ethnic affinity. The MNC-L won 21 of 24 seats in Orientale Province. Ten of its remaining 12 seats were in Sankuru, Maniema, and Tshuapa districts, where the Ankutshu-Anamongo populations were found. Eight additional seats were won by small parties competing in direct alliance with the MNC-L. See Gérard-Libois and Verhaegen, *Congo 1960*, 1:262–63.
21. Willame, *Patrice Lumumba*, 54.
22. Kanza, *Conflict in the Congo*, 119, 151.
23. Urquhart, *Ralph Bunche*, 304.
24. Ibid., 317.
25. Bunche, *Selected Speeches*, 189–204.
26. Urquhart, *Ralph Bunche*, 304.
27. Willame, *Patrice Lumumba*, 209.
28. Serge Michel was a French journalist of Polish extraction who had been a publicist for the Front de Libération Nationale in Algeria. Frantz Fanon, originally from Martinique, likewise was associated with the Algerian revolution. Félix Moumié was a Cameroonian nationalist of extremist reputation. Andrée Blouin, a Guinean mulatto, was an intimate of Vice Premier Antoine Gizenga as well as Lumumba, an excellent speaker with a remarkable gift for languages. Maryse Hockers was a Belgian scholar, once attached to the Institut Solvay in Brussels.
29. For a careful analysis, see Willame, *Patrice Lumumba*, 219–32.
30. Illustrative of the complexities of Hammarskjöld's legal reasoning was the draft memorandum for Lumumba explaining his interpretation of the UN mandate Hammarskjöld brought to Kinshasa on August 11, 1960. The UN staff worked feverishly all night trying to translate the relatively brief memorandum into French, with enormous difficulty. Urquhart, *Ralph Bunche*, 326.
31. Kalb, *Congo Cables*, 44.
32. I rely here on the account by Urquhart, *Ralph Bunche*, 325–28.
33. Henry, *Ralph Bunche*, 199.

34. Ibid., 201.
35. Urquhart, *Ralph Bunche*, 332; emphasis in Urquhart.
36. Kalb, *Congo Cables*, 53.
37. Ibid., 64–65.
38. Ibid., 71–80.
39. Willame, *Patrice Lumumba*, 388–96.
40. Dayal, *Mission for Hammarskjöld*, 28, 31–32.
41. Urquhart, *Hammarskjöld*, 446.
42. Urquhart, *Ralph Bunche*, 334.

CHAPTER NINE

Ralph Bunche, Patrice Lumumba, and the First Congo Crisis

GEORGES NZONGOLA-NTALAJA

RALPH BUNCHE was sent to the Congo in late June 1960 to represent the UN secretary general Dag Hammarskjöld at the independence ceremonies and to stay for a few weeks to advise the new government and explore the requirements for UN assistance. Instead of a few weeks, Bunche stayed on for over two months, becoming in the process the first UN special representative in the Congo and interim force commander of the United Nations Operation in the Congo (ONUC).[1] As a member of the secretary general's inner circle of trusted advisers dealing with the Congo question, Bunche did take part in the decisions whose ultimate result was the fall of Patrice Lumumba, the Congo's first democratically elected prime minister.

Based primarily on the cable traffic recorded in the United Nations archives in New York,[2] and the few available writings on Bunche's role in the Congo crisis,[3] this chapter is a brief analysis of Bunche's antagonistic relationship with Lumumba and its negative consequences for the Congolese leader and his country. The conflicting interpretations of the Security Council mandate on the Congo by Lumumba on the one hand, and Hammarskjöld, Bunche, and their colleagues on the other, combined with Bunche's contempt for Lumumba and the latter's impatience to create a hostile relationship between the two men. In spite of his active support for the African independence struggle and the civil rights movement in the United States, Bunche shared the common cold war outlook within the UN Secretariat, in which Lumumba was perceived as being too influenced by radical

Pan-Africanism to accommodate Western interests. As a contributing factor to Lumumba's demise, Bunche's contempt for the first Congolese prime minister will be analyzed with respect to three major events between June and August 1960: (1) Lumumba's independence day speech, (2) Lumumba's handling of the crisis, particularly the Katanga secession, and (3) Soviet assistance to Lumumba.

Lumumba's Independence Day Speech

Bunche arrived in the Congo with a generally negative attitude toward Lumumba. This was based at least in part on Bunche's own reported hostility to African nationalism, particularly the radical and anti-imperialist type represented by the likes of Kwame Nkrumah, Ahmed Sékou Touré, Gamal Abdel Nasser, and Patrice Lumumba, which was dismissed in Secretary General Hammarskjöld's entourage as "emotional pan-Africanism."[4] It was also based on the briefings Bunche had received on Lumumba from the Belgians. These briefings had obviously painted Lumumba in the most negative light possible, given the Belgians' hostility to him and their failed attempt to prevent him from becoming prime minister.

In spite of having won a plurality in the parliamentary elections of May 1960 and having put together a coalition of political parties with a majority in the parliament, Lumumba was not the first choice for prime minister–designate by the Belgian minister in charge of the transition. W. J. Ganshof van der Meersch had entrusted the task of forming the government to Joseph Kasavubu, leader of the Alliance des Bakongo, whose party had won only twelve seats in the House of Representatives, as opposed to thirty-three by the Mouvement National Congolais–Lumumba (MNC-L), out of the 137 seats in the lower chamber. It is only when Kasavubu failed to gain a working majority that the Belgians reluctantly turned to Lumumba.

Once Lumumba became prime minister and agreed to have Kasavubu as the ceremonial head of state, their different temperaments and ideological positions would be exploited by the Belgians in particular and Lumumba's enemies in general to prevent a harmonious working relationship and create hostility between them. While Lumumba and Kasavubu were to collaborate admirably to stay on top of the situation during the first two weeks of what will be designated here as the first Congo crisis, the first sign of division between them came on independence day, June 30, 1960, with Lumumba's now-famous speech against Belgian colonialism.

Lumumba's speech, which has become a classic text of African nationalism, only reinforced the contempt that Bunche and Western officialdom and media in general had for him. Brilliantly improvised by Lumumba at the independence day ceremonies, the speech came with a view to setting the historical record straight in reaction to a very patronizing speech by Baudouin I, king of Belgium, and Kasavubu's timid and lackluster response. With a paternalistic tone bordering on insult, the Belgian king had declared that Congolese independence was the culmination of the civilizing mission that his great-granduncle Leopold II had begun in 1885. Lumumba responded to the king's litany of Belgium's charitable deeds in the Congo with a historically correct reading of heinous crimes committed under the Leopoldian system, as well as the repression and the humiliations suffered by the Congolese under colonialism.

Like most Western diplomats, international civil servants, and journalists, Bunche characterized Lumumba's behavior and speech as impolite. While it is true that Lumumba's speech did not obey the canons of diplomacy, none of those who have accused him on this ground ever stop to question to what extent the king's own speech was diplomatic. How inappropriate could it be for the Congolese to be told that the man responsible for nearly ten million deaths in their country between 1885 and 1908 was only interested in saving them from the Arab slave trade and uplifting them from backwardness to civilization! That a single event, undiplomatic though it might be, should become a major factor in the Western strategy to remove Lumumba from power shows the arrogance of the major powers and their ideologues in academia, international organizations, and the media, all of whom feel entitled to write our history from the perspective of the West rather than that of its former colonial subjects.

Lumumba's Handling of the Crisis

The major issue around which the antagonism between Bunche and Lumumba was centered was the role of the United Nations in removing Belgian troops from the Congo and helping the Congolese government restore the territorial integrity of the country by ending the Katanga secession. Elsewhere, I have described the first Congo crisis as "a period of political instability and civil war that began with the mutiny of the armed forces on 5 July 1960 and ended with the military coup of 24 November 1965," and including, "among other major events, the Katanga secession, Lumumba's assassination, and the consolidation of political power by Congolese moderates under the tutelage of Washington, New York, and Brussels."[5]

The independence settlement had left the Force Publique under the command of its white Belgian officers, the highest-ranking Congolese being noncommissioned officers. With an arrogant commander in chief insisting that no change would result from independence, Congolese soldiers responded to this provocation with a mutiny that degenerated into widespread violence and the flight of white civil servants, military officers, professional cadres, and business operators. Bunche himself apparently escaped injury on July 8, when he was fired at while standing on the balcony of his hotel in Kinshasa (then known as Léopoldville).[6] On July 10, Belgian metropolitan troops stationed in the Congo intervened, supposedly to protect the lives and property of whites. A day later, Katanga Province declared its secession from the Congo.

On the same day, the American ambassador to the Congo, Clare Timberlake, had advised the Congolese government to call upon the United Nations for a peacekeeping force to help resolve the crisis. Two days later, President Kasavubu and Prime Minister Lumumba dropped their appeal for U.S. assistance and addressed an urgent request for help to UN secretary general Dag Hammarskjöld. Bunche, who was not consulted before this appeal, was surprised at how fast the UN responded to this request.[7] Two days later, the UN Security Council, via resolution 143, authorized the deployment of the UN Congo mission, and the secretary general appointed Bunche as head of the entire operation as well as interim force commander before the arrival of Gen. Carl von Horn of Sweden.

The antagonism between Bunche and Lumumba, as between Lumumba and the UN Secretariat in general, arose in connection with the interpretation of the Security Council mandate for ONUC. I have maintained that although Hammarskjöld and his staff might have written the Security Council authorization, it is Lumumba who is correct as to the literal meaning of the authorization itself:

> The Security Council directed the secretary-general to provide military assistance to the Congolese government to ensure the withdrawal

of Belgian troops, to end the Katanga secession, and to restore law and order throughout the country. It also directed the Secretariat to provide technical assistance to the government for ensuring the smooth running of essential services. For Lumumba, then, what ONUC was supposed to do was crystal clear: help his government send the Belgian troops home; end the Katanga secession, which was made possible by Belgian support; restore law and order; and train Congolese civil servants in running essential services. Hammarskjöld, on the other hand, saw matters differently. The most charitable explanation of his position is that he was convinced that the Belgians would leave without confrontation once UN troops had restored law and order and brought the situation under control. While this was true for the rest of the country, it could not apply to Katanga, where Belgian soldiers and white mercenaries were backing the secession. Hammarskjöld was unwilling to use force to expel Belgian military advisers and white mercenaries from Katanga.[8]

A recipient of the Nobel Peace Prize for his role in negotiating a truce to the Israeli-Arab war of 1948, Bunche in the Congo was still operating according to the original rules of peacekeeping, under which UN intervention deals with monitoring a ceasefire or a truce between two well-designated belligerents. Hammarskjöld, for his part, saw in the Congo situation an opportunity to implement his grandiose plan of world government, with a strong UN involvement in nation building. On the other hand, the two colleagues were in total agreement on not using force against Belgian military advisers and white mercenaries in Katanga. This infuriated Lumumba, because he could not understand why the UN was attempting to take over the administration of the rest of the Congo while leaving Katanga Province to Belgian control and tutelage. Under the circumstances, it is incredible that Bunche and Hammarskjöld could not understand why Lumumba would be upset when Hammarskjöld visited Katanga in August 1960 without the approval of the Congolese government. For Lumumba and Congolese nationalists, the UN was behaving as though it were in a conquered territory, and not in a sovereign state. Bunche's reaction to Lumumba's position is typically condescending. He wrote to Cordier, "Reaction verged on rage. . . . Vigorously challenged validity of SecGen's interpretation, held him to be unsympathetic to Central Govt. and threatened to seek unilateral military support from Ghana and Guinea for Katanga action.... He was particularly incensed that SecGen came to Léo[poldville] 'unannounced' and then left for Katanga early next morning. Also that SecGen cabled Tshombe and not Lumumba."[9]

If Hammarskjöld's calculations were clearly made in terms of global politics in the context of the cold war, Bunche's reasoning was just as superficial as it was based on an erroneous understanding of the Katanga secession: "I advised Mr. Hammarskjöld not to send the force to Katanga for the time being. I greatly doubt that a United Nations peace force could be stationed for very long in any country if, even in self-defense, it would have to turn its guns on civilians rather than military forces."[10]

Bunche's argument here simply makes no sense. First, Katanga was not a country but a province of the Congo, in which a UN military presence had already been established. Second, there was no indication whatsoever of any likely civilian resistance to UN intervention, as subsequent events were to show. The groups opposed to UN intervention were Belgian troops and white mercenaries, not Congolese civilians. As Madeleine Kalb has pointed out, "Bunche had been taken in by 'Tshombe's bluff,'" and "it seems likely that there would have been less resistance at that early point and fewer lives lost than there eventually were in the series of UN military operations in Katanga during the next two and a half years."[11] Third, and contrary to Bunche's argument, there was an active popular resistance against the secession in the northern part of Katanga Province, led by a major political party allied with Lumumba's MNC-L, namely, Jason Sendwe's Balubakat. The amazing thing is that Bunche was well aware of this reality, which was later underlined by Ambassador Adlai Stevenson, then the U.S. permanent representative to the United Nations, in a television interview featuring Bunche as a guest in January 1963:

> Had it not been for intervention from the outside, the secession of the province of Katanga probably could have not been sustained. For when Tshombe proclaimed his province an independent country, he invited two foreign governments to send troops to help him put down local mutinies against his policies. And at the same time people often forget that the party which polled the greatest number of votes in Katanga was the Balubakat Party, which proclaimed its loyalty not to Tshombe but to the Central Government.[12]

But why did Ralph Bunche, too, seem to forget this fact in August 1960? My argument is that in addition to having taken seriously Tshombe's empty threat of resisting the deployment of UN troops by force, Bunche as a senior US diplomat was consciously or unconsciously acting "to advance American policy in Africa," as Stevenson summarized the convergence of US policy and UN action in the Congo.[13] However neutral Bunche and his Swedish, British, and American colleagues in the UN secretary general's office may have considered themselves in their actions as international civil servants, it is true, as Kalb has written, that "there is no doubt that their preconceptions, attitudes, and beliefs caused them to see the [Congo] situation in much the same way that the American government did."[14] In looking at the Congo through a cold war perspective, Bunche the UN official had the same apprehensions about Soviet penetration as the greatest threat to the political independence of African countries as Bunche the U.S. diplomat, and he saw Lumumba as a potential instrument of that penetration in the Congo.

Soviet Assistance to Lumumba

Facing the prospects of the consolidation of the secession, even in the presence of a UN peacekeeping force, Lumumba decided to rely on his own army to crush it. To do this, he requested and received some military supplies from the Soviet Union, particularly trucks and military transport aircraft for logistic purposes. In the eyes of Washington, its Western allies, and those international civil servants like Ralph Bunche who saw their job as maintaining the existing balance of power in the world, this marked a serious threat of Soviet penetration in central Africa. This strategic perspective was strongly held by Hammarskjöld, Bunche's boss, who wrote to his executive assistant from Kinshasa in August 1960, "The Congo should not be permitted to become a Korea, nor should it become a Hungary—or a Munich."[15] For those who had already perceived Lumumba as the African equivalent of Fidel Castro, the time had come to deal with him in a decisive way. Three days later, in an action unrelated to this cable but sharing the same mindset, President Dwight D. Eisenhower gave his "implicit authorization" to the Central Intelligence Agency for the assassination of Patrice Lumumba.[16]

Bunche would later state that Lumumba "may have been subject to leftist influence, but I did not regard him as anyone's stooge and felt that he was not greatly concerned with ideology."[17] Independently of this position, Bunche's biographer Charles Henry writes that "Bunche's reports left UN officials questioning the mental stability of the prime minister" in a context in which U.S. officials were convinced that Lumumba "was a Communist and not to be trusted."[18] Bunche, who used the communications facilities of the U.S. embassy in Kinshasa for his reporting to New York, thus contributed in no small way to the general negative disposition of U.S. and UN officials toward Lumumba. Several of his cables contain derogatory references to Lumumba, such as "the gutter-sayings of the Congo demagogue," whose behavior seems "irrational" and even "racist";[19] the "utterly cheap and vulgar reaction of PM";[20] and Lumumba being incapable of taking "sensible advice from any source" and prone to "constant recrimination, suspicions, unfounded charges and in general airing criticism of UN."[21]

In Bunche's assessment, the one person from whom Lumumba received "much advice" was Nathaniel Welbeck, the Ghanaian ambassador to the Congo, whom Bunche described as "a fool but dangerous,"[22] and most of whose advice was bad.[23] Like Hammarskjöld, who describes Ghanaian leader Kwame Nkrumah's Pan-African vision and unification plan as an "African Hitler-Mussolini drive,"[24] Bunche was greatly obsessed with Nkrumah's Ghana. Emotionally, he was hurt by the fact that despite his being an African American with a record of anticolonial and antiracism activism, he was simply dismissed as a representative of Yankee imperialism by the Ghanaian ambassador and his entourage, who, in Bunche's view, were "trying to undercut me in playing vigorously the Nkrumah game of all-African politics."[25] For Bunche, that game was all the more dangerous, inasmuch as it involved active cooperation with Sékou Touré's Guinea and Nasser's Egypt, in addition to close ties with the Soviet Union.[26]

According to Rajeshwar Dayal, the Indian diplomat who replaced Bunche as the UN secretary general's representative in the Congo in September 1960, Hammarskjöld "had little respect for the Soviet [UN] Under-Secretary, G. P. Arkadiev, and though Arkadiev's functions were political, he was rather pointedly excluded from participation in the Congo discussions."[27] For Hammarskjöld apparently believed that a UN official from the Soviet Union would remain loyal to the foreign policy of his country, while those from the West would act as neutral international civil servants. That is why the Congo discussions were dominated by the secretary general's senior American aides:

Ralph Bunche, his deputy; Andrew Cordier, his executive assistant; and Heinrich Wieschhoff, his éminence grise.[28] While Bunche and Wieschhoff were more diplomatic in following the secretary general's line on being extremely careful not to create the impression that they were "out to get Lumumba,"[29] Cordier the cold warrior had no such scruples. During his brief tenure as acting head of the UN Congo mission between Bunche's departure, on August 28, and Dayal's arrival, on September 8, 1960, he helped engineer and execute the illegal removal of Lumumba from power.

―◦―

The general conclusion I reached in my book on the Congo concerning the responsibility of the United Nations in Lumumba's demise does apply to all prominent members of the so-called Congo Club, including Ralph Bunche. The secretary general and his chief collaborators on the Congo "shared a common Cold War outlook with Western policymakers, and saw their mission in the Congo as that of preserving the then existing balance of forces in the world."[30] Wittingly or unwittingly, they provided to those seeking Lumumba's demise the justification and the opportunities they needed to remove a democratically elected leader from office by illegal means.

Notes

1. ONUC is the acronym for the mission's name in French, Organisation des Nations Unies au Congo, renamed the Opération des Nations Unies au Congo in 1963.

2. United Nations Archives, Incoming Code Cable, Dag-1/2.2.1–27, file: Congo—Cables, Code, vol. 1, June 17 to August 23, 1960, UN Archives, New York. The principal cable senders and recipients were Dag Hammarskjöld, the secretary general; Ralph Bunche, the undersecretary general for special political affairs; and Andrew Cordier, executive assistant to the secretary general. The letter and number of each archival document are those so indicated in the UN Archives.

3. Mostly from Ralph J. Bunche, *Selected Speeches and Writings*, ed. Charles P. Henry (Ann Arbor: University of Michigan Press, 1995).

4. Hammarskjöld to Cordier, B472, August 15, 1960.

5. Georges Nzongola-Ntalaja, *The Congo from Leopold to Kabila: A People's History* (London: Zed Books, 2002), 95–96.

6. Bunche, *Selected Speeches*, 182.

7. Ibid., 194

8. Nzongola-Ntalaja, *Congo*, 113–14.

9. Bunche to Cordier, B433, August 12, 1960. Moïse Tshombe was the provincial president of Katanga and leader of its secession.

10. Bunche, *Selected Speeches*, 198.

Ralph Bunche, Patrice Lumumba, and the First Congo Crisis

11. Madeleine G. Kalb, *The Congo Cables: The Cold War in Africa—From Eisenhower to Kennedy* (New York: Macmillan, 1982), 43.

12. "Transcript of 'Adlai Stevenson Reports,' ABC-Television, January 20, 1963: Interview with Mr. Ralph J. Bunche," UN Archives, New York, Dag-1/2.2.1–90, Congo—United States, book 4 (January 1–December 31, 1963), 3–4.

13. Ibid., 4. According to Stevenson, "Our object, the object of the United States in supporting the United Nations in this long and trying ordeal has been to advance American policy in Africa. . . . So it has seemed to us that our policy and the United Nations policy have coincided exactly in the Congo."

14. Kalb, *Congo Cables,* 24.

15. Hammarskjöld to Cordier, B472, August 15, 1960.

16. Kalb, *Congo Cables,* 53–55.

17. Bunche, *Selected Speeches,* 193.

18. Charles P. Henry, *Ralph Bunche: Model Negro or American Other?* (New York: New York University Press, 1999), 197.

19. Bunche to Hammarskjöld, B570, August 20, 1960 (typo in original—year recorded as 1950).

20. Bunche to Hammarskjöld, B545, August 19, 1960.

21. Bunche to Cordier, B439, August 13, 1960.

22. Bunche to Hammarskjöld, ONUC 19, July 20, 1960.

23. Bunche to Hammarskjöld, B157, July 21, 1960.

24. Hammarskjöld to Cordier, B472, August 15, 1960.

25. Bunche to Hammarskjöld, B157, July 21, 1960.

26. In a cable dated August 18, 1960 (B515) to Cordier, Bunche reports that Maj. Gen. Henry T. Alexander, the British commander of the Ghanaian ONUC contingent, "said that Accra last week purchased six Ilyushins" from Moscow.

27. Rajeshwar Dayal, *Mission for Hammarskjöld: The Congo Crisis* (Princeton: Princeton University Press, 1976), 308.

28. According to Kalb, Wieschhoff "was in theory Arkadiev's subordinate," but it is he, not Arkadiev, who had the Congo files under his control, and his boss did not have access to them. Kalb, *Congo Cables,* 21. "Others who played key policymaking roles on the Congo included General Carl von Horn, Hammarskjöld compatriot who served as force commander in the Congo, and the secretary-general's British assistant, Brian Urquhart." Nzongola-Ntalaja, *Congo,* 115.

29. Kalb, *Congo Cables,* 137.

30. Nzongola-Ntalaja, *Congo,* 114.

PART THREE

Reflections on Bunche's Legacy in Global Perspective

CHAPTER TEN

Africa in the Global Decolonization Process
The Road to Postcoloniality

RALPH A. AUSTEN

THE SUBJECT of decolonization has taken a roller coaster ride through the relatively short lifetime of Africanist historiography. This entire field first came into its own near the end of the colonial era, and much of its energy drew upon the promise of impending independence. Decolonization was seen at that time largely from the perspective of African political movements and their preparation for the impending task—so ominous during the present Iraq and Afghanistan situations—of nation building. In the ensuing decades, tellingly labeled postcolonial rather than national, disillusionment with the performance of new African states made the moment of their birth appear less significant. In a 1987 book I could thus assert, "It is even possible to write an economic history of Africa without designating the shift to independence as a major turning point."[1]

In preparing the present chapter in 2004, I was surprised to see what a vast amount of scholarship had been dedicated specifically to decolonization over the past two decades, including two "decolonization readers" published over the previous year.[2] To be sure, most of this literature gives at least as much attention to Asia as to Africa. Much of it can also be explained less by an analytic interest in the topic than by the new availability of European and American archives for the 1950s and 1960s. These records have, however, added more nuance than major revisionist revelations to existing narratives. Moreover, the topic of African nationalism remains pretty much off the radar screen.[3]

The shift to a more metropole-centered account of African decolonization does represent a major change in perspective and sometimes explicit interpretation. For Africanists, moreover, the central questions to be answered have taken a radical turn. Instead of asking, how did Africans overcome and incorporate the experiences of colonialism in order to regain their independence? the new goal, as stated by Frederick Cooper, is "understanding how Africa ended up with the kind of independence which it, for the most part, got."[4] The clear implication here is that this has not been a very happy independence. "The past of the present"—to cite the subtitle of a more recent work by the same author[5]—is linked very particularly to the terminal phase of colonialism, which must therefore be reexamined. Likewise we need to extend the story beyond the 1960s to understand the degree to which decolonization was ever fully achieved.

Frederick Cooper holds a deserved position as one of the preeminent historians of modern Africa, so I will use him as a point of departure for suggesting the kind of framework I think we need to comprehend the role of colonialism and decolonization in shaping contemporary Africa. There can be no quarrel with Cooper's assertion of considerable continuity between the colonial development efforts of the post–World War II era and the state projects of the early independence era. He also shows how the failure and high cost of these projects induced Europeans to abandon them, leaving African governments to work out the problems for themselves.

The present argument will depart from Cooper by placing the transformations of Africa in a more global process. Cooper himself has very effectively shown some of the limitations of the concept of globalization for understanding African history. This critique is consciously linked to his analysis of the "modernization theory" that inspired colonial development managers in the 1940s and 1950s.[6] In both cases the "particularities and complexities" of African society and its dynamics are reduced to abstracted versions of (or deviations from) what is supposed to be going on elsewhere. When such concepts are turned into policy, whether in the form of late-colonial development schemes or structural adjustment policies of the International Monetary Fund (IMF), they often impose great damage on African capacities for effective transformation.

The problem with such an analysis is not that Cooper is wrong in his attacks on modernization and globalization theory but rather that

Africa in the Global Decolonization Process

he makes such a critique the center of his historical analysis. It is the general instinct of Africanists, when faced with "lay" accounts of African problems, to take on the faulty, ethnocentric analysis rather than the problem itself. To some degree that is our job, especially when we are historians or anthropologists rather than political scientists or economists. We have a duty to criticize bad policy and suggest better premises for its execution but not, ultimately, to formulate alternative solutions. However, we are also obligated to look beyond the poor fit between externally imagined policy and African reality toward the larger context that produces this mismatch in the first place. Colonialism, decolonization, and structural adjustment are all such mismatches, but they have their own history of "particularity and complexity," which is as important to African development as the African social orders and wide-ranging networks that they usually misunderstand.

The dimension of that history that I want to stress here is the global—that is, shifts in regimes of international politics and political economy that drove Europeans to involve themselves in Africa as colonizers, decolonizers, and postcolonial patrons.[7] This set of engagements has not, generally, worked out to the advantage of Africans, particularly in their efforts to live within the historical form bequeathed to them, the nation-state. In my conclusions I will return some African agency to my own narrative by indicating (very briefly) some alternatives to the nation-state found within the postcolonial global order.

Both *decolonization* and *postcoloniality* are terms heavily implicated in their reference to a prior condition: colonialism. Our analysis must thus begin with a discussion of the relationship between globalization, very broadly understood, and the establishment of colonial rule in Africa. By globalization I mean a regime of international political economy in which large areas of the world are integrated through market mechanisms (as measured not only by flows of trade goods but also price convergence and dispersed but centrally managed divisions of labor) with relatively little interference from political authorities. Colonialism is here defined as the formal occupation and governance of African territory by European powers.

It is often argued that colonialism was a means for bringing non-European regions like Africa more fully into the global economy.[8] There is certainly some truth to this contention, since colonial regimes provided the infrastructure for greater flows of goods, people, and information within Africa and between it and the outside world.

However, a central point of this chapter will be to argue that the colonization of Africa at the end of the nineteenth century constituted one aspect of a lengthy "policy backlash" against globalization in the latter 1800s.[9] From that point on, but especially after World War I, the dominant states of the world retreated from open and international markets to nationally centered *regulation* of their internal and external economies. African decolonization, some two decades after World War II, then forms part of the movement back toward globalization. Thus, "the kind of independence which ... [Africa], for the most part, got" was shaped by the relationships between global market logic and the efforts to use colonies as a tool against such forces.

Historians are generally agreed that the free-trade era of the mid-nineteenth century represents an earlier—perhaps the first and possibly still the most complete—period of globalization.[10] Throughout this whole time and even during the "mercantilist" seventeenth and eighteenth century which preceded it, Africa participated on an ever-increasing scale in the world economy. The key breakthrough here was the opening of the Atlantic maritime frontier, although this commerce built on earlier trans-Saharan and Indian Ocean connections to global trading partners. None of these linkages required colonialism. Africans themselves organized the movement of commodities to and from coastal and Sahelian entrepôts where foreign merchants resided and exercised sovereignty, at most, over the immediate environs of their trading posts.

There is certainly something pathological about the fact that for much of this period the most important African export was slaves. However, with the abolition of the Atlantic slave trade, African merchants and rulers were able to adjust without any general crisis to the provision of "legitimate" goods (mainly vegetable oils and kernels).[11] The only problem with this transition, at least from a global perspective, is that tropical Africa[12] now became more marginal to the world economy than it had been in the earlier slave trade era and in its even earlier role as major gold supplier.[13]

The colonial partition of Africa in the last decades of the nineteenth century could not have occurred without the previous history of international trade and resulting European stations around Africa. However, given the position of Africa within the global economy (especially in the 1880s, when vegetable oil prices moved sharply downward), it might be expected that Europeans would continue their earlier policies of negotiating trade rivalries (or even withdrawing from coastal stations altogether, as did the Dutch) rather than abruptly expanding their holdings to encompass virtually the entire continent.

Partition, therefore, was driven less by positive interest in Africa than a set of political and socioeconomic anxieties developing within Europe itself. The political anxiety arose from the emergence of a newly unified Germany as the most powerful and yet insecure state in Europe. As with the superpower cold war of the decolonization era, the Great Power rivalry of 1871–1914 meant that disturbances anywhere in the world had to be perceived as potential opportunities for one side to gain advantages over the other. From a political perspective, Africa was colonized because it could be (the weapons and other technology of Europeans made this relatively easy) and because no power wanted to be cut off from the possible advantages that just might be gained from such territorial possessions.

The social and economic anxieties of the late nineteenth century arose most immediately from the processes of globalism and industrialism themselves. The competitive aspect of integrated and expanding world markets meant that no country felt secure about the viability of its producer sectors, particularly in agriculture but also in industry. A market crisis like the Long Depression of 1873–96 also appeared to vindicate Marxist theories about the collapse of capitalism and ensuing class warfare. As a response to both international and domestic tensions, Atlantic industrialized states (European and American) retreated from the market liberalism of the mid-nineteenth century. The new "regulation" order involved a mix of economic nationalism abroad and welfare capitalism at home.[14] Its specific measures included tariffs, restrictions on immigration, empowerment of labor unions, social security, direct government investment in various industries, and *colonialism*.

Within this new system colonies were supposed to counter the insecurity of globally integrated markets by guaranteeing each metropole its own closed source of strategic raw materials, an expanded export outlet for its domestic production, and a secure base for capital investment. Until World War II, Europe's African territories did not meet most of these needs and little was invested in them. The only significant development projects were railroads and harbors. For the most part these did not spur capitalist transformations of African economies but rather provided an outlet for greatly expanded peasant cash-crop production. In terms of economic policy, African colonies were treated as holding operations. Only modest "night watchman" administrative structures were put into place and the export of commodities like cacao, peanuts, coffee, and cotton were mainly designed to cover the costs of such governance. Since the commodities were neither strategic nor scarce, they were sold to any buyers who might appear.[15]

If the African colonies seem, in this period, to have played little active role in the regulatory order of the new international economy, it is equally difficult to see in them the roots of decolonization. Certainly few nationalist or protonationalist organizations can be found. There was plenty of resistance to European impositions of various sorts, but these actions were mainly localized and often in the nonpolitical form identified by James Scott for Malaysian peasants.[16] European education created what would later become the basis for systemic anticolonial leadership, but it remained very weak at the time. The level of schooling was still generally limited and mainly designed to produce African subalterns within the colonial bureaucracy itself.

Men in these positions, more than the somewhat aloof and segregated European administrators themselves, foreshadow what Cooper has called the "gatekeeper" function of later postcolonial regimes. As clerks and interpreters, they literally served as intermediaries between the alien regime and the general population. In this role they often built up clienteles and thus engaged in a kind of politics. But it was not a mobilization of forces that threatened colonialism itself, the very system that allowed such figures to flourish. This situation was not invisible to either Europeans or Africans, who both depended on clerk-interpreters, so that they often aroused as much suspicion and resentment as admiration.[17]

A much smaller group of more highly educated Africans did—mainly while abroad—connect with international circuits of Pan-Africanism and anticolonialism. When employed within the colonial system as teachers and technicians they usually received higher formal salaries than clerks but lacked the same opportunities to profit from local governance as gatekeepers. Some of them would gain such positions after independence.

The vision of African decolonization began to take on serious shape only after World War II. It is true that some African protesters evoked it earlier and colonial regimes gave it lip service. In categorizing the former German colonies handed over to Belgium, Britain, and France as class B mandates, whose populations were "not *yet* able to stand by themselves under the strenuous conditions of the modern world," the League of Nations implied some eventual independence for African colonies, but at too great a distance to be of immediate concern.[18]

In retrospect, the changes after World War II in both Africa and the larger world make decolonization seem almost inevitable. In political terms, colonialism was under assault from well-developed Asian nationalist movements (India became independent by 1947), by the generally antiracist and pro-national autonomy sentiments of the victorious antifascist alliance, and specifically by the now-dominant superpowers, the United States and the Soviet Union, each claiming in its own way to be the champion of "peoples liberation." Within Africa colonial regimes were pressured to undertake reforms, including opportunities for electoral politics that quickly gave voice to demands for complete self-rule. At the very least (as again officially expressed in the UN trusteeship system that replaced the League of Nations mandates) the horizon for self-rule of some kind had now become more explicit and foreshortened.

The global political economy of this era, however, pointed toward a very different evolution of African-European relations. The 1940s and 1950s represent the high point of the regulation order. Indeed, for many leftist scholars who lived through it as critics, this time has now become something of a lost Fordist paradise characterized by relatively homogenous living standards, welfare legislation, and secure trading relations under the shelter of the Bretton Woods agreements.[19]

Bretton Woods did, however, replace the gold standard with the U.S. dollar as the stable basis for international transactions and that caused considerable anxiety to the one-time Great Powers Britain and France. Despite the generosity of Marshall Plan aid, both war-torn countries owed considerable debt to the United States that could be repaid only if they found new means of earning hard currency and sources of imports within nondollar currency zones. Two choices were available for regaining such autonomy: integration into a larger European entity or the creation of more active ties to their colonial empires. There was also some talk of a "Eurafrican" solution that would combine both options, but this took on real meaning only after the formation of the Common Market and decolonization, as will be seen. However, in the immediate aftermath of a war that had been fought against Hitler's attempt to unify Europe around Germany, Britain and France first chose to protect their own currencies and national status by investment in the colonies.

By the 1950s, colonies meant essentially Africa, since the Asian territories were all moving toward independence. Because little indication of African nationalism occurred before World War II, European rulers imagined that gradual political reforms would stave off rather than accelerate demands for independence. In the French case, the great reform document of 1944, the Brazzaville Declaration, actually denounced "self-government" (English in the original) in favor of a Union Française that would bring elected African representatives to Paris. The most immediate expression of British and French reinforced incorporation of African colonies into postwar metropolitan economies came in the form of regulations.[20] These included, in varying mixes, restrictions on currency conversion, government control over exports purchases and their prices, and preferential treatment of colonial and metropolitan goods in their respective markets. Such controls were only extensions, or in some case simple continuations, of policies that had been in place before World War II, and especially since the Great Depression of the 1930s. In the British case, the regulations actually forced the colonies to subsidize sterling during the critical years up to the mid-1950s. The French system shared its burdens more equitably between home and colonies, consumers on each side paying more for commodities than they would have under conditions of free international trade.

What was entirely novel in the postwar period and somewhat offset the self-interested imposition of colonial regulations was the high degree of investment made by both Britain and France in their African territories. This flow of funds (much of it outright aid rather than loans) came mainly under two programs, the British Colonial Development and Welfare Act and the French FIDES (Fonds d'Investissements pour le Développement Économique et Social). As their names imply, both efforts combined economic projects of some presumed interest to the metropole with social ones (education, medical care, support of labor unions) that offered immediate benefits to African subjects. In principle there was no conflict between such objectives: economic development would provide the basis for continued support of social services and Africans with better education, and health and wages would become more robust economic partners within each currency zone. However, the unintended consequences of all these undertakings was less to develop either colony or Europe than to push them toward the "divorce" of decolonization.[21]

The forces of separation came from three directions: African political movements mobilized by new colonial interventions; European disillusionment with the poor, often disastrous, economic results of investments in Africa; and the shift in the international economy toward globalization rather than regulatory nationalism. I will deal very briefly with the first two and dwell somewhat more on the third.

The initiation of territorywide electoral politics in African colonies might have had the modest impact predicted by European planners if the European regimes had likewise maintained the low-key night watchman role of the pre–World War II period. Development projects, however, sometimes referred to as a second colonial occupation, touched Africa much more intimately than had previous efforts merely to encourage peasant cash cropping. Farmers and herders were now expected to undertake arduous and costly antierosion measures or destroy crops identified as diseased by government authorities; others were encouraged to move under new settlement schemes with high costs of their own. The more positive aspects of development also moved people with new levels of education or merely awareness of new opportunities away from rural sites to cities, which grew exponentially from the very small sizes of the 1930s. Ethnicity and patron-client networks, previously working to support the localized and collaborationist identities favored by colonial regimes, now converged in urban settings. Here political leaders could use them (and the grievances of their still-rural families) as the basis of "mass" nationalist parties.

From a European perspective, investments in Africa soon came to appear highly wasteful. The major Tanganyika (Tanzania) groundnut scheme became a British watchword of misguided planning as early as 1949. In France during the mid-1950s, *cartierisme* (after the editor of the popular weekly *Paris Match*) signified right-of-center objection to more general misallocation of funds for African colonial projects. For both Britain and France, trade with the colonies reached its peak, in both absolute and relative terms, during the early 1950s but then began a steady decline. This shift indicated a general change in the international economy that again marginalized Africa.

In simple economic terms, the brief prominence of Africa in British and French calculations from 1945 to about 1955 had been based on very temporary conditions. These included the general weakness of the metropoles after the war, a scarcity of tropical primary goods induced by wartime Japanese conquests in Asia (a situation briefly revived in 1950 by the Korean War), and fear of German domination in any European union. By the mid-1950s the French and British economies had overcome their "dollar crisis" largely due to trade with other European countries; tropical export prices had returned to the highly competitive situation that had prevailed since the opening of the Suez Canal, in 1869; and a truncated, Catholic-dominated West Germany proved to be an amenable partner in a burgeoning European Common Market. As Britain and France (and eventually even Belgium and Portugal)[22] gave up varying degrees of their national autonomy for a European identity, they also found it economically convenient to give in to nationalist demands and turn at least political responsibility for African development over to independent African governments.

But the link between decolonization and globalization is not just an issue of pre–Common Market European economic interests. For Europe and Africa it involves a relationship continuing beyond decolonization; for international politics it involves the cold war and the nature of American hegemony; and for economics itself it involves a shift from regulatory, or Fordist, regimes to globalized neoliberalism. These issues are not entirely separable but I will treat them serially in order to consider the ever wider perspectives from which one might view transitions within Africa.

Eurafrica is a term from the era of late colonialism that seems particularly irrelevant to the postcolonial era. However, like decolonization, it has again become the focus of historical efforts to trace the past of Africa's present.[23] The concept of Eurafrica dates from the interwar era, when its function was as much to promote the idea of a European unity as to alter an unabashedly colonial relationship with Africa. The concept was also taken up very early by French colonial spokesmen as a justification for their national efforts in Africa.[24] There was little ambiguity (if much mandates-style idealism) about the colonial aspects of Eurafrica, but the question of whether it was a European or mainly a French project continued throughout this term's history.

In the postwar era Eurafrica was presented within a general vision of Western Europe as a third force in opposition to the bipolar US-USSR regime.[25] The intercontinental relationship would be one of "integration and complementarity," implying something of a reformed colonialism in the manner of the French Union.[26] In practice, colonial development policies up to the mid-1950s remained entirely national projects, while the first steps toward European integration were taken with no more than occasional rhetorical concern for collective links to Africa.

The realization of Eurafrica thus came only at the moment when the 1957 Treaty of Rome established the Common Market, thus committing France (although not yet Britain) to a European rather than a colonial basis for its economic future. By this time French disillusionment with the results of colonial investment had already set in, reinforced by awareness of the "Dutch complex," in which decolonization proved to be a basis for enhanced prosperity.[27] With the Loi Cadre (Overseas Reform Act) of 1956, France had already set its African territories on a path toward the once dreaded "self-government" and was thus prepared, along with Belgium, to surrender its exclusive control over colonies to the more important project of Europe.

In the Treaty of Rome, France effectively managed to have its cake—whatever advantages remained in colonialism—and also eat the benefits of decolonization. The treaty gave the not-yet-independent African territories of France and Belgium associated status with the Common Market, thus recognizing their ties to their metropoles but also sharing trading privileges with the rest of the Six (Italy, Luxembourg, Netherlands, West Germany). At the same time these noncolonial European partners (especially Germany) would share the costs of providing development aid to what became known as the Eurafrica fund.[28]

From an African perspective, the Treaty of Rome was a classic version of Eurafrica as reformed colonialism, since its negotiation did not involve any participation by overseas subjects. However, following the independence of most of tropical Africa, the first of a new set of agreements with the EEC (European Economic Community) was signed in Yaoundé, Cameroon, in 1963 (renewed in 1969). These pacts guaranteed the African signatories continued access to both European markets and EEC aid. In return the EEC was allowed preferred access to the markets of the African partners.

The English-speaking African states refused to participate in arrangements that they understandably viewed as neocolonial. However, it soon became evident (especially after Britain joined the EEC, in 1973) that exclusion from the trade advantages of such agreements would also be very costly. In 1975 a whole new partnership was established through a treaty signed in Lomé, Togo. It joined the now more unified and enlarged European Community (EC) to a much expanded group of ex-colonies—in Africa, the Caribbean, and the Pacific (the

ACP countries)—that included virtually all tropical African territories (those that gained independence after 1975 joined under subsequent Lomé agreements).

Lomé I, as it came to be known, was closest among all these conventions to achieving the stated goals of a more egalitarian "Eurafrica." This agreement had been drawn up in the mid-1970s, a brief period of renewed raw material (especially petroleum) shortages when the United Nations Conference on Trade and Development was attempting to design a New International Economic Order, more favorable to societies in the third world and the South. In the case of Lomé, the new advantages offered to the ACP signatories were guarantees of aid, export price stability, and no reciprocal privileges for EC goods coming into Africa. *Equality* here can only refer to the bargaining process, since all the concessions made to the ACP imply continued weakness. However, the stated aims of the (mainly African) ACP negotiators was to use such medium-term preferences to provide their economies with a basis for substantive equality at some future date.

As things turned out, the neocolonial aspects of Lomé I have been transformed, through further agreements and practices between 1990 and 2002, into a neoliberal "decline of Eurafrica."[29] The guarantees of European markets were undone by World Trade Organization rulings on free trade; price stability is no longer upheld; and aid to Africa has been cut in favor of more critical Mediterranean and Eastern European partners (even now, members) of the European Union (EU). The funds still going to Africa are tied to the "conditionality" of structural adjustment programs. We can view this new order as both the final stage of decolonization (represented by continuing formal ties with former European rulers) and also the beginning of *re*colonization (through the domestic African policy reforms dictated by aid donors). But before examining what this may mean for African participants, it is necessary to move a step beyond Europe and see the new global economy from a wider perspective.

Globalization has been alternatively viewed as a project of American empire or an economic force well beyond the control of the United States and even damaging to its international hegemony. Formal decolonization is more obviously tied to the politics of the immediate postwar decades, in which the United States certainly exercised considerable hegemony, so this must be the first context in which to examine the transformations of Africa (and of Eurafrica).

The strongest representation of decolonization as an element (even a critical one) of U.S. hegemony is presented by Kelly and Kaplan, two students of a non-African ACP country, Fiji.[30] "Decolonization as actually experienced," they insist, was entry into a new world order already tooled for purposes at best differing from the aims of the anticolonial movements, and at times clearly obstructive of them.

This argument is based on two premises: the role of the United States in dismantling the colonial empires of Europeans and the construction of the postcolonial nation-state as an instrument of subsequent American power. Neither of these authors is a historian, so it is very easy to show how the narrative of American involvement in the colonial process is much more complicated" than they contend. Even the key role of the United States, particularly in the ending of the British colonial empire, was not very direct.

The major historians of this "Anglo-Saxon" anticolonial partnership are William Roger Louis and Ronald Robinson, who concur that America's intention during and immediately after World War II was to eliminate colonies in favor of an international free-trade order, that is, immediate globalization. However, this story is strongly qualified by the exigencies of the cold war, which led the United States to shift its position in favor of strengthening Western Europe by whatever means possible, including the defense of sterling and franc zones against the dollar.[31]

More generally, as Ebere Nwaubani has shown, U.S. African policy during most of the decolonization era was rather vague and focused more on maintaining the stability of its West European allies than worrying about Africa itself.[32] After 1957 both American and British strategies for Africa (with Britain taking the lead) sought to steer a balance between overrigid opposition to nationalists (whom both powers mistrusted) and hasty concession: "If the Western Governments appear to be reluctant to grant independence.... They may turn [African opinion] towards the Soviet Union; if... they move too fast, they run the risk of leaving large areas ... ripe for Communist exploitation."[33]

In any case, Britain's economic ties with African territories and the commonwealth in general were declining during this period. One problem here was the formation of the Common Market in Europe, a project pushed very energetically by the United States as a bulwark against communism. By the mid-1950s both Britain and its African territories (not covered by commonwealth preferences) were increasingly trading more with continental Europe than one another. The ultimate solution to all this, a decade and a half later, was for Britain to enter the Common Market and anglophone Africa to join the Lomé version of Eurafrica. But such a move was not possible at the moment of decolonization because of both the complications of British and commonwealth relations with Europe and, as already seen, African sensibilities about neocolonialism.

In political terms the United States did not appear very concerned with replacing European colonial empires in Africa with formally independent nation-states. The main issue was stability, so as to avoid crises that might provide opportunities for Soviet or (after 1956) Nasserist/Pan-Arab subversion. Nonetheless, the nation-state was the political form that emerged from this process, and it can be argued from both a radical" and more conservative position that it is less an expression of African politics and identity than an artifact of an American-dominated international order.

The conservative (or classical liberal) version of this argument has become a central theme of recent political science inquiry into postcolonial Africa. In echoes (if usually more sensitive) of European and American cautions on the eve of independence, scholars have labeled these new entities "collapsed," "gatekeeper," or "weak" states, exercising only a "juridical," "quasi," or "negative" sovereignty over their populations.[34] Such critiques identify international recognition as the only attribute of statehood enjoyed by such regimes but do not stress the agency of the post–World War II international system and its hegemony, the United States, as the main cause or beneficiary of the outcome. Instead, Africa is simply seen as marginal, left in its present form out of negative convenience (it would be more costly to intervene than tolerate things as they are) rather than to gain any positive advantages.

Of course during the cold war era the West (as well as the Eastern Bloc) offered significant aid to African governments, allowing them to continue the development projects of the late colonial era. However, by the 1980s, with the evident failure of these projects and the end of the cold war, aid became less generous and tied to "conditionalities" that required the dismantling of the development state. Thus the "decline of Eurafrica" is synchronous with decisions of the United States and the international institutions that it dominates, the World Bank and the IMF, to draw still further back from involvement with

African regimes that have proven themselves incapable of living up to their nationalist pretensions.

The more radical view of this transformation, as expressed by John Kelly and Martha Kaplan, is to argue that the nation-state concept is itself a construct of the post–World War II era, designed to maintain systems of local and global subjugation under a myth of equality among and within these territorial entities. The argument here is largely theoretical, directed particularly at Benedict Anderson rather than any globalist arguments. However, it does suggest a global basis for "failed" national conditions and also some global means of realizing "ambition[s] . . . much higher than independence."[35] But to deal with these issues we need to examine the transformations of the global political economy that I have proposed as the framework for my own presentation.

Here the argument will have to be very sketchy and more tentative than the style of writing might suggest.[36] The major issue is to identify the point (or elements) of transition from a "regulated" to a "global" economy and then see how these changes help us understand African decolonization in its fullest sense.

The immediate decades after World War II, when African territories achieved political independence, certainly do not constitute the moment of this change. As already indicated, the development programs in Africa that began in this era and continued well beyond it represented state-initiated and state-regulated economies with high commitments to welfare reform. Production in this period, whether under capitalist or socialist regimes, was heavily concentrated in Fordist systems of mass production. One of the great problems of African development efforts in the 1960s and after was to imitate these industrial models when they were already becoming outdated in the core of the world economy.

Sometime in the 1970s this core of the world economy shifted into something today identified as globalization. The United States, whose political power expanded after this era, lost its regulatory control over international economies when the Bretton Woods system (tying the dollar to a fixed gold value as the standard of international exchange) collapsed in 1973. This moment is simultaneous with the rise of Western Europe (then the EEC) and a Japan-centered East Asian economic sphere as world economic poles competitive with the United States. Manufacturing systems now began to shift from a Fordist to a "flexible" model, with operations decentralized around the globe and tuned closely to a variety of demands and product variants. These operations were greatly enhanced by the development of digitized-information technology, allowing the integration of widely scattered operations, with manufacturing moved farther and farther from the historical centers of industrialization. Capital, in this system, became almost entirely detached from national identities. Its free movement and access to labor and markets throughout the world was enhanced by the enforcement of free-trade regimes, both internationally (EU, NAFTA, WTO) and nationally, as governments felt pressure to deregulate their domestic economies.

Africa has not been a very active partner in these global transformations and yet is very powerfully influenced by them. In tandem with "negative sovereignty," it may be said to be experiencing "negative globalization." The effects only began to be felt, moreover, after globalization had already established itself in other parts of the world. If the colonization of Africa can be seen as an aspect of the shift from nineteenth-century globalization to a new system of regulation, decolonization only represented the failure of one version of this system rather than its general abandonment. In granting political independence to their African colonies, the European powers recognized that they were not risking the loss of very valuable assets but also understood that they maintained the means to assert economic control over these territories. Such control was exercised through Eurafrica as well as the patronage of the United States, World Bank, and IMF. However, even more than in the late-colonial era, this investment did not produce significant, if any, economic returns and was maintained more for the political reasons of national prestige and cold war rivalry as well as moral economy.

Globalization arrived in Africa in the form of neoliberal reforms that may be seen as both attacks on postcolonial states and the final phase of decolonization. The attacks are most obvious, since the structural adjustment programs imposed by the IMF and the Lomé IV/ii (1995) and Cotonou (2000) Eurafrica agreements explicitly demanded that African states limit their interventions in the market by privatizing many of their functions, allowing currencies to float, and deregulating prices for food and other commodities. The decolonization aspects took two more nuanced forms: first, the possible dismantling of Eurafrica privileges and second, the real termination of the South African apartheid state. The latter was a clear if delayed and racially skewed example of Fordism now replaced by a decidedly and much-disputed neoliberal order.[37]

South Africa has now taken its place as a leading force in affairs across the entire continent. In particular, it plays a major role in the New Partnership for Africa's Development (NEPAD), an initiative and organization that seeks to move all of sub-Saharan Africa forward on neoliberal and democratic lines, with renewed support from outside sources of capital. NEPAD represents the greatest possible African engagement with the world on the terms of the first stage of decolonization. The world has changed through globalization and Africa needs to accept new models of domestic political economy in order to maintain external support, but the actors are still postcolonial nation-states and the outside patrons are still mainly Western Europe and the United States with a growing but not very transformative involvement of China. It is too early to insist that such models will not work, but the experience of the recent past suggests the need for at least some consideration of alternatives.

Kelly and Kaplan's challenge to the nation-state form itself represents a more radical departure from the limits of decolonization than any of the formal politics currently engaged in by African leaders. The only historical basis for their argument is a rather loose gesture toward the models of Gandhi and South Asian subaltern studies scholarship. They do, however, point to elements in the global situation that allow Africans as individuals and communities to access international arenas without the mediation of the state. These include movements for human rights, indigenous rights, feminism, and the ecology. Historians and others might associate these efforts, which depend heavily on the patronage of First World–based nongovernmental organizations (NGOs), with colonialism in its moral economy mode.[38] But, at the very least, they are linkages to the outside world that follow globalist rather than traditional national patterns and perhaps offer agency to Africans other than government gatekeepers. Thus if Africa has not benefited from the early stages of globalization, the best opportunities for change or at least amelioration may have to follow global lines. If this is true, it may thus also be useful to rethink the colonial and immediate postcolonial African past—as I have attempted here—in global terms.

Notes

1. Ralph A. Austen, *African Economic History: Internal Development and External Dependency* (London: James Currey, 1987), 197. See this book also for additional assertions about African economic history not cited here.

2. Prasenjit Duara, ed., *Decolonization: Perspectives from Now and Then* (London: Routledge, 2004); James Le Sueur, ed., *The Decolonization Reader* (New York: Routledge, 2003).

3. See the hesitant and sparse (five out of 489 text pages) treatment of this topic in Paul Nugent, *Africa since Independence: A Comparative History* (Basingstoke, UK: Palgrave Macmillan, 2004).

4. Frederick Cooper, *Decolonization and African Society: The Labor Question in French and British Africa* (Cambridge: Cambridge University Press, 1996), 5.

5. Frederick Cooper, *Africa since 1940: The Past of the Present* (New York: Cambridge University Press, 2002).

6. Frederick Cooper, "What Is the Concept of Globalization Good For? An African Historian's Perspective," *African Affairs* 100, no. 399 (2001): 189–213.

7. One historian who has taken a similar position is William G. Clarence-Smith, "The Modern Colonial State and Global Economic Integration, 1815–1945," in *States and Sovereignty in the Global Economy,* ed. David A. Smith, Dorothy J. Solinger, and Steven C. Topik (London: Routledge, 1999), 120–37. However, this article does not focus on Africa and stops before the era of decolonization.

8. Niall Ferguson, *Empire: The Rise and Demise of the British World Order and the Lessons for Global Power* (New York: Basic Books, 2003); A. G. Hopkins, introduction to *Globalization in World History,* ed. Hopkins (London: Pimlico, 2002).

9. Jeffrey G. Williamson, "Globalization, Labor Markets and Policy Backlash in the Past," *Journal of Economic Perspectives* 12, no. 4 (Fall 1998): 51–73.

10. Ronald Findlay and Kevin H. O'Rourke, "Commodity Market Integration, 1500–2000," in *Globalization in Historical Perspective,* ed. Michael D. Bordo, Alan M. Taylor, and Jeffrey G. Williamson (Chicago: University of Chicago Press, 2003).

11. See Robin Law, ed., *From Slave Trade to "Legitimate" Commerce: The Commercial Transition in Nineteenth-Century West Africa* (Cambridge: Cambridge University Press, 1995).

12. I use the qualifier *tropical* here because South Africa has, of course, continued to be a major world source of gold. It has also had a very different history of colonialism and of economic and political development than tropical Africa. Throughout this chapter, unless otherwise stated, the term *Africa* will refer exclusively to the tropical regions of the continent.

13. I am omitting from this discussion the entire issue of Africa as the object of a European "moral economy of colonialism," beginning with the antislavery movement and continuing into contemporary NGO initiatives. This is a critical factor in understanding the global position of the continent and even its present political economy (q.v. below) but perhaps less important in the process of decolonization. See Ralph A. Austen, "Human Rights," in *Encyclopedia of Western Colonialism since 1450,* ed. Thomas Benjamin (Detroit: Thomson Gale, 2007), 556–63.

14. *Regulation* as a term to describe this phase of capitalist development was coined by a group of French theorists. For a lucid presentation, see David Harvey, *The Condition of Postmodernity: An Enquiry into the Origins of Cultural Change* (Oxford: Blackwell, 1989), 119–71.

15. One interesting exception is the research and investment in cotton production by all colonial powers that followed the U.S. boll weevil crisis of the 1890s. In the end there was little European demand for this cotton, much of which went to domestic African or Asian cloth industries. See Ralph A. Austen, "'The Premier Colonial Crop': Cotton and the Meaning of European Rule in Africa," *Historian* 59, no. 4 (1997): 862–66.

16. James C. Scott, *Weapons of the Weak: Everyday Forms of Peasant Resistance* (New Haven: Yale University Press, 1985).

17. Cooper, *Africa since 1940;* Benjamin Lawrance, Emily Lynn Osborn, and Richard Roberts, eds., *Intermediaries, Interpreters, and Clerks: African Employees in the Making of Colonial Africa* (Madison: University of Wisconsin Press, 2005).

18. League of Nations, Covenant, article 22; emphasis added.

19. William H. Sewell Jr., "The Political Unconscious of Social and Cultural History, or, Confessions of a Former Quantitative Historian," in *Logics of History: Social Theory and Social Transformations* (Chicago: University of Chicago Press, 2005), 22–80.

20. For more detail, see Austen, *African Economic History*, 205–6; David K. Fieldhouse, *Black Africa, 1945–80: Economic Decolonization and Arrested Development* (London: Allen and Unwin, 1986), 6–21.

21. The term *divorce* comes from one of the key works on decolonization, Jacques Marseille, *Empire colonial et capitalisme français: Histoire d'un divorce* (Paris: A. Michel, 1984).

22. Portugal is obviously a more complicated case of much-delayed decolonization and entry into the EU. However, the basic pattern is surprisingly similar; that is, by the late 1960s it too found that the cost of forcing African cotton production was not worth the returns, even to its much weaker metropolitan economy. See M. Anne Pitcher, "From Coercion to Incentives: The Portuguese Colonial Cotton Regime in Angola and Mozambique, 1946–1974," in *Cotton, Colonialism, and Social History in Sub-Saharan Africa*, ed. Allen Isaacman and Richard Roberts (Portsmouth, NH: Heinemann, 1995), 121.

23. Thomas Moser, *Europäische Integration, Dekolonisation, Eurafrika: Eine historische Analyse über die Entstehungsbedingungen der eurafrikanischen Gemeinschaft von der Weltwirtschaftskrise bis zum Jaunde-Vertrag, 1929–1963* (Baden-Baden: Nomos, 2000); see also Marie-Thérèse Bitsch and Gérard Bossuat, eds., *L'Europe unie et l'Afrique: De l'idée de l'Eurafrique à la convention de Lomé I: Histoire d'une relation ambiguë* (Brussels: Bruylant, 2005).

24. Moser, *Europäische Integration*, 96–111.

25. This concept was also endorsed by the late American cold war guru George Kennan; see Chidiebere Augustus Nwaubani, *The United States and Decolonization in West Africa, 1950–1960* (Rochester, NY: University of Rochester Press, 2001), 30–31.

26. Marc Michel, "Néocolonialisme éclairé," *Relations internationales*, no. 34 (1983): 100–106.

27. Marseille, *Empire colonial*, 357–65.

28. Catherine R. Schenk, "Decolonization and European Economic Integration: The Free Trade Area Negotiations," in Le Sueur, *Decolonization Reader*, 146.

29. Trevor Parfitt, "The Decline of Eurafrica? Lomé's Mid-Term Review," *Review of African Political Economy* 23, no. 67 (March 1996): 53–66. Parfitt, tellingly, expresses regrets about the transformation of a system that he once denounced as "neo-colonial."

30. John D. Kelly and Martha Kaplan, "'My Ambition Is Much Higher than Independence': U.S. Power, the UN World, the Nation-State, and Their Critics," in Duara, *Decolonization*, 140–51.

31. William Roger Louis and Ronald Robinson, "The Imperialism of Decolonization," *Journal of Imperial and Commonwealth History* 22, no. 3 (1994): 462–511. Ironically, this article is reprinted right after Kelly and Kaplan's article under the title "Empire Preserv'd: How the Americans Put Anti-Communism before Anti-Imperialism" in Duara, *Decolonization*, 152–61. It is also found, with its original title and full footnotes, in Le Sueur, *Decolonization Reader*, 49–79.

32. Nwaubani, *United States and Decolonization*.

33. June 1959 British Foreign Office memo, cited in Louis and Robinson, "Imperialism of Decolonization," in Le Sueur, *Decolonization Reader*, 68–69.

34. See (in order of the adjectives quoted in text) I. William Zartman, ed., *Collapsed States: The Disintegration and Restoration of Legitimate Authority* (Boulder: L. Rienner, 1995); Cooper, *Africa since 1940*; Jeffrey Herbst, *States and Power in Africa: Comparative Lessons in Authority and Control* (Princeton: Princeton University Press, 2000); Robert H. Jackson and Carl G. Rosberg, "Sovereignty and Underdevelopment: Juridical Statehood in the

African Crisis," *Journal of Modern African Studies* 24, no. 1 (1986): 1–31; Robert H. Jackson, *Quasi-states: Sovereignty, International Relations, and the Third World* (Cambridge: Cambridge University Press, 1990); Christopher Clapham, *Africa and the International System: The Politics of State Survival* (Cambridge: Cambridge University Press, 1996).

35. John Kelly and Martha Kaplan, "My Ambition Is Much Higher Than Independence"; see also Kelly and Kaplan, *Represented Communities: Fiji and World Decolonization* (Chicago: University of Chicago Press, 2001).

36. There is no authoritative literature on this controversial subject, but for a convenient and reasonably informed source who pays some attention to Africa (although less than its title suggests), see Ankie Hoogvelt, *Globalization and the Postcolonial World: The New Political Economy of Development*, 2nd ed. (Baltimore: Johns Hopkins University Press, 2001).

37. Pádraig Carmody, "Between Globalisation and (Post)Apartheid: The Political Economy of Restructuring in South Africa," *Journal of Southern African Studies* 28, no. 2 (2002): 255–76.

38. Makau Mutua, *Human Rights: A Political and Cultural Critique* (Philadelphia: University of Pennsylvania, 2002).

Epilogue

CHARLES P. HENRY

MARKING THE centenary of any historical figure can be a delicate exercise. Does one simply laud the accomplishments of the individual that made him or her a part of history? This is a safe but often boring choice. Does one attempt to show how relevant a figure's life is to the contemporary scene? This is a more stimulating option but runs the risk of making assumptions that have no way of being supported. For a historical individual who is also an intellectual, there is a further complication. Ideas have a life of their own that often extends beyond that of their originator. Is, for example, our conception of race the same today as fifty or a hundred years ago?

I am happy to conclude that the contributions to this volume—celebrating the centenary of the birth of Ralph Johnson Bunche—manage to avoid all the above obstacles. It is a volume that Bunche himself would be pleased with. That is, it gets to the heart of his work with a minimum of adulation. In fact, there is significant criticism of Bunche. Even better, it raises crucial contemporary issues pointing out how lessons from the past—Bunche's past—might lead to improved solutions. In short, the legacy of Bunche, especially for Africa, is on full display here and contemporary policymakers would do well to take note.

Four themes emerge from the preceding articles: opportunity, theoretical sophistication, practical application, and constructive criticism. Several contributions point out the rare opportunity afforded to Bunche as an African American to do fieldwork in the colonial world in the 1930s. There was little interest on the part of most American scholars and virtually no chance for academics of color to do field research in Africa until the 1950s. Although he wrote about Africa, W. E. B. DuBois never conducted fieldwork there, and the early black Africanist William Leo Hansberry was discouraged from applying for a place on British archeological expeditions in Egypt.

The fact that Bunche was able to gain both the financial support and the permission to conduct field research in colonial Africa tells us something about the man and the context in which he operated. Of course, Bunche's stellar student career at Harvard at least opened the door of major foundations. Yet it is a tribute to his emerging diplomatic skills that Bunche was able to conduct his research with the relative independence that eluded figures such as James Aggrey. That Bunche never had the opportunity to turn his voluminous field notes into a major publication is the price we pay for his rapid ascent in the world of politics.

Not only would Bunche's observations and analysis of colonialism have been an invaluable perspective but they would have added to the theoretical sophistication of the literature on Africa. Bunche was a political scientist with training in anthropological field research, not a historian. He was always interested in philosophy and theory.

One contributor compares his work to that of Raymond Buell but argues that the latter was more positive about the mandate system and British rule than Bunche. Another contributor suggests that Bunche's work may be compared to Karl Deutsch's social mobilization thesis and Immanuel Wallerstein's theoretical work on capitalist world systems. This is high praise indeed and even if only partly true hints at the potential Bunche held as a scholar.

In the battle between Bunche's dual identities as a bourgeois-pragmatist or a leftist, one would have to say the pragmatist dominated his later years. The decision was probably an easy one with the unique opportunity presented to him to help shape the post–World War II world through the instrumentality of the United Nations. Of course, the UN itself was an expression of idealism in search of practical grounding. In the person of Ralph Bunche it found the nearly perfect public servant. As that rare American who was not tainted with European colonialism but expert in its characteristics, Bunche found a laboratory for the practical application of his scholarly learning and his democratic ideals. With Dag Hammarskjöld, Bunche believed the UN could play a crucial role in the transition of Africa from colonialism to independence. Whether this opportunity amounts to a vision of world government, as one contributor writes, is open to debate.

What is not open to debate, as several other contributions state, is Bunche's role in devising a trusteeship system far superior to the mandate system that was the subject of his Harvard dissertation. By almost all accounts the trusteeship system and the UN peacekeeping forces are Bunche's most lasting legacy. In fact, in the face of "failed states," which some argue never had a chance to succeed, there have been calls for a revival of the trusteeship system in some form.

Beginning with Namibia, the UN's role in transitional administration has begun to resemble a type of trusteeship. Yet, as one contributor rightly warns us, some trusteeship safeguards are absent from transitional administration. If the UN is to play the positive role in African development that Bunche and Hammarskjöld foresaw nearly fifty years ago, Bunche would insist on not only keeping but updating those safeguards. First and foremost, Bunche believed in democracy and human rights and therefore opposed imperialism, whether exercised by a state or by the UN itself.

This last point leads to the major criticism of Bunche in this volume— his role in the Congo crisis. Whether you believe that Bunche was placed in an impossible situation or that he and his UN colleagues manipulated the situation, it is clear in retrospect that mistakes were made. Perhaps the principle mistake was Bunche's falling for the bluff of Tshombe and the Belgians in regard to the "hostile" greeting UN forces would receive in Katanga. The failure to introduce UN forces led directly to Lumumba's appeal to the Soviets for assistance and his final break with the UN and Western powers. The consequences of that action and the limits of Bunche's authority are vigorously discussed in this volume. The consequences of the failure to develop an independent and stable Congo are still with us today. They are destabilizing all of central Africa at the cost of millions of lives. As one contributor points out, the United States tends to underestimate the influence it has and could have on African states with "backward" colonial traditions, such as the Congo.

Perhaps the greatest tribute one could pay Ralph Bunche would be a national and international recommitment to Africa in general and the Congo in particular. The events of September 11, 2001, were a shocking reminder of the dangers of avoiding international engagement. Yet if we are to engage it must not be solely to protect our national security. It must be as Bunche said, "that man will survive, but he has much to overcome in himself in order to do so. The best answer to dangerous alienation, I think, is change for the good, progress."[1]

Note

1. Ralph J. Bunche, "Race and Alienation," in *Ralph J. Bunche: Selected Speeches and Writings,* ed. Charles P. Henry (Ann Arbor: University of Michigan Press, 1995), 306.

APPENDIX

United Nations Charter

The Trusteeship System

CHAPTER XI

DECLARATION REGARDING
NON-SELF-GOVERNING TERRITORIES

Article 73

Members of the United Nations which have or assume responsibilities for the administration of territories whose peoples have not yet attained a full measure of self-government recognize the principle that the interests of the inhabitants of these territories are paramount, and accept as a sacred trust the obligation to promote to the utmost, within the system of international peace and security established by the present Charter, the well-being of the inhabitants of these territories, and, to this end:

a. to ensure, with due respect for the culture of the peoples concerned, their political, economic, social, and educational advancement, their just treatment, and their protection against abuses;

b. to develop self-government, to take due account of the political aspirations of the peoples, and to assist them in the progressive development of their free political institutions, according to the particular circumstances of each territory and its peoples and their varying stages of advancement;

c. to further international peace and security;

d. to promote constructive measures of development, to encourage research, and to co-operate with one another and, when and where appropriate, with specialized international bodies with a view to the practical achievement of the social, economic, and scientific purposes set forth in this Article; and

e. to transmit regularly to the Secretary-General for information purposes, subject to such limitation as security and constitutional considerations may require, statistical and other information of a technical nature relating to economic, social, and educational conditions in the territories for which they are respectively responsible other than those territories to which Chapters XII and XIII apply.

Article 74

Members of the United Nations also agree that their policy in respect of the territories to which this Chapter applies, no less than in respect of their metropolitan areas, must be based on the general principle of good-neighbourliness, due account being taken of the interests and well-being of the rest of the world, in social, economic, and commercial matters.

CHAPTER XII

INTERNATIONAL TRUSTEESHIP SYSTEM

Article 75

The United Nations shall establish under its authority an international trusteeship system for the administration and supervision of such territories as may be placed thereunder by subsequent individual agreements. These territories are hereinafter referred to as trust territories.

Article 76

The basic objectives of the trusteeship system, in accordance with the Purposes of the United Nations laid down in Article 1 of the present Charter, shall be:

a. to further international peace and security;

b. to promote the political, economic, social, and educational advancement of the inhabitants of the trust territories, and their progressive development towards self-government or independence as may be appropriate to the particular circumstances of each territory and its peoples and the freely expressed wishes of the peoples concerned, and as may be provided by the terms of each trusteeship agreement;

c. to encourage respect for human rights and for fundamental freedoms for all without distinction as to race, sex, language, or religion, and to encourage recognition of the interdependence of the peoples of the world; and

d. to ensure equal treatment in social, economic, and commercial matters for all Members of the United Nations and their nationals, and also equal treatment for the latter in the administration of justice, without prejudice to the attainment of the foregoing objectives and subject to the provisions of Article 80.

Article 77

1. The trusteeship system shall apply to such territories in the following categories as may be placed thereunder by means of trusteeship agreements:

a. territories now held under mandate;

b. territories which may be detached from enemy states as a result of the Second World War; and

c. territories voluntarily placed under the system by states responsible for their administration.

2. It will be a matter for subsequent agreement as to which territories in the foregoing categories will be brought under the trusteeship system and upon what terms.

Article 78

The trusteeship system shall not apply to territories which have become Members of the United Nations, relationship among which shall be based on respect for the principle of sovereign equality.

Article 79

The terms of trusteeship for each territory to be placed under the trusteeship system, including any alteration or amendment, shall be agreed upon by the states directly concerned, including the mandatory power in the case of territories held under mandate by a Member of the United Nations, and shall be approved as provided for in Articles 83 and 85.

APPENDIX

Article 80

1. Except as may be agreed upon in individual trusteeship agreements, made under Articles 77, 79, and 81, placing each territory under the trusteeship system, and until such agreements have been concluded, nothing in this Chapter shall be construed in or of itself to alter in any manner the rights whatsoever of any states or any peoples or the terms of existing international instruments to which Members of the United Nations may respectively be parties.

2. Paragraph 1 of this Article shall not be interpreted as giving grounds for delay or postponement of the negotiation and conclusion of agreements for placing mandated and other territories under the trusteeship system as provided for in Article 77.

Article 81

The trusteeship agreement shall in each case include the terms under which the trust territory will be administered and designate the authority which will exercise the administration of the trust territory. Such authority, hereinafter called the administering authority, may be one or more states or the Organization itself.

Article 82

There may be designated, in any trusteeship agreement, a strategic area or areas which may include part or all of the trust territory to which the agreement applies, without prejudice to any special agreement or agreements made under Article 43.

Article 83

1. All functions of the United Nations relating to strategic areas, including the approval of the terms of the trusteeship agreements and of their alteration or amendment shall be exercised by the Security Council.

2. The basic objectives set forth in Article 76 shall be applicable to the people of each strategic area.

3. The Security Council shall, subject to the provisions of the trusteeship agreements and without prejudice to security considerations, avail itself of the assistance of the Trusteeship Council to perform those functions of the United Nations under the trusteeship system

relating to political, economic, social, and educational matters in the strategic areas.

Article 84

It shall be the duty of the administering authority to ensure that the trust territory shall play its part in the maintenance of international peace and security. To this end the administering authority may make use of volunteer forces, facilities, and assistance from the trust territory in carrying out the obligations towards the Security Council undertaken in this regard by the administering authority, as well as for local defence and the maintenance of law and order within the trust territory.

Article 85

1. The functions of the United Nations with regard to trusteeship agreements for all areas not designated as strategic, including the approval of the terms of the trusteeship agreements and of their alteration or amendment, shall be exercised by the General Assembly.

2. The Trusteeship Council, operating under the authority of the General Assembly shall assist the General Assembly in carrying out these functions.

CHAPTER XIII

THE TRUSTEESHIP COUNCIL

COMPOSITION

Article 86

1. The Trusteeship Council shall consist of the following Members of the United Nations:

    a. those Members administering trust territories;

    b. such of those Members mentioned by name in Article 23 as are not administering trust territories; and

    c. as many other Members elected for three-year terms by the General Assembly as may be necessary to ensure that the total number of members of the Trusteeship Council is equally divided between those Members of the United Nations which administer trust territories and those which do not.

2. Each member of the Trusteeship Council shall designate one specially qualified person to represent it therein.

FUNCTIONS and POWERS

Article 87

The General Assembly and, under its authority, the Trusteeship Council, in carrying out their functions, may:

   a. consider reports submitted by the administering authority;

   b. accept petitions and examine them in consultation with the administering authority;

   c. provide for periodic visits to the respective trust territories at times agreed upon with the administering authority; and

   d. take these and other actions in conformity with the terms of the trusteeship agreements.

Article 88

The Trusteeship Council shall formulate a questionnaire on the political, economic, social, and educational advancement of the inhabitants of each trust territory, and the administering authority for each trust territory within the competence of the General Assembly shall make an annual report to the General Assembly upon the basis of such questionnaire.

VOTING

Article 89

1. Each member of the Trusteeship Council shall have one vote.

2. Decisions of the Trusteeship Council shall be made by a majority of the members present and voting.

PROCEDURE

Article 90

1. The Trusteeship Council shall adopt its own rules of procedure, including the method of selecting its President.

2. The Trusteeship Council shall meet as required in accordance with its rules, which shall include provision for the convening of meetings on the request of a majority of its members.

Article 91

The Trusteeship Council shall, when appropriate, avail itself of the assistance of the Economic and Social Council and of the specialized agencies in regard to matters with which they are respectively concerned.

Contributors

David Anthony is professor of African and African American history at the University of California, Santa Cruz. His research explores African and African American history, art, music, literature, and cinema as well as eastern and southern Africa, African languages, and African and African American linkages. His most recent book is *Max Yergan: Race Man, Internationalist, Cold Warrior* (2006). He is coeditor, with Robert R. Edgar and Robert T. Vinson, of *Crossing the Water: African American Historical Linkages with South Africa* (forthcoming). He has also written several articles on Max Yergan and the history of the YMCA in Africa.

Ralph A. Austen is professor emeritus of African history at the University of Chicago. He received his PhD from Harvard University in 1966 and served as a member of the board of directors of the African Studies Association (1980–83). His current research focuses on the political economy and cultural dimensions of European overseas expansion (including autobiographical writings by "colonial subjects") and African literature. He is editor of *In Search of Sunjata: The Mande Oral Epic as History, Literature, and Performance* (1999) and author, with Jonathan Derrick, of *Middlemen of the Cameroons Rivers: The Duala and Their Hinterland, ca. 1600–ca. 1960* (1999). He has recently completed *Trans-Saharan Africa in World History* (2010), which deals with North African, Saharan, and west-central Sudanese history, mainly in the era of Islamic caravan trade. He is also working on an autobiographical study of the Malian intellectual and writer Amadou Hampâté Bâ (1901–90). Austen is also working, with Woodruff Smith, on a longer book, *The Road to Postcoloniality*.

Abena P. A. Busia is associate professor in the English department of Rutgers, the State University of New Jersey, where she has taught since 1981. Born in Accra, Ghana, she completed her BA in English language and literature at St. Anne's College, Oxford, in 1976, and a PhD in social anthropology (race relations) at St. Antony's College in 1984. Busia is codirector of the groundbreaking Women Writing

Africa Project, a multivolume anthology published by the Feminist Press at CUNY. She is coeditor, with Stanlie James, of *Theorizing Black Feminisms: The Visionary Pragmatism of Black Women* (1993) and has published numerous articles on black women's literature and colonial discourse. She is currently completing *Song in a Strange Land: Narratives and Rituals of Remembrance in the Novels of Black Women of Africa and the African Diaspora*. Her poems have appeared in several anthologies, including *Summer Fires, New Poetry of Africa* (1983), *Mandela Amandla, A Seventieth Birthday Tribute to Nelson Mandela* (1989), and *Daughters of Africa: An International Anthology of Words and Writings by Women of African Descent from the Ancient Egyptian to the Present* (1992).

Neta C. Crawford is an adjunct professor at the Watson Institute for International Studies at Brown University. She was a peace fellow at Radcliffe's Bunting Institute (1998–99) and a postdoctoral fellow at the Watson Institute (1994–96). She is the author of *Argument and Change in World Politics: Ethics, Decolonization, and Humanitarian Intervention* (2002). She is coeditor, with Audie Klotz, of *How Sanctions Work: Lessons from South Africa* (1999). In addition to publishing articles in scholarly journals such as *International Organization* and *International Security,* Crawford has also published in newspapers and popular journals, such as *Christian Science Monitor, Newsday,* and *Boston Review.* She received her doctorate in political science from the Massachusetts Institute of Technology.

Robert Edgar is professor of African studies at Howard University, where he is also director of graduate studies in the Department of African Studies. His research interests include southern Africa and African religious and political movements. He is author of *Sanctioning Apartheid* (1990) and coauthor, with Hilary Sapire, of *African Apocalypse: The Story of Nontetha Nkwenkwe, A Twentieth-Century South African Prophet* (2000). He is also editor of *An African American in South Africa: The Research Diary of Ralph J. Bunche, 1937* (1992) and coeditor, with Luyanda ka Msumza, of *Freedom in Our Lifetime: The Collected Writings of Anton Muziwakhe Lembede* (1996). Edgar was also an adviser on a 2001 documentary film about Ralph Bunche.

Charles P. Henry is professor of African American studies at the University of California, Berkeley. In 1994, President Clinton appointed him for a six-year term on the National Council on the Humanities.

CONTRIBUTORS

Former president of the National Council for Black Studies, Henry is the author or editor of six books and more than seventy-five articles and reviews on black politics, public policy, and human rights. His recent publications include *Ralph Bunche: Model Negro or American Other?* (1999), *Foreign Policy and the Black (Inter)national Interest* (2000), and *Long Overdue: The Politics of Racial Reparations,* (2007). Before joining UC Berkeley in 1981, Henry taught at Denison University and Howard University. Henry was chair of the board of directors of Amnesty International USA from 1986 to 1988 and is a former NEH Post-doctoral Fellow and American Political Science Association Congressional Fellow. Professor Henry was Distinguished Fulbright Chair in American History and Politics at the University of Bologna, Italy, for the spring semester of 2003. He holds a doctorate in political science from the University of Chicago.

Robert A. Hill is director of the Marcus Garvey and Universal Negro Improvement Association Papers Project in the African Studies Center at the University of California, Los Angeles, where he is also professor of history. Hill is internationally recognized as a leading authority on the life of Garvey and the history of the Garvey movement. In recent years he has received invitations to speak on Garvey from institutions throughout the United States, as well as the Caribbean, England, and Africa. He was guest curator of the NEH-funded Marcus Garvey Centenary Exhibition at the Schomburg Center for Research in Black Culture of the New York Public Library and was an adviser to the government of Jamaica on its Garvey centennial. He has lectured and written widely on the Garvey movement and has edited several documentary collections, including *The Black Man,* the complete run of Garvey's final journal, and *The Crusader,* a facsimile reprint of Cyril Briggs's influential, but hitherto inaccessible, journal of the African Blood Brotherhood. Hill also wrote the introduction to the reissue of *Philosophy and Opinions of Marcus Garvey* (1992).

Edmond Keller is professor of political science, director of the UCLA Globalization Research Center–Africa, and former director of the James S. Coleman African Studies Center at the University of California, Los Angeles. He specializes in comparative politics with an emphasis on Africa, and his research focuses on political transitions, cultural pluralism and nationalism, and conflict and conflict management in Africa. He is author of two monographs: *Education, Manpower and Development: The Impact of Educational Policy in Kenya* (1980) and *Revolutionary Ethiopia: From Empire to People's Republic* (1988) and has coedited, with Donald Rothchild, *Afro-Marxist Regimes: Ideology and Public Policy* (1987) and *Africa in the New International Order: Rethinking State Sovereignty and Regional Security* (1996). He has also coeditor, with Louis Picard, of *South Africa in Southern Africa: Domestic Change and International Conflict* (1989). His most recent publication is a coedited volume, with Donald Rothchild, *Africa-US Relations: Strategic Encounters* (2006).

Martin Kilson is the Frank G. Thomson Professor of Government emeritus at Harvard University. He earned his PhD in political science from Harvard University. He was a visiting professor at the University of Ghana (1964–65). In 1968, Kilson became the first African American to be granted full tenure at Harvard. He has written numerous social and political articles on black life, as well as several books, including *Political Change in a West African State: A Study of the Modernization Process in Sierra Leone* (1966). He is also editor of *Crisis and Change in the Negro Ghetto* (1973).

Georges Nzongola-Ntalaja is director of the United Nations Development Programme (UNDP), Oslo Governance Centre, and professor emeritus of African studies at Howard University. As an expert on governance, conflict, and capacity-building issues, Nzongola served as senior UNDP adviser for governance in Abuja, Nigeria (2000–2002). He has done consulting work for the UN Secretariat, the UNDP, UNESCO, and many other organizations. Past president of the African Studies Association and of the African Association of Political Science, he is the author of several books and numerous articles on African politics, development, and conflict, including *Revolution and Counter-Revolution in Africa* (1987), *Nation-Building and State Building in Africa* (1993), and *Le mouvement démocratique au Zaïre, 1956–1996* (1997). His major work, *The Congo from Leopold to Kabila: A People's History* (2002), won the 2003 Best Book Award of the African Politics Conference Group, a study group of both the American Political Science Association and the African Studies Association.

John Olver entered public service in 1941 as personnel officer with the U.S. government in Washington, D.C., following completion of an MS degree in public administration at the Maxwell School of

Syracuse University. He worked in the newly constituted Secretariat of the United Nations, assisting with establishing the organization in New York. In 1957 he became chief administrative officer of the UN Emergency Force in the Gaza Strip, for the first of the peacekeeping forces, and in 1960 filled a similar post in the UN operation in the Congo, under Ralph Bunche. Subsequently, he became responsible for management operations at the Palais des Nations, in Geneva, followed by a similar posting with the Food and Agriculture Organization of the UN, in Rome. He returned to New York in 1966 as secretary of the International Civil Service Advisory Board. Olver joined the UN Development Programme in 1968 as director of finance and continued in various management positions until retirement from the career service in 1980, as assistant administrator (assistant secretary general).

Pearl T. Robinson is associate professor of political science at Tufts University. She is coauthor, with Peter M. Lewis and Barnett Rubin, of *Stabilizing Nigeria: Sanctions, Incentives and Support for Civil Society* (1998), coauthor and coeditor, with Elliott P. Skinner, of *Transformation and Resiliency in Africa* (1983), and has published more than twenty-five articles and book chapters. A member of the Council on Foreign Relations and a senior adviser to the Boston Pan-African Forum, she has served as a board member of Oxfam America, a member of the advisory board of the Center for Preventive Action of the Council on Foreign Relations, chair of the SSRC/ACLS Joint Committee on African Studies, adviser to the African Academy of Science's research project on the education of women and girls, and consultant for the PBS film series *The Africans: A Triple Heritage* (1986) and the PBS documentary *Hopes on the Horizon* (2001). From 1994 to 2001, Robinson was director of the Program in International Relations at Tufts. She has been Ford Foundation Visiting Professor at Makerere University, Uganda; visiting professor in political science at the University of Dar es Salaam, Tanzania; and research affiliate with the Université Abdou Moumouni, Niger.

Elliott P. Skinner held the Franz Boas Chair of Anthropology at Columbia University and was U.S. ambassador to Upper Volta. In granting him their Distinguished Africanist Award, the African Studies Association said, "He has been an ardent and vigorous defender of the interests of both Africa as a region and African studies as a discipline. On the African continent, the field of African studies in America is as much identified with Elliott Percival Skinner as with any other American scholar." His books include *A Glorious Age in Africa* (with Daniel Chu, 1965), *African Urban Life: The Transformation of Ouagadougou* (1973), and *Roots of Time: A Portrait of African Life and Culture* (with Margo Jefferson, 1974). Unfortunately, Skinner passed away on April 7, 2007.

Crawford Young is the H. Edwin Young and Rupert Emerson Professor emeritus of Political Science at the University of Wisconsin, Madison, where he has taught since 1963. His major books include *Politics in the Congo: Decolonization and Independence* (1965), *The Politics of Cultural Pluralism* (1976), *Ideology and Development in Africa* (1982), *The Rise and Decline of the Zairian State* (with Thomas Turner, 1985), and *The African Colonial State in Comparative Perspective* (1994). He has also taught in Congo-Kinshasa, Uganda, and Senegal. He is a former president of the African Studies Association (1984) and a fellow of the American Academy of Arts and Sciences.

Index

ACP countries, 172–73
Adoula, Cyrille, 144
Africa, African, 10, 17, 22, 45–58, 74–82, 127, 130, 161; American attitudes about, 13, 45, 46, 65; bourgeoisie, 11; colonial government officials, 13, 99–113, 134, 136, 168; conversion to Christianity, 9, 96; culture, 14, 55, 56, 63, 74, 80; descent, 43, 45, 46, 47, 48, 52, 60, 65; development assistance to, 15, 81, 82, 97, 104–13, 134, 137, 139, 148, 168–75; education, 29, 55, 56, 80, 166; elites, 14, 15, 31, 37, 52–57, 80, 86, 99, 128, 129, 177; fable about, 35; intellectuals, 4–17 passim, 19–23, 47–63 passim, 72, 81; languages, 56, 75; late-colonial, 19, 71, 84, 165, 170, 174; masses, 5, 7, 14, 22, 34–38, 55, 77, 82, 113, 169; nationalism, 14, 15, 37, 38, 57, 85, 161–76 passim; self-determination, 12, 37, 56, 61, 79, 80, 86, 94–111 passim, 162; students in Europe, 22, 27–29, 53, 54, 129, 166, 168; views of African Americans, 19, 25; in world history, 46
Africa gloriana, 52
African Americans, 31, 39, 50–65, 70–83 passim
African Genesis (Frobenius), 53
African Journey (Robeson), 21
African National Congress (ANC), 17, 33–39, 51; Defiance Campaign against Unjust Laws, 39; Program of Action, 38; Silver Jubilee conference, 35; Youth League, 37, 38. *See also* South Africa
Afrikaner, 30, 35, 82
African studies, 19–23, 25, 27, 42–66, 71–83 passim, 161–74 passim, 181
Afro-Caribbean intellectuals, 22, 23, 53, 54, 58, 74, 130
Agenda for Peace, An (UN), 106
Aggrey, James, 29, 182
agriculture, 165, 166, 169, 178n15
Alexander, Henry, 136
All African Convention (AAC), 32–37
Alliance des Bakongo, 133, 149

American Dilemma, An (Myrdal), 39, 42, 63
American Negro Academy, 5, 43
American Political Science Association, 39
American South, 30
Anglo-American Caribbean Commission, 43
Annan, Kofi, 95
anthropology, 20, 21, 25, 26, 51, 52, 53, 57, 58, 60, 62, 63, 75
anticolonialism, 17, 28, 61, 74, 85, 95, 128–42 passim, 149, 155, 166, 167
apartheid, 38, 61, 105, 176
Arab states, 43, 63, 116, 122, 130, 152
Arkadiev, G. P., 155
Armstrong, Henry, 31
Asia, 38, 44, 57, 58, 65, 161, 167, 169
Asiatic, 29, 44, 46
assimilation, 55, 80–82
assimilés, 14, 55
Azikiwe, Nnamdi, 84, 90n81

Baker, Josephine, 54
Ballinger, Margaret, 34
Balubakat Party, 153
Banks, William, 4
Banneker, Benjamin, 46, 47
Barnes, Leonard, 28
Baudouin, King, 129, 134, 150
Belgians, 64, 80, 101, 116–26, 128–40, 149, 150, 166, 183
Benin, 20, 99
Berlin West Africa Conference, 96
Bernadotte, Count Folke, 43
black, blacks: chauvinism, 5, 38, 49, 53, 84; colleges, 72, 73; urban communities, 5; working class, 5–6
Black Jacobins, 58
Black Power movement, 65
Black Reconstruction, 53, 83
Bloemfontein, 34
Boas, Franz, 51, 58, 75
Bondelswarts, 101
boycott, 34, 36, 38
Brazil, 19, 53, 73
Brazzaville, 118, 120, 168
Bretton Woods agreements, 167, 175
Britain. *See* England

199

INDEX

British Colonial Development and Welfare Act, 168
British empire, 22, 27, 28, 80, 81, 173
Brown, Sterling, 20
Brussels World Exposition, 129
Buell, Raymond Leslie, 3, 4, 51, 54, 67n37, 74–86 passim, 89n43, 89n60, 182
Buisseret, Auguste, 128
Bunche, Ralph J.: in Africa, 59–64, 76, 80, 99, 116, 130; as Africanist, 19–23, 25, 51, 63, 70–84 passim; on black African leadership, 31, 33–36, 38, 62; on black civil rights activism, 6, 39, 52, 83; as Congo force commander, 119, 120, 137, 151; dissertation of, 3–18, 20, 25, 26, 42–57 passim, 71–85 passim, 93–102 passim, 114n14, 129; economic determinism of, 71, 77, 84; in Europe, 27, 53, 58, 59, 76; fieldwork of, 3, 13, 19–21, 25, 57, 71–79 passim, 181; as first African American Nobel Prize recipient, 43, 152; as first African American political science doctorate, 25; government service of, 39, 71; graduate studies, 3, 20, 21, 50; grandmother of, 44–50; as international civil servant, 22, 43, 64, 86, 93, 119–29, 131–44, 150, 182–83; on League of Nations, 84, 99; on modern colonial rule, 9, 11, 56, 61; as Palestine mediator, 43, 63, 105; passing for white, 45, 50, 64; peers of, 4, 5, 72–75; policy prescriptions of, 70–86; on race, 53, 54, 57, 66n12; religious views of, 59; on South Africa, 30, 38–39, 58–62, 130; system-remedial perspective of, 11–14; at UCLA, 49–50, 69; worldview of, 18, 64, 65, 70, 84; writings of, 6, 7, 8, 9, 12, 13, 16, 26, 29, 72, 73, 83, 84; as young man, 3–18, 44, 48, 69–73

Cameroun, 79
Cape Town, 26, 28, 29, 60, 61; African liberals of, 37; provincial delegates of, 36, 82
capitalism, 10, 15, 20, 26, 58, 84, 106, 128, 165, 176
Caplan, Richard, 94, 111, 112
Carey, Rev. Lott, 47
China, 74, 177
Chopra, Jarat, 111–12
Christianity, 9, 59, 60, 96
CIA, 132, 142, 154
circumcision, 62–63
citizenship, 5, 37, 55, 81–82, 108–9

civilization, 10, 16, 37, 43, 45, 54, 60–84 passim, 94–112 passim, 150
civilizing mission. *See* Europeanization
civil rights activists, 5–6
Clark, Kenneth, 4, 52
class conflict, 8, 56
Coalition Provisional Authority in Iraq, 106, 109, 110
cold war, 64, 94, 106, 113, 118, 128–38, 148–56, 165–74
colonialism: accountability, 11, 21, 98–113; exploitation, 12, 16, 26, 46, 55, 77, 86, 96, 99, 105, 117, 128, 165, 168, 175; governance, 3–18, 28, 38, 39, 64, 71, 80, 86, 93, 105, 111, 129, 133, 134, 151, 162, 165; impact on African societies of, 9–12, 21, 25, 26, 45–54, 78–86, 96, 112
colonial studies, 43, 55, 61, 62, 66
Coloured, 29, 38, 60, 61, 82, 89n67
Columbia University, 36, 51, 52, 58, 72, 75
Commager, Henry, 46
communism, 52, 57, 74, 128, 131, 138, 142, 155, 173
Communist Party, 22, 39
Congo, 63, 64, 71, 101, 116–25, 128–45, 183; army, 118–26, 136, 151; elites, 128; government, 128–44, 149, 151; Kasai Province, 136, 142; Katanga secession, 118, 132–42, 149–53, 183; Loi Fondamentale, 143; Tetela-Kusu ethnic group, 134; treaty with Belgium, 118
Cook, Mercer, 74
Cooper, Frederick, 162
Coppin, Bishop Levi Jenkins, 60
Cordier, Andrew, 143, 144, 152, 156
Crisis magazine, 51, 69
Crockett, George, 6
Crummell, Alexander, 5
Cuffe, Paul, 47

Dahomey, 3, 6, 10, 20, 25, 42, 53–59 passim, 71–85 passim, 99, 129
Davis, John Aubrey, Sr., 4, 5, 6
Davis, John P., 4
Dayal, Rajeshwar, 120, 129, 143, 155
decolonization, 12, 15, 16, 22, 39, 47, 63, 94–110 passim, 116, 117, 121, 130, 136, 137, 150, 161–77
de Crèvecoeur, Hector, 46
Delafosse, Maurice, 53
democracy, 11, 94, 99, 106, 111, 112, 113, 183
DeMond, Albert, 5
Detroit, 43, 48
Deutsch, Karl, 15, 182

200

INDEX

Devlin, Lawrence, 142
Diagne, Blaise, 14, 77
diaspora, 21, 22, 45, 47, 57, 59, 131
Dingane (Zulu king), 35
Dorsey, Emmet, 74
double-consciousness, 44, 63, 65
Douglass, Fredrick, 70
Drake, St. Clair, 4
Dube, John, 33
DuBois, William E. B., 5, 20, 43–65 passim, 69–86 passim, 181
Dulles, Allen, 142
Dunham, Dows, 76
Dutch colonialism, 38

East Africa, 19–21, 25–39 passim, 59, 62, 71, 101
East Timor, 94, 111
Edgar, Robert, 20, 21
education: need for, 5, 70; philosophy of, 31, 55, 56, 80, 85, 86; programs, 53, 55, 83, 98, 99; Tuskegee model, 55–56
Edward VIII, King, 27
Egypt, 44–52 passim, 76, 105, 116, 122, 152, 155
Eisenhower, Dwight, 154
elections, 5, 32, 34, 35, 104–8, 167, 169
Ellington, Duke, 31
Embree, Edwin R., 19, 73
Emerson, Rupert, 3, 4, 50, 85
Engels, Frederic, 52, 59
England, 15, 20, 47, 58, 61, 137, 166–70; politics of, 59; strikes in, 27; Unionist government of, 27
Enlightenment values, 7, 8, 78, 112
Ephebian Society, 49
equality, 7, 12, 37, 47, 83, 172, 175
Equiano, Olaudah, 47
Ethiopia, 17, 27, 57, 74, 76, 125
Ethiopian Research Council, 52
Eurafrica, 170–76 passim
Europe, European, 12, 22, 35, 46, 53, 74; attitudes about Africa, 13, 45, 53, 55, 66n16, 80, 99, 112, 136, 150; colonial elites, 10, 15, 33, 44, 55, 80; Common Market, 170–74; conquests, 46, 93, 163, 165; descent, 47, 48, 65; Economic Community, 171–75; languages, 45, 132, 171; leftists, 139; nation-states, 7, 10, 51, 77, 113, 164, 171; natives in Africa, 33, 34, 37, 113, 135, 136; philosophers, 45, 46, 52; Union, 172, 176
Europeanization, 12, 54, 62, 63, 81, 112, 143
évolué, 128, 133

failed states, 94, 95, 175, 183
Fair Employment Practices Committee, 6
fascism, 12, 27, 57
Fiji, 173
Filmer, Robert, 71, 87n16
Fitzhugh, H. Naylor, 5
Fonds d'Investissements pour le Développement Économique et Social, 168
Force Publique. See Congo: army
Foreign Policy Association (FPA), 75
Fou Chin-Liu, 132
foundations (research funding), 26, 53, 72
France, French, 15, 20, 47, 53, 54, 74, 132, 137, 166–70 passim; administration, 3–14, 25, 42–57, 75, 77, 80, 98–100, 129, 168; attitudes about Africa, 13, 56, 80; colonial office, 75, 77; culture, 56, 112; parliament, 77; Revolution, 12; Soudan, 53
Franklin, John Hope, 4
Frazier, E. Franklin, 4, 6, 20, 51, 72–74
free trade, 172–76
Frelinghuysen, Frederick, 47
French Soudan, 53
Frobenius, Leo, 53

Garvey, Marcus, 21, 31, 50, 61, 64, 131
Gaus, John, 4
General Education Fund, 53
Geneva, 53, 74–76, 98–101
genocide, 93, 111
George VI, King, coronation of, 27, 28
German colonialism, 11, 20, 53, 54, 79, 93, 96, 99, 166
Germany, 12, 57, 74, 96, 110, 165, 170, 171
Ghana, 17, 29, 116, 133, 136, 153, 155
Gizenga, Antoine, 142
globalization, 162–77
Godlo, Richard, 33
Gold Coast, 17, 55
Golden Jubilee, 28
Gool, Goolam and Jane, 34
grassroots mobilization, 6, 8, 15–17, 33–39, 61, 62
Great White Fleet, 48
Guinea, 133, 137, 153, 155

Haiti, 58, 75
Hall, H. Duncan, 101
Hammarskjöld, Dag, 115n24, 116–27 passim, 130–44 passim, 148–54 passim, 182, 183
Hansberry, Leo, 52, 76, 181
Harlem, 30, 50, 60
Harris, Abram, 4, 6, 20, 51, 52, 72–74

INDEX

Harvard University, 3, 4, 50, 52, 57, 69, 70, 72–85 passim, 129, 182
Hastie, William, 5
Hayford, J. E. Casely, 17
Hegel, Wilhelm, 46
Helman, Gerald, 94
Hemmings, Sally, 46
Henderson, Elmer, 5, 6
Henry, Charles, 4, 84, 145n1, 155
Herskovits, Melville, 20, 26, 27, 30, 52, 57, 58, 74, 75, 89n43, 130
Hertzog, J. B. M., 32, 82
Hofmeyr, Jan, 29
Holcolme, Arthur, 3, 4, 73, 85
Houston, Charles, 4, 5, 6
Howard University, 4, 5, 20, 25–27, 38, 39, 51–63 passim, 71–76
Huggins, Nathan, 50, 57
Hughes, Langston, 4
humanitarianism, 8, 95, 96, 113
human rights, 97, 99, 103, 108, 109, 111, 177, 183
Hume, David, 45, 46
Hunton, William A., 20
Hurston, Zora Neale, 52

Ileo, Joseph, 144
immigrants, 48
imperialism, 8–10, 17, 71, 84–86, 96–112 passim, 128, 155, 163–65, 183
Imvo zabantsundu, 33
independence, 12, 16, 21, 94, 101–6 passim, 117, 124, 132–35, 148, 161–76 passim
India, 26, 28, 38, 74, 120, 167
indirect rule, 38, 80, 81
Indonesia, 26, 38, 58, 63
industrialization, 9, 10, 56, 77, 165; Fordist, 167, 170, 175, 176
Indyk, Martin, 94
Institute of Pacific Relations, 42
international affairs, 72–86 passim, 98, 102, 116, 135, 163, 177
International Committee on African Affairs (ICAA), 22
International Court of Justice, 105
International Institute of African Languages and Cultures, 75
International Labor Organization, 43
International Military Advisory and Training Team, 108
International Monetary Fund (IMF), 162, 174, 176
International Relations with Special Attention to the Government of Dependencies, 77

interwar period, 4, 6, 21, 101, 170
Iraq, 106–10 passim, 161
Israel, 43, 63, 94, 116, 122, 130, 152
Italy, 12, 27, 57, 74
Ivory Coast, 77

Jabavu, Alexander, 33–37, 61
Jamaica, 46
James, C. L. R., 27, 58, 130
Japan, 57, 110, 169, 175
Jefferson, Thomas, 46, 47, 66n17
Jefferson High School, 44, 49
Jews, 60
Jim Crow, 30
Johnson, Charles, 85
Johnson, Mordecai, 27, 53, 72, 74, 87n18
Johnson, Mrs. (Nana), 44–50 passim
Johnson, Paul, 94
Joint Committee on National Recovery, 20
Jones, Thomas Jesse, 55
Journal of Negro Education, 85
Journal of Negro History, 76, 85
Just, Ernest, 74

Kanza, Thomas, 64, 131, 132
Kasavubu, Joseph, 64, 117, 118, 119, 133–44 passim, 149, 150, 151
Kenya, 62, 64, 71, 82, 130
Kenyatta, Jomo, 27, 59, 63, 130
Kikuyu tribe, 62, 63
Kinshasa. *See* Léopoldville
Kipling, Rudyard, 46, 63
Kirby, John, 4
Kisangani, 133, 134, 143
Kosovo, 94, 108

labor: civilized, 30; forced, 56, 99, 101; movement, 6, 56
language, 55, 56, 62, 80, 132, 171
law, rule of, 50, 98, 99, 105–8 passim, 152
Lawson, Belford, 5
League of Nations, 11, 20, 25, 51–54, 73–84, 98–102, 167; Charter, 97, 101; Permanent Mandates Commission, 76, 98–102 passim
leftist, 20–22, 28, 84, 154, 167; and pragmatist, 3–18, 26, 53, 84, 182
Lembede, Anton, 37
Le Neveu, Charles, 75
Lenin, 52
Leopold II, King, 150
Léopoldville, 64, 117–25, 129–41, 151–54
Lewin, Julius, 28, 39, 40n8
Liberia, 47, 51, 67n26, 74, 80, 84

INDEX

Lie, Trygve, 39, 43
Linnaeus, Carolus, 45
Linner, Sturo, 121
Livingstone, David, 96
Locke, Alain, 51, 53, 57, 72–75, 88n23, 88n24
Logan, Rayford, 51–53, 76
Lomé agreements, 171–76
London, 27, 74, 130; South African embassy in, 28, 60
London School of Economics, 20, 21, 26, 28, 58, 59
Los Angeles, 43–63 passim, 69
Louis, Joe, 31
Lubumbashi, 140
Luce, Henry, 44
Lumumba, Patrice, 64, 117–20 passim, 128–45, 148–56, 183

Macmillan, William, 28
Mahabane, Rev. Z. R., 36
Makonnen, T. Ras, 27
Malcomess, Carl, 34
Malinowski, Bronislaw, 20, 26, 27, 58–63 passim, 130
mandate: compared to colony, 55, 56, 67n43, 79, 84, 95, 98; compared to trusteeship, 94, 103, 104, 110, 182; system, 11, 53, 76, 93, 96, 97, 100, 102, 103, 112, 170; territories, 20, 25, 52, 71, 75, 97, 103, 166
mandate countries: British, 11, 12, 38, 74; French, 11, 12, 77, 79, 86, 112
Mandela, Nelson, 17, 37, 62
manifest destiny, 46, 96
Mapikela, T. M., 33
Marshall, Thurgood, 4
Marx, Karl, 52, 59
Marxist, 4–9, 51–58, 165
Matthews, Z. K., 39
Mauritania, 77
McCarthy, Joseph, 39
Mda, A. P., 37
Middle East, 43, 105, 116, 122, 130, 152
Millennium Development Goals, 108
Minnesota, 72
missionary efforts, 22, 26, 28, 31, 32, 56, 96
Mitchell, Clarence, 6
Molema, Silas, 31
Morgan, Lewis Henry, 52, 59
Moroka, James, 31
Mortimer, Edward, 111, 112
Mouvement National Congolais-Lumumba (MNC-L), 133, 134, 149, 153
Mozambique, 62, 63
Mpondo, 33

Mugabe, Robert, 17
Mussolini, 52, 57, 155
Myrdal, Gunnar, 39, 40n1, 42, 58, 63, 130

Nabrit, James, Jr., 4–6
Namibia, 93, 105, 106, 183
Nardal, Paulette and Jane, 74
Nasser, Gamal Abdel, 149, 155, 174
National Association for the Advancement of Colored People (NAACP), 4, 50, 51, 70
National Congress of British West Africa, 17
nationalist movements, 15–17, 74, 85, 105, 129–39, 148, 150, 161–74
National Negro Congress, 20, 22
National Urban League, 4, 5, 72, 84
native affairs, 22, 32, 33, 36, 77, 82, 99
native leaders, 13, 16, 33, 55, 81, 99
Native Problem in Africa, The (Buell), 51, 74–80 passim
Native Representative Council (NRC), 32–37
native viewpoint, 79, 82, 86, 100–111, 135, 171
Ncome (Blood) River, 35
negritude, 55, 64, 74
Negro, 30, 43–65 passim, 70–84 passim, 130; Associates in Negro Folk Education, 84; journals, 61, 71; New, 50–51; spirituals, 48
Negro National Congress, 52, 56
Negro Problem, The, 70
neocolonialism, 64, 110, 140, 171–74
New Negro Alliance (NNA), 5, 6
New Partnership for Africa's Development (NEPAD), 177
New World, 19, 45–47
New York City, 39, 43, 50, 72, 75, 119, 120, 143
NGOs, 96, 109, 177
Niger, 77
Nigeria, 17
Nkrumah, Kwame, 17, 133, 138, 149, 155
Nobel Peace Prize, 43, 130, 152
Northwestern University, 20, 26, 27, 57, 58, 75

occupation, 93, 110, 113, 163, 169
Office of Strategic Services (OSS), 39, 42, 128, 130
Olver, John, 119, 126
Organisation des Nations Unies au Congo (ONUC), 119–27, 129, 144, 148, 151
Ottoman Turkey, 96

INDEX

Overseas Reform Act (Loi Cadre), 171
Owens, Jesse, 31
Oxford University, 36, 51, 58, 74

Padmore, George, 27, 58, 130
Palau, 104
Palestine, 43, 63, 94, 105
Pan-African Conference, 129, 133
Pan-African Congress, 50
Pan-Africanism, 16, 17, 18n10, 27, 129, 132–39, 149, 155, 166
Paris, 13, 14, 53, 54, 74–77, 129, 168
Paris Peace Conference, 53, 96
Park, Robert, 72
Parti National du Progrès, 134
Pate, Maurice, 121
paternalism, 33, 95–113 passim, 125, 136
patriotism, 47
Peabody series, 51
peacekeeping, 105, 106, 110, 116–25, 130–44, 152, 154, 182. *See also* United Nations
Phelps-Stokes Association, 29, 53, 55
philosophy, 52
political economy: capitalist, 8, 167–77 passim; colonial, 20, 59, 71, 163, 168
political science, 3, 4, 20, 23, 25, 39, 49, 57, 61, 63, 69–73, 93, 163, 174
Portuguese colonialism, 101
postcolonialism, 15, 17, 94, 106, 161–74 passim
postconflict governance, 95, 106–10, 168
Poto, Victor, 33
Pretorius Hall, 33

race, racial: conflict, 10, 11, 25, 50, 69, 81, 82; consciousness, 13, 17, 30, 49, 61, 65; cooperation, 29, 50, 70; mixing, 19, 53, 58, 73, 75
racism, 4–11 passim, 29, 31, 44–55 passim, 128
radicalism, 5, 6, 19, 26, 34, 41n31, 51–53, 128–40 passim, 148
Ralph Bunche Day, 43
Randolph, A. Philip, 4, 22
Rappard, M., 79
Ratner, Steven, 94
realpolitik, 7, 8
Reid, Ira, 4
Rhodesia, 82
Robeson, Eslanda Goode, 21, 27, 28, 58
Robeson, Paul, 22, 23, 27, 28, 31, 58
Roosevelt, Franklin, 6
Roosevelt, Theodore, 46
Rosenwald Fund, 19, 53, 73
Rwanda (Ruanda), 101, 111

Sakwe, C. K., 33
Schapera, Isaac, 20, 26, 29, 58, 60, 130
Scramble for Africa, 47, 93
segregation, 13, 25, 29–31, 38, 49, 50, 61, 73, 81–83
self-rule, 11, 12, 21, 43, 55, 64, 80, 86, 94–113 passim, 121, 133, 135, 167–71
Seme, Pixley, 33, 36, 51, 61, 62
Sendwe, Jason, 153
Senegal, 59, 77
Shepperson, George, 23
Sierra Leone, 108, 109
Simons, Jack, 28, 35, 40n8
Sisulu, Walter, 37
slavery, 7, 46–58 passim, 66n17, 70, 73, 97, 164
Smit, Douglas, 33
Smyth, Henry, 47, 67n26
Social Darwinism, 78
Social Science Research Council, 20, 26, 40n1, 75, 129
social sciences, 18, 21, 25, 70–77 passim, 85
Sojourner Truth, 70
Souls of Black Folk, The (DuBois), 5, 43
South Africa, 17, 19–22, 25–39, 56–64, 71–82, 103–6, 176, 177; African vote in, 32; black majority in, 30, 32, 82, 83; Bondelswarts, 101; civilized labor, 30; Day of the Covenant, 35; fable about, 35; Hertzog bills, 32–37, 82; National Party, 32, 38; Native Affairs Department, 33; Native Land and Trust Act, 32; Native National Congress, 51, 61; Natives' Land Act, 62; non-European politics of, 21, 29, 33, 36, 61, 62; Parliament, 32; Representation of Natives Act, 32; restrictions on African Americans, 29, 60; townships, 38; UN commission on, 39; United Party, 32; Vereeniging riots, 33; Voortrekker march, 35; whites of, 29, 33, 37, 60, 61, 82. *See also* Cape Town
South Africa Party, 32
South-West Africa People's Organization, 105
Soviet Union, 8, 74, 138, 140, 142, 148–55 passim, 167–74 passim, 183
Spain, 12, 27, 57
Stanley Hotel, 117, 119
Statistical Information Concerning Territories under Mandate, 76
Stevenson, Adlai, 153, 154, 157n13
Sudan, 76
Suez crisis, 116
Swahili, 27
Switzerland, 20

204

INDEX

Talented Tenth, 70, 83, 86. *See also* DuBois, William E. B.
Tambo, Oliver, 37
Tanzania, 169
Tauxier, Louis, 53
Thema, R.V. Selope, 33, 35
Thirtieth Street Intermediate School, 48
Timberlake, Clare, 131, 143, 151
Togo, Republic of, 20, 53–56, 85, 99, 129; *Conseils des Notables*, 100
Togoland, 3, 6, 10, 20, 25, 42, 54–59, 71–79, 99–112
Touré, Ahmed Sékou, 133, 138, 149, 155
transitional administration, 94, 105–13, 183
Treaty of Rome, 171
Treaty of Versailles, 54
tribal leadership, 15, 38, 55, 61, 81
trusteeship, 37, 64, 93–113, 167, 182; discourse about, 110–12, 145n8; for failed states, 94
Tshombe, Moise, 118, 120, 140, 153, 154, 183
Turkey, 96

Union Coloniale Française, 75, 168, 170
Union Theological Seminary, 39
United Nations, 21, 42, 63, 102, 110; Afro-Asian caucus, 39, 137–40; Charter, 95, 102, 103, 111; Conference on Trade and Development, 172; in the Congo, 117–26, 128–45; Council for Namibia, 106; Dept. of Trusteeship and Information from Non-Self-Governing Territories, 43, 95, 103; General Assembly, 39, 43, 95, 105, 137; Integrated Office for Sierra Leone, 108; Palestine Commission, 43, 105; peacekeeping role, 105, 116–22, 131–44, 151, 183; representatives, 64, 110; Secretary General, 39, 43, 95, 106, 116–22, 130–39, 153, 155; Security Council, 94, 106, 119–27, 136–40, 148, 151; Transition Assistance Group, 106; Trusteeship Council, 39, 71, 93–111, 130, 167
United Negro Improvement Association, 61
United States, 19, 27, 29, 38, 44–63 passim, 77, 131–38, 167–77; Department of State, 42–57 passim, 77, 102, 128, 130; foreign policy of, 22, 81, 132, 151–54, 170, 173; in Iraq, 106, 109, 110; race relations in, 42–58, 69, 73, 78, 83, 130, 148; Senate, 39

Universal Negro Improvement Association, 31
University of Cape Town, 20, 26
Urquhart, Brian, 4, 115n24, 119, 132, 142, 144

van der Meersch, W. J. Ganshof, 149
Victoria, Queen, 28
von Horn, Carl, 120–22, 136, 151
voting. *See* elections

Wallace-Johnson, I. T. A., 27
Waller, Fats, 31
Wallerstein, Immanuel, 15, 182
Washington, Booker T., 31, 50–56, 70
Washington, D.C., 5, 6, 63
Weaver, Robert, 4, 6
Welbeck, Nathaniel, 155
Wesley, Charles, 51
West, the, 7–16, 56, 128–40, 150–56, 174
West Africa, 12–16, 20, 25, 53–59, 74–86 passim, 99–109 passim, 132
Wheeler, Raymond, 121
white, whites: Americanism, 44, 45; antagonism among, 30; mercenaries, 152, 153; riots against black officials, 6; supremacy, 5, 48, 49, 53, 62; working class, 5, 6, 8
white man's burden, 9, 30, 46, 54, 63, 66, 96
Wieschhoff, Heinrich, 156, 157n28
Wilkerson, Doxey, 4, 20
Willame, Jean-Claude, 132, 134, 138, 139
Williams, Eric, 27, 58
Williamstown Institute of Politics, 75
Wilson, Woodrow, 21, 52
women, 28, 50, 70, 119
World Trade Organization, 172, 174, 176
World View of Race, A (Bunche), 6, 7, 8, 9, 12, 13, 16, 26, 84
World War I, 21, 50, 96, 99, 164
World War II, 6–16, 25, 39, 42, 63, 101, 102, 125, 128, 162–75 passim
Wright, Quincy, 98

Xuma, Dr. A. B., 35, 41n33

Year of Africa, 23
Yergan, Max, 22, 23, 28
YMCA, 22, 26, 28
Young, Donald, 20, 26, 27, 40n1

Zimbabwe, Republic of, 17
Zulu, 61

www.ingramcontent.com/pod-product-compliance
Lightning Source LLC
Chambersburg PA
CBHW031244290426
44109CB00012B/424